If you have dysfunction in your family, if you are challenged with a difficult family, you can develop relationships that fill your life with love, companionship, joy, good times, and humor. But, be prepared for the death of your parents. They say Karma is a bitch but Death makes Karma look tame, even in good families. In bad families, all bets are off so the more prepared you are, the less painful it may be.

-from *Tales From The Family Crypt*

Tales From The Family Crypt

Deborah Carroll

Contents

Dedication

To Ned who is and will always be my true companion. To my daughters, Alexis, Tamra, and Shira who bring more love and joy than can be described in these pages. To my son-in-law John who married all of us happily and is a great addition to our family. To our first grandchild Avery who is simply a bundle of love. To family members in the past who brought us to the good place we are today. To family members in the present and future who fill our hearts with unconditional love that will live on. And finally, to those friends who have become our family. We love you and if we haven't said it often enough, thanks.

Prologue: Life Before Death

A friend once sent me a cartoon, perhaps from the *New Yorker* magazine. It showed a picture of a ballroom with a banner that read, "Functional Family Convention." There was one person in the room.

That person couldn't have been me…or my husband.

It has taken almost a lifetime to understand how the dysfunction that derailed our families played out. Despite the fact my husband Ned and I had four siblings and four parents between us, our three lovely little girls grew up with virtually no aunts or uncles and only one loving grandparent. We aren't completely blameless but Ned and I lived what we believed were compassionate and ethical lives. It wasn't easy dealing with our siblings throughout our adult lives but it got astronomically awful when our parents' deaths rolled around.

If you have dysfunction in your family, if you are challenged with a difficult family, you can develop relationships that fill your life with love, companionship, joy, good times, and humor. But, be prepared for the death of your parents. They say Karma is a bitch but Death makes Karma look tame, even in good families. In bad families, all bets are off so the more prepared you are, the less painful it may be.

I know our dysfunctional families don't make us special. Lots of people have issues with their siblings. About 80% of Americans have siblings so there are quite a few relationships out there that could go wrong. A few years back Ned and I were having dinner with five couples, a few of whom we didn't know. They were friends of our friends. In discussing sibling relationships we discovered almost every person at the table, at least one person in each couple, had what we lovingly referred to as a "bad sister." That is a sister who caused conflict in the family--one who tried to control other family members to an extreme. We also agreed that maybe every family had one such sibling and if you didn't know who it was, it was likely you. One of the attendees at the dinner called her mom the next day to report the conclusion at dinner. She said, "Mom, I don't think we have a bad sibling but," she added humorously, "they say if I didn't know who it is it might be me." Her mother's silence was deafening. Our friend is concerned about that silence but I think if you are concerned about being the bad sibling that is your first clue that you're not it.

I worked hard to understand how my extended family evolved. I want my daughters to understand how *not* to live the way we did. That way when Ned and I die, our daughters will feel only love and will be able to come together in their loss and then move on to continue living good lives. I want our deaths to be a time when our family can gather together to look back with love and ahead with optimism. I realize this is the ultimate "Do as I say and not as I do," but it's important they see how we all got here so their future families will be different and, yes, better. Our girls assure us they don't need to learn this lesson; they value family and know how to nurture those relationships. They were the first readers of my first draft of this story. Their reaction was that I was so focused on describing the saga in detail I didn't tell enough of the funny parts or enough of as they phrased it, "the good stuff" about our family. Although our family situation was painful at times and pathetic in parts, the five of us did survive and thrive and found ways to live joyfully despite the challenges. We weathered the four deaths and the five of us came out of the storms stronger and closer.

Writing is a cathartic experience. I was able to write this story because I remember the details vividly. The memories, though, are just that – memories. As such they are subject to the vagaries of time. Every story I tell and every person I describe is true and real to the best of my recollection. (But I did change names to protect privacy.) Were you to ask the players involved what they remember of the incidents I describe perhaps they would differ with my account. Friends tell me my memory of seemingly minor aspects of this story is uncanny. But we've spent thousands of hours (and I mean that literally) talking ad nauseum about the family saga. Ned and I speak to each other about it, we speak to our friends, even to strangers. Yes, we're fun at parties!

Seriously, we are fun at parties when we talk about our family because we do it with humor. Some of the details are bizarre. Our siblings are characters who *could* be found in fiction but readers might find them unrealistic and unbelievable. They are, however, real. Over the years we've cried an ocean of tears but in the end it's laughing about it when we could that got us through reasonably healthy mentally and emotionally. Our family members challenged us but they did not defeat us. That is of paramount importance. Here's the other interesting thing about telling this story. Almost every time we share parts of our story with strangers or with friends, they come back to us with a story of their own involving a dysfunctional way of dealing with a family member's death. It is astounding how many people have gone through similar situations. We haven't yet heard too many that top ours, if we had foam fingers we'd still raise them and chant, "We're number one, we're number one." But, we've heard some that come close in being pretty depraved and sad. Our friends once gave Ned a T-shirt that read, "If there's a will… I want to be in it." While it was mildly amusing, it was more comforting. First, it showed our friends understood the difficulty of dealing with selfish siblings. Second, if such a T-shirt existed, clearly we were not alone in suffering these problems in dealing with the impending death of aging parents. Considering death is the one thing we all know for sure we'll face some day, in particular the death of our parents, we are overall remarkably unprepared for dealing with it in a healthy way. That can and should change.

I wrote this book because I wanted to document the truth about our family. But I also wanted to help other people who have to deal with death in the family and the surrounding cruelty and competition it brings out in some people. If you have a loving family, even with flawed members, you are one of the lucky ones. Chances are if you have a great relationship with your siblings, you may get through the death of a parent together, enveloped in love. You may be able to help your parent have a "good death" that is peaceful. If you have a bad sibling or a weak parent, you may be looking at very tough times in dealing with death. Families are complex webs in constant flux. It is hard work to weave them into successful long-lasting relationships. It's worth the work but it's vital to know that the work, much like the relationships, never ends. And, if you don't have family relationships that make you happy, you can still have happy and fulfilled lives.

Author Pat Conroy could be considered an expert on dysfunctional families. The author of 11 books including, "The Great Santini," about his abusive father, knows firsthand the power of parents to make or break a family. His situation was so bleak, given the violent abuse his father showered on his wife and children, Conroy says the word dysfunction can't come close to describing it adequately. He thinks a more apt moniker might include the words supersonic or nuclear disaster. Our family issues are not of that caliber. (Although some who know our story might think I'm understating how bizarre it all got.) But, Conroy does have an interesting take on families. He believes when people gather in groups like a family it's unlikely any are without the "crazies." Sometimes at book signings when people say to him, "Boy, your family's nuts," he responds, "Yes they are. How far do you have to go to hit crazy in your family?"

In my family and Ned's you don't have to go far at all to hit crazy. If Ned and I were to stand in a room with my sister on our right and Ned's parents and siblings on our left, we could strike right and hit crazy. Then we could strike left and hit crazy. Then we could continue to strike left again and again and, yes, again and again, until we touch every person in the room. But the thing is, we didn't always know they were crazy. Both Ned and I thought we had normal childhoods. We thought we had normal siblings. Maybe we were the crazy ones. You be the judge.

Conroy believes the families that work best are those that work together to "soften" the crazies. This is the story of how Ned and I and our daughters worked together to succeed as a family. We tried to "soften crazies" on both sides of the family. But then our parents died and with each death a bit more of the family fell apart until the last parent died and the extended family died with her. But we moved on and found happiness. I believe it is possible for most people to do that if they are willing to work at it.

Understanding how our families imploded begins with learning how our families were built. Here are our stories. Buckle your seat belt. Like a roller coaster our stories begin gently, roll along smoothly and sometimes pleasantly uphill and then plunge wildly careening downhill before slowly coasting to a peaceful and happy ending.

Chapter One: The Family Portrait

As a child I enjoyed those drawings in magazines where you have to find the errors in the picture. You had to look closely to see little details that don't make sense. The raccoon is wearing a bow tie. The cat has gloves on. There's a fish floating in a glass of milk. I believe these puzzles were meant to test the acuteness of your vision but I think they're more a test of how mundane is your mind. If you can't imagine a raccoon in neckwear, you pass the test.

So it was with my family photos. Look quickly and we appear to be a normal family of the late '50s-early '60s. Take a lingering look and you might notice something amok. On closer inspection perhaps you see the parts that don't make sense. Photographs are graphic representations of who we are at a given moment. They provide insight into details about the people, places, and things that create, as the Kodak ad campaign once touted, "the times of your life." So, poring over them, I'm now looking for details that may spark a memory and illuminate an understanding of who I am, who my parents were, and who my sister may be, because I've never really been sure.

When I was about eight years old my parents hired a professional photographer to shoot a family portrait. In those days families who could afford it and were into preserving memories got movie cameras with screens and projectors. My family rarely even took a snapshot. In fact, being the second child in the family there are almost no baby pictures of me. There are plenty of pictures of my older sister Linda, but I guess the thrill was gone the second time around. But on this one occasion my parents must have felt motivated to capture us for posterity. Probably a photographer offered them a cheap family portrait, maybe even a free one, thinking he could make a good profit selling them other sizes like wallet photos. He obviously had no clue with whom he was dealing. My father was definitely the person who would take just the cheap or free picture and not one item more. The photographer might figure most mothers and fathers couldn't possibly turn down adorable pictures of their kids. And it's not that our parents didn't love us, it's just that when it came to money, emotions never entered into the decision-making process. Well, that and the fact that my parents were cheap.

The formal picture of the four of us dressed up is posed in the living room of our split-level home on Long Island in New York. My parents bought this house when my sister Linda was about 5 and I was a baby. I loved that house, situated on the corner next to a big empty lot where my imagination and my best friend and I ran free. So much of my childhood was spent roaming among the cattails that grew there or nearby the brackish water we called the creek. I don't remember Linda playing there. She didn't play outside much at all. When Linda had free time, she stayed in. She read books, and sometimes she did that just for fun. She was the kind of student who, when assigned a ten-page paper, would write thirty-five pages. I was the kind of student who would write eight pages in really big handwriting with large margins so it would seem like ten. Plus, I'd hand it in late. My sister would probably hand her work in before it was due.

Anyway, on formal portrait day we got all dressed up. This is the first thing that's wrong and misleading in the picture. We were not a fancy family. If we wanted a representative picture we should have been dressed in much more casual clothes. My father is wearing a suit and tie, and I'm pretty sure that's the only time I saw him dressed like that when I was a child. My sister and I are wearing matching black-and-white taffeta dresses and we have the same haircut. I should have been wearing a rumpled polo shirt and mismatched, wrinkled, dirty pedal pushers exposing scraped knees. My sister should have been wearing a button-down shirt and neat slacks. Then we would have looked like our authentic selves.

Linda and I are nothing alike. She's almost five years older and always seemed like she was from another generation entirely. I would not have chosen her as a friend, yet I had to live with her. It's an odd consequence of having siblings – sometimes you live with people who feel a bit like strangers. Still, I liked her and basically we got along. We didn't have that much to do with each other. We didn't interact so much as coexist. Side by side, each in our own room. Hers blue, mine pink. Hers orderly, mine messy. Hers filled with books and notebooks and a collection of violin music. Mine filled with dolls, stuffed animals, a killer marble collection, and AM radio playing top 40 hits. I often wondered how two girls raised in the same home by the same parents could be so very different.

I have researched that question about how siblings grow to be so different from each other. I found that in the 1980s, Robert Plomin published a research paper about the similarities and differences between siblings. He studied three aspects of siblings: physicality, intelligence, and personality. He concluded that in two of these three siblings were quite similar, but in the third aspect – personality – vast differences occurred. He said that in only 20 percent of the time are siblings similar in personality. In his studies, the conclusion was the differences were developed in part, as a result of the "non-shared environmental factors." Those might be factors in the environment encountered outside the home but also include the reality that even inside the home, the difference in times when each child grows up changes the environment. Thus, children raised by the same parents in the same house aren't raised in the same environment because the times are different.

Another explanation for personality differences is competition. Siblings compete for their parents' affections. That competition might actually foster differences in personality. If you have a sibling you see as strong in an area in which you are weak, you might be motivated subconsciously to develop in a different area in order to differentiate yourself from your sibling. So, for example, if your sister is a terrific singer and you can't carry a tune, you might start playing tennis and put your energies into being wholly different than your sister. Or, as it played out in my case, perhaps I saw my sister succeeding in school and being very smart so I put my energies into being more social.

My parents didn't foster togetherness all that much. Linda and I weren't encouraged to play together. I don't remember my mother ever suggesting we do anything together at all, not play or do chores around the house. While we did sometimes play board games, I have no memory of ever playing with any other toys with my sister. I don't recall ever going outside to play with her and we never went anywhere just the two of us. Those are activities I remember doing with friends. With a friend I'd go ice-skating, or to a movie, or we'd walk to a candy store. But I never did that with Linda and my parents never suggested we do so. On a daily basis, the only time we did something together at the urging of my parents is when Mom called us to dinner.

I guess my mother thought it would be very cute if we dressed alike for the formal photo. Our Aunt Becky used to send us matching outfits each year. My sister hated those annual clothing gifts because they were always geared to the younger sibling - me. Actually, I did look pretty cute in that dress, but Linda didn't look happy. She must have hated having to look just like her sister who was only eight when she was 13. The picture does make her look juvenile, which is the last thing you want when you are a teenager. I've tried to figure out why my sister resents me and I think these pictures could hold one of the answers. The haircut we both had was one they used to call the "pixie." (Come to think of it, when did they stop naming haircuts? It's actually a pretty good idea.) The name alone should have been enough of a clue that this was no style for anyone over the age of eight. Also my sister's personality was about the furthest thing from pixie-ish. Don't even start me on how her middle name being "Joy" is unbelievably ironic.

That particular dress probably didn't appeal to Linda in any way. The white taffeta top had cap sleeves. The bottom was black and white four-inch checks with a big black velvet belt that tied into a bow in the back. I thought it was the most beautiful dress ever made. And the coolest, too, because when you walked, the taffeta made this neat swishy, rustling noise. I suspect, however, my sister was less than impressed with this same feature. I have a feeling that when you are 13 you don't particularly enjoy wearing clothes that make more noise than you do. And my sister was not the type who wanted her clothes to announce her entrance into a room. She would much prefer not being noticed at all. Or, better yet, not being made to enter any room where there were people. Linda never had the "gift of gab." In social situations she was very quiet, almost to the point of withdrawn. If my parents took us to visit friends Linda was okay with that. She'd talk to people she was comfortable and familiar with. But, at larger gatherings, she would appear uncomfortable. She'd speak up if the topic of conversation interested her but she did not make small talk. I believe that made it difficult for her to engage new people. On topics about which she was knowledgeable, particularly religion, she could speak at length. She'd get exasperated with anyone who disagreed with her or told her she was mistaken about anything, though. At that point she'd often cut off conversations, almost to the point of being impolite, but stopping just short of rudeness.

In the formal photo Linda is posed with her arms around me. The hug is not convincing. I don't think she wanted a little sister to begin with. I know this because she told me so many times. As far back as I can remember, Linda told me the story about how much she wanted a little brother like my cousin Stevie. I couldn't blame her for that. Stevie was cute and charming. I liked him a lot, too.

"You know, I didn't want a little sister. I had my heart set on a little brother like Stevie. I asked Mommy to bring home a brother just like him and when she brought you instead I didn't know why," she'd say frequently.

That sentence was often followed with this one:

"You were a bad baby. I remember one time," Linda would recount, "you were in your playpen and you hit me over the head with a broomstick."

I never thought of this when I was a kid but in retrospect thinking back on that story, I do wonder, what was a broomstick doing in my playpen? Who handed me a broomstick in the first place?

Despite our differences I have a handful of whimsical and fun memories of life with my sister. Once her pet turtle disappeared. We spent weeks looking for it together. We all believed the search would end in tragedy but amazingly, we found the nameless turtle under the sofa in the den. Although missing for weeks he was still alive. We put him back in his bowl and although he was no longer the same color as the plastic palm tree he used to match, he continued to live for many more months. And, he got a name – Fuzzy – because when we found him he was coated with some kind of white fuzz. It seemed the turtle search brought my sister and me closer together for a while.

I wanted to be close with my sister but I wasn't sure how. My parents worked hard at treating the two of us equally. This wasn't always easy because I was a fairly sick little kid. I had a ureter that was too short causing urine to "reflux" back up into the kidneys. That causes urinary tract infections. Those infections would begin with fevers of 103 and higher and they might also cause hemorrhaging so I'd often get rushed to emergency rooms. Eventually my condition required a few lengthy hospitalizations, some surgery, and many doctor visits. My condition lasted for several years and was a constant source of conversation around the house. I guess my sister felt left out. From my perspective, my sister always got her share of attention from being smart and doing well in school. But I guess she wanted to just be more like me. Not that she wanted to be sick, but perhaps she would have liked to be more the center of attention and concern.

Linda often behaved more like a parent than a sister. When I was four or five years old I stole a pair of white lace doll socks from the "Five and Ten" store (where, presumably, once upon a time, everything was five or ten cents). My sister found out about it – because I was stupid enough to show her the socks. She explained to me she would *have* to tell my parents for my own good and I suppose it was, but I was angry with her for getting me into trouble. I resented her acting like my mother and not my sister.

The next thing I knew my father was marching me into the store.

"Tell the man what you did," Dad commanded, as he ushered me forward toward the counter. I craned my neck to see the storekeeper's face to assess his level of meanness. Then I glanced down toward the floor. He didn't look that mean so I figured I could survive the confession. Plus, I had no choice.

"I took these doll socks," I reported sheepishly and a brief second later I added, "and this packet of Chiclets." I handed him the socks from my jacket pocket with my right hand and with my left hand I passed over the packet of gum I produced from my other pocket. I hadn't told my sister that along with the socks I had also taken a small pack of gum. But I figured while I was confessing, I might as well reveal all.

Linda also made me attend synagogue services. I don't think anyone else in town had a sibling who monitored his or her religious attendance. I guess Linda thought she could make it fun for me because it was fun for her. Linda discovered religion when she was about ten years old. Here's how that happened. When my mother was diagnosed with diabetes in the 1930s the medical world didn't know much about the disease. The doctors told her she could pass out at any time. The thought of losing consciousness behind the wheel frightened her so much she never learned to drive. Later, as medical advances were made in the field of diabetes research, doctors told Mom she could learn to drive without fear of lapsing into diabetic coma, but by then she believed she was too old to learn.

Mom wanted us to have some religious education at after-school Hebrew school. Because she couldn't drive and my father didn't get home from work until 6:30 PM, my mother had to find a synagogue within walking distance. My mother was not the kind of person to ask favors of other people, so she wouldn't ask anyone to drive us if she was unable to participate in the carpool. The orthodox -- most religious -- synagogue was the only one we could walk to so we became members. The rabbi was young, probably in his twenties, and he was really nice. He taught the kids Linda's age. I think Linda loved religion almost immediately because it gave her a community where she felt accepted. And, at the risk of sounding sacrilegious, I think she thought the rabbi was cute. I may be putting my own spin on this because I thought the rabbi was cute but I know Linda liked him a lot. What's not to like about a 20-something kindhearted rabbi with blond hair and blue eyes? Perhaps you've heard the expression "*shiksa* goddess," which describes a stereotypical Jewish guy's view of the perfect non-Jewish female, one with blond hair and blue eyes. Well, this rabbi was the *shiksa* goddess of rabbis. Again, I know that's my perspective, but you get the idea.

About that time Linda was having a hard time in public school. The kids made fun of her because she was weird. Where they were social, Linda was shy. Where they were comfortable with their peers, Linda was awkward. She was passionate about her schoolwork while other kids cared more about having fun. She played the violin and they would tease her about that. I remember one day in junior high she ran home from the school bus crying hysterically because two girls on our block had chased her down the street trying to grab her violin case and shooting the rubber bands from their braces at her. Not even taking the bands out and aiming them at her, but rather, shooting them, all wet, directly from inside their mouths. I think it was the part about the saliva that bothered Linda the most. Or, at least that's what she claimed. I thought at the time that having two neighbor girls who *should* be your friends mercilessly teasing you was probably worse than getting hit with a little spit. But it was kind of disgusting; it's true.

At Hebrew school Linda was not so odd. The group of kids her age was small. I guess it was easier for her to get to know them and for them to get to know her. Mostly, the rabbi was kind to her and took her under his wing. Whatever the reason, she loved being there and took the teachings to heart. The more she learned, the more religious she became. As Linda became more religious, so did our family. As she learned more about the rules of keeping kosher, our kitchen became more rigid in organization. I didn't mind or even notice until Linda found out that cheese had to be kosher. Mama Rosa's restaurant, our usual Sunday night destination, did not use kosher cheese on its pizza so we had to stop eating there. They served my favorite chocolate pie and I couldn't believe my sister was stopping me from being able to eat that pie ever again.

Other than that, my sister's religion did not affect me in too many negative ways. We went to synagogue much more than any of my friends did but I didn't mind so much a lot of the time. The walk took about 15 minutes. We would spend the time talking and playing little games. Those walks were probably the best times we ever had together. I recall there were some fierce-looking, barking Rottweiler dogs we passed along the way. I was worried one day they would jump their fence and bite me. My sister assured me God protected people on their way to synagogue. While I hoped that was true and even found it somewhat comforting, I wondered how the dogs knew we were going to synagogue. But no dogs ever bit me so I guess she was right.

The professional photographer's family portrait was taken right about the time my sister started going to synagogue and kids began teasing her. I can see in her eyes in this picture she is not happy. Anyone looking carefully at the picture could see that, but they might think it was because of the dress or the funny haircut. And although Linda and I seem to be a matched pair, closer inspection could reveal we were a mismatch at heart.

I haven't seen this picture for years. In fact I had forgotten it had ever been taken. With this being our sole professional family portrait you might think my parents would have hung it prominently on a wall and by now it would have been a fixture in my life. But after it was delivered I rarely saw it. My mother couldn't stand the sight of it so she put it away at the bottom of a drawer in the china closet of our dining room. She hated the picture because it forced her to accept an unacceptable truth. My mom was fat.

My mother had a hard time accepting herself as fat. Although she was a size 18 she just did not, could not, and would not, think of herself as a fat person. And I think she was all the more upset about it because she had done nothing to make herself fat. My mother did not overeat. If anything she under ate. Because she was diabetic, she was on a really Spartan diet. She ate Puffed Rice for breakfast and cottage cheese and fruit for lunch and then a regular dinner of meat, starch, and vegetable. No dessert, not ever. At least not until they found a way to make sugar-free treats; but that came later in her life.

She was fat because she also had a thyroid condition that somehow caused her to gain weight for no apparent reason. She had never been bigger than a size 4 so blowing up to size 18 was a shock. She didn't let us take pictures of her often. I guess the professional photographer offer was such a good one she couldn't resist, but when she saw the picture I don't think she could deal with it. I don't think she looks that fat in the picture. I guess she just felt big because she wasn't used to it. It may have caused her to feel uncomfortable in her own skin; similar to the way my sister felt much of her life. Perhaps that's one of the reasons my mother and sister felt a kinship; they were both a bit dissatisfied with their lives.

So that's another hidden aspect of this picture. My mom is smiling but she probably felt more like crying. I imagine if I could view this picture from inside her head I would see the tiny, petite woman she was disfigured by an oversized body. My mom was not a complainer. I never once heard her lament her lot in life, challenged by her disease. She accepted her limitations gracefully and for the most part, quietly and resolutely. Growing up watching her do what she had to do to survive and stay healthy probably taught me many lessons about how to tackle challenges head-on and how not to be defeated by obstacles. Given the family challenges and obstacles I encountered later, those lessons were probably invaluable.

So there you have it--the family portrait of us and our secrets. My father is in the picture too, but when I was a little kid my dad wasn't much of a presence in my life. How could he have been so little of a presence in what appears to be such a close, happy family? I was later to get to know him better and appreciate him too, but at that time, he was just there, nothing impressive. I could not have known he would turn out to be the most memorable of us all, leaving the greatest legacy.

Chapter Two: Vacation Paradise

One of the best birthday gifts my parents ever bought for me was a Brownie Midget camera. I loved taking pictures and I especially loved the "pop" of the flashbulb that snapped onto the top. The problem, though, was beyond paying for the camera, film cost money, developing the film cost even more, and flashbulbs had to be replenished regularly. Although the Eastman Kodak company starting pitching the "Kodak Moment" in 1961, in my family those were few and far between. The expense of film and developing made picture taking a luxury limited to very special occasions or vacations.
So, our family photos are valued artifacts.

There's one snapshot of Linda and me in shorts. Actually they were skorts, not shorts. Skorts were one of the fashion highlights of the 60s. They were a combination of a skirt and a pair of shorts. Actually they were baggy shorts that were pleated, but I guess no one would have bought them if they called them baggy, pleated shorts. Anyway, my sister and I are wearing these things, with the matching shirts. The shirts are white but they have sleeves of the same print as the skort. Again, one of us looks fine and one of us looks uncomfortable. The question is why would Linda wear these clothes if she detested them so much?

She probably wore them to please my mother. They were very close and understood each other well. My mother never really fit in with her peers in the neighborhood. I was born when my mom was 39. That made her quite a bit older (by about 15 years on average) and much more conservative than most of the mothers on the block. Consequently, Linda, also being socially awkward, became more like a friend for our mother. They were kind of a mutual admiration society. While I knew my mother loved me, I also knew she did not feel about me the way she felt about Linda. I don't think their closeness bothered me. I understood my mother and sister needed each other. I knew I could not fulfill their social needs, and no one else could either, so I was glad they had each other. Thus, if my mother wanted Linda to wear these outfits, I don't think my sister would have refused even if she felt awkward or thought she looked stupid.

In retrospect, although it wasn't conscious on my part, maybe I was envious of the way my mother and sister related to each other so effortlessly. Again, I knew my mother loved me unconditionally and I knew she liked me and was proud of me. But I also knew I was not as much like her as my sister was. Because she was older than most of the other mothers, Mom was less in tune with the culture. For example, Mom couldn't stand the rock and roll music I loved. I had to listen to the radio in my room with the door closed because she objected to the noise. When Linda took up guitar playing, she chose to study classical guitar. When other kids her age were mimicking folk singers of the 60s, Linda's musical style was more along the lines of Andrés Segovia. Whose music do you think my mother would have been more likely to enjoy?

So, in this skorts photo we're on vacation in Lake George. These yearly vacations were our family tradition. Dad worked five and sometimes six days each week. Each day he would be gone when I got up at 7:00 AM. He would get home from the factory around 6:30, eat dinner, watch a little TV, and go to bed in order to get up early the next day and do it all again. His life was typical of the dads around the neighborhood. I guess some of the fathers had professional jobs but as a child I could see no difference between my father's life and any other dad's. From my vantage point all I could see is the fathers left early, were gone all day and came home in time for dinner, newspaper reading, and TV.

A great deal of my life was fashioned around my father's work. He worked hard so we weren't supposed to bother him when he got home. He worked hard so we shouldn't have expected him to play with us at home. He worked hard so we weren't supposed to wake him early on Sunday, which was the only day he could sleep. His work, although I knew what he did, was like some mysterious entity that determined our day-to-day existence and even our destinies. So, since he worked hard, he earned two weeks vacation each year. My parents would pick a destination and off we'd go. Usually, we'd go off after a certain amount of fighting and crying. Vacation planning was very tense. I'm not sure if it was the packing or the getting ready to leave and all that goes with that, or simply the stress of worrying about whether the vacation would be worth the expense, but we never left for a trip happily.

In later years I learned my mother's diabetes and related mood swings were probably the underpinning of the travel woes. The hormones related to insulin were highly receptive to stress. Thus, the stress of the trip would impact greatly on her blood sugar level. As a result, my mother would normally get kind of crazy just before we left. It happened in the blink of an eye. Her mood would go with lightning speed from calm to hysterical, from breezy to full-flown tornado. That frenetic mood would inevitably result in a fight of some kind, often involving my father or me, but usually not my sister. With my dad it was often a case of my mother making sure he had taken care of the things he was supposed to do to get ready.

"Sidney!" Mom would shriek, her mood already altered to a hysterical annoyance level that didn't match the circumstance, "Did you get directions to the hotel? How do you expect us to get there if you didn't ask for directions? We're never going to get there. We'll get lost. We always get lost."

"Sidney!" slightly louder as Mom's mood had already risen to a state of minor panic, "Did you gas up the car? You didn't? Oh God, now we have to stop for gas, too? We'll never get there."

Those minor blips would result in Mom yelling at him and then just yelling in general. Or it could be me who was the problem. I must have been a real pain in the ass when we were in a hurry. I have always been a procrastinator and also somewhat forgetful. This is a bad combination when people are relying on you to be ready. If my dad was loading up the car and at that point I'm still collecting toys to take with me or I had to run back upstairs to get the white Orlon sweater that Mom had told me ten times to be sure to take but after I got into the car I realized I had never packed, that sort of thing could set Mom off. Forgetting to pee right before getting in the car and then running back into the house to do so (remember I had kidney issues so peeing was a big deal) would make my mother angry. My mother, probably being in a high state of getting-ready-to-travel stress, would not respond well to my last-minute activities. That resulted in yelling, screaming, threats to cancel the trip, punishment, and door slamming as my mom walked back into the house and swore she would not travel with us that day or ever again. Ultimately, we'd all get into the car and head to vacation paradise. The vacation destination varied, the departure horror rarely did.

But, every year, off we'd go.

You might think the vacations would have provided time for me to get to know my father better, maybe even bond with my sister and my mother, but I didn't really see them once we reached our destination. My parents chose vacation places that had programs for kids. I'm sure they thought that was what we wanted-- to be provided with constant activity. We'd eat breakfast together in the hotel dining room and go our separate ways. My sister and I would go to whatever kids' program was offered, but as soon as we got there we'd be separated into our age groups so we wouldn't see each other all day. My day would be filled with arts and crafts, swimming, horseback riding, and similar activities. I suppose my sister would be doing the same kind of thing, but I have no idea what my parents did. When I was a kid I suppose I didn't care, and now that I'm older I do wonder about it, but there's no one to ask. So, we lived somewhat parallel lives during these vacations, making them not entirely different from what we did at home. We existed side by side but managed to artfully avoid interaction. The vacation pictures show us all having a great time. We're in pools, we're riding in horse-drawn sleighs, we're sightseeing in interesting places, but we're rarely all in the same picture.

A photo from one vacation in Florida fills in one more piece of the puzzle of differences between my sister and me. The picture is of me in a pool with a young girl, about my age. I met Nina the first day of the trip in the children's day camp program. She was Cuban and did not speak English. I didn't speak Spanish, so we must have made an interesting pair. We played together each day. Considering the language barrier, I have no clue how we did this. Linda met Nina too, but after a few minutes she wearied of trying to make herself understood. Nina had an older sister and the four of us could have hung out together, but Linda did not want to stay with us. I guess she had a hard enough time communicating with peers who spoke the same language. Maybe she just wasn't up to doing the work of trying to reach someone who spoke a different language.

My parents loved telling the story about my vacation friend, Nina. They thought watching us together was quite funny. I suppose we must have been gesturing wildly and were hilarious to watch. I like to think they were proud of my ability to communicate so well but maybe it was just funny to watch. They would say Linda tried too, but probably she was too old to pull off the non-verbal communication. Even then it was easier for them to deny Linda's inability to connect than to recognize it and try to deal with it. I suppose if Linda couldn't communicate verbally or non-verbally, that explained why it was hard for her to make a lot of friends. I made friends wherever I was. Maybe this was painful for my sister to watch. She never said. I can't even be sure she was upset about her lack of friends. I don't know what my parents could have done to help Linda be more comfortable in social situations. As parents we learn to accept our children, or at least we have to, even if they are different than we are. Perhaps they thought the best thing they could do to help her was to accept her the way she was. It's also possible, since Linda was so much like my mother that neither of my parents found her odd or sad.

It's important parents value and respect their children, even when they turn out differently than they envisioned. I guess my parents were trying to show my sister they loved and respected her regardless of how many friends she had or how well she interacted. They might have been worried about bruising her ego, but I think they may have been better off if they had hurt her a little bit in order to help her. Perhaps if they told her early on that human interaction is important and worth working hard to achieve, Linda may have done better with people. She was so smart in school; she was willing to work so hard to succeed. What if she had put that energy into revealing herself to people and trying to make friends? Maybe our sisterly relationship would have turned out better if someone had taught Linda to value people. While she didn't speak about wanting to have more friends, she would talk about how much it hurt when other kids rejected her. To explain why they treated her poorly she would say other kids were mean or were cliquish or not as smart as she was. My parents were sympathetic but I don't recall either of them ever talking to Linda about what she could have done to make things any better for herself so she could be happier.

Our vacations continued through the years. Lake George followed by Lakewood, NJ, followed by Florida and a cross-country train trip to California. The pictures are always the same. My sister and I smiling in front of the giant redwood trees, smiling in front of the giant orange display at Cypress Gardens, smiling in front of the giant statue of Mickey Mouse. We are smiling in the photos. And even now I'd like to believe that sometimes we must have been happy to be together.

Chapter Three: Pink Sunglasses

One picture is of my sister and me getting into our 1963 convertible red Chevy Impala. Normally, a ride in that car was a treat, especially when the top was down, but not on the day in this photo. I'm wearing pink sunglasses; you might think I was headed to a day at the beach. But this was the day from Hell. I was leaving my home, never to return. We were moving from New York to Philadelphia.

A few months earlier I heard my parents talking about the factory where my father worked and how they were looking for a new location. They needed more space, in a less expensive area, one with reasonable business taxes, near train tracks to facilitate their shipping needs. As with anything that didn't pertain directly to 10-year-old me, I paid little or no attention to what I overheard. Perhaps if I had listened more closely I would have had advanced warning of the doom to come.

The result of those conversations was the dog food factory was moving lock, stock, barrel, and dog food cans, to Philadelphia. And so was my family. Philadelphia! What did I know about it? Some called it the city of brotherly love. They named a cream cheese after it. That was it. I had no brothers and no interest in cream cheese. Needless to say, this was not a place I wanted to go. And then there were my friends. I had lived all of my almost eleven years in Oceanside in the only home I could remember with the only friends I ever cared about. And, since my sister had been not easy to be close with, I had kind of created my own family with my friend Patti, declaring her honorary sister. So, I was not just being uprooted from my home, but from my family as well. I was devastated.

We started looking for a house. We spent weekends driving the 90 or so miles to Philadelphia to check out potential new homes. My mother always said the best time to go house hunting was in December. That way you could tell if you were looking in Jewish neighborhoods without having to ask the real estate agent. In those days, in December families either put up Christmas lights or displayed electric Chanukah menorahs in the windows. This was a great way to distinguish the Jews from the Goyim. (Yiddish word for non-Jews) God forbid (almost literally) we should look for a home in a neighborhood with too much of the latter and too little of the former.

As far as I was concerned, it didn't matter what kind of neighborhood we chose. I fully intended to be miserable no matter where we ended up. I was emotionally attached to my house, my room, my friends, and to the brick wall outside my house, all of it. How was I going to know how deep the snow was in Philadelphia without the brick wall outside my house? Snow came in two depths, higher than the brick wall and not. Higher than the wall usually meant no school and definitely determined the necessity for boots and snow pants. Life as we knew it was going to be changed forever, along with any chance for happiness. So thought 10-year-old Debby.

I don't remember moving being an issue for Linda and probably it wasn't. She may even have been looking forward to a fresh start. Maybe people in Philadelphia, the city of brotherly love, could find a place in their hearts for one weird sister. Maybe they didn't wear braces and would be unable to shoot the rubbery, slimy things in her direction.

I told my friends I had to move. They were genuinely upset. We spent most weekends together. We'd go miniature golfing or ice-skating or to a movie. We organized scavenger hunts. One of us would make up a list of items to find. The list would have things like safety pins, baby bottles, a two-cent stamp, everyday items people would have in their homes. We'd pair off and go from house to house asking for items. The couple who collected all of the items on the list first would win. The neighborhood was safe. We didn't have to worry about knocking on the doors of strangers. Every weekend was filled with fun and friends. Beginning in fifth grade, if we had nothing else to do someone would have an impromptu get-together with music, dancing, and kissing games like Spin-the-Bottle or Seven Minutes in Heaven.

My friends threw me a going away party, complete with the ritual signing of the "autograph hounds," stuffed dogs made of material suitable for writing on with a permanent marker.

They all signed the hound with the customary warm autograph book wishes of the early 60s:

2 Sweet
2 Be
4 Gotten, Love Randy

Or:

Don't kiss behind the garden gate.
Love is blind but your neighbor's ain't. Love, Mark
(Coincidentally, many years later I came across an autograph book of
my mother's from about 1934 with this same message.)

The party was simultaneously one of the happiest and saddest days of
my life. I felt enveloped by their love and convinced I'd never find
another group of friends quite like this one. While I did go on in my
life to be surrounded by many loving friends, the combination of the
innocence of that group and the way we interacted at such a young age
was never really duplicated. I don't recall my sister being thrown a
similar party. There was no autograph hound moving to Philadelphia
with her. Having that dog in my room comforted me in the first few
years after the move. I don't know where my sister found comfort after
the move. That was sad because in some ways, Linda was losing even
more than I was in this move. I was likely to be able to make new
friends. The likelihood my sister would find another small religious
community to surround her was not good. In fact, she never did find
one near our new home.

If it seems to you I had a perfect childhood, then you have the correct
picture. So, when I had to move away from that perfect life, I was
devastated to say the least. On top of everything else, I got some kind
of eye infection, maybe pink eye, and had to put drops in my eye and
avoid direct sunlight. Hence the pink sunglasses in the photo. And my
mom said crying would only worsen the condition and wash the
necessary medicine from my eye. She strongly suggested I avoid crying.
In fact, she forbade it. To add insult to injury—literally-- my highly
contagious eye meant I couldn't even give my best friend Patti a hug
goodbye.

Chapter Four: The Circle Game

When we moved to Philadelphia I was entering 6th grade. Linda was going into 11th grade. She immediately proved herself to be one of the smartest kids in school and I immediately proved myself to be one of the popular ones. I had a very cute accent, as all New Yorkers do. While that was no big whoop on Long Island, here in Philadelphia, I was a hit. Kids just liked hearing me talk.

"Say chocolate," they'd implore, and I'd oblige with "chalk-let" instead of the Philadelphia treat pronounced "chock-let." "Say winter," they request and I'd reply with "wint-ah." You wouldn't think that would be much of a political platform but you'd be surprised because the accent got me elected 6th grade president. New friends from school came to the house all of the time. My sister brought home only one new friend that year.

Linda studied hard to get all A's as she always did. I can still hear her walking around the house reciting lines from Lady Macbeth that she had to memorize.

"Out, blank spot! out, I say!—One; two: why, then'tis time to do't."

Imagine my surprise years later when I learned that the line was actually, "Out damn'd spot." My sister censored herself because she didn't want to say "damn."

She even studied on weekends, highlighting what she read by affixing Bobbie pins to the pages she needed to note. Because she was religious she couldn't write on the Sabbath so the Bobbie pins served as highlighters. I also got all A's that year, the only year I was to do so. I hadn't suddenly gotten smarter. Seems schools in New York were way ahead of those in Philadelphia. So, I had already learned most of the Philadelphia 6th grade curriculum in 5th grade in New York. I sailed through the review year with nary a moment spent studying.

Ultimately I adjusted to the move to Philadelphia pretty well. Linda seemed okay too as she was busy preparing for and applying to colleges. I still missed my hometown and my friends but my parents were pretty good about letting me go back for visits. At a fairly young age I'd take the train from Philadelphia to New York and then take the Long Island Railroad to Oceanside. I'd go a few times a year and that enabled me to stay in touch with the people I cared about. My sister went back once or twice as well. As Joni Mitchell wrote in "The Circle Game," "So, the years spun by and now the girl was 20." By the time my sister was 20 and I was 15, we lived in peace. We weren't friends; we weren't enemies. We were more like housemates who got along fine.

Throughout my high school years my life was pretty typical. I wasn't the most popular kid. I didn't hang with the coolest kids. My friends could aptly be described as the runners-up to cool. The coolest kids drank more than we did, smoked some pot (we did not at that time smoke any pot), dressed in better clothing and were generally wilder than we were. We had lots of fun but still did well in school as most of us were A and B students. The "cooler" kids were more likely B and C students but were perhaps more talented in the arts than we mostly-academics were.

My sister's friends, on the other hand, could aptly be described as almost non-existent. She lived at home for some of her college years but she didn't bring home many friends. I don't recall her going out on any dates. My friends didn't hang out at my house much but it was obvious I had friends, as they'd often come to pick me up to go out. Once in a while, I'd have a boyfriend or at least a date. While I did sit home alone on a lot of Saturday nights and never felt like the most attractive girl, I did have a social life.

My sister and I rarely talked about our dating lives. I remember she told me once she had met a boy named Gary. She said he was just a friend but from the way she spoke about him it seemed as though she was hoping he'd eventually be more than a friend. He even came to the house once or twice and I recall her being nervous just before he arrived. They never dated, though, and he stopped coming by. In looking back I wish I had told her more about what I was going through around that same time. I was invited to a friend's "dated" Sweet Sixteen party. I didn't have a boyfriend like most of my girlfriends did at that time so I had to ask out a guy out I hardly knew.

I approached him in the hall and simply said, "Hi, Louie. Franny's Sweet Sixteen party is Saturday night. Do you want to go with me?"

"No," he said, and turned and walked away.

Perhaps if I hadn't told everyone I was going to ask him, it wouldn't have been quite so mortifying. But I had, so then I had to tell everyone what he said and, suffice it to say, I don't know when I've had a more embarrassing moment. Well, okay, I've probably had many, but this one stands out in my memory as pretty devastating. So maybe I should have told my sister about this dating debacle. I could have told her how painful it was for me to have to go to that party alone and be the only girl to do so. But, then again, at least I was invited to a party and that was more than she had going on socially so maybe it wouldn't have helped bring us any closer.

After college, Linda moved to New York to attend grad school at Columbia. She rented an apartment in 1968, which she still lives in today, as far as I know. We entered our best years of siblinghood. During high school and into my college years, I'd occasionally take the train to New York to visit her. We'd go shopping or hang out and when she came home to Philadelphia, we'd do the same. Occasionally, Linda would surprise me with something special. We'd visit museums or get facials. Linda would encourage me to try on outfits in stores and then when my birthday would roll around the box she'd give me would have one of the outfits I tried and liked, everything from sweater to skirt to matching socks. We laughed some, we talked some, and we got along. We didn't fight or disagree. We were on the same side politically. As I got older and more interested that was something we shared. She knew a great deal more than I did as she was studying for a doctoral degree in political science. I didn't always understand what she was talking about, but I knew she was smart and I respected that.

Linda started dating a bit during her early years in New York. Eventually she had a first boyfriend named Michael. While I was in college, I met Ned and we were pretty serious and heading toward marriage. During those years, my sister and I talked more than we had before and we planned that I would join her on a trip she was scheduled to take to Israel and Egypt. I didn't end up going on that trip

26

because I decided I wanted to spend that summer with Ned and I did not want to be away for so long a time. But Linda and I were friends and probably closer as sisters than ever before or since. Eventually, Ned and I got married and my sister was my maid of honor. Michael and Linda were engaged for a time, too, but then he broke it off. Michael had introduced Linda to his mother, with whom he was very close. His mother did not support his plan to marry my sister. He told Linda he couldn't marry her after all because he couldn't upset his mother in that way. Although my mother told me Linda talked to her at great length about how heartbreaking this was, Linda never said much to me about it. I didn't feel comfortable talking to her about it either although I did tell her I was sorry it didn't work out. It was sad because he seemed like a nice guy and we all felt bad when Linda had her heart broken.

Plus, in those days, it was pretty embarrassing when your 22-year-old sister got married and you were already 27 and still single. But, a short time later, Linda did find someone to love who loved her too. When she was 29, she married Natan. Natan was an Israeli who had been in America for a few years. He was religious, even more so than Linda, but that was okay as she was pretty committed to the Orthodox religious way of life. He was cute and charming and friendly. We all liked him. My mother loved him because he was a talker. When Linda and Nat would come for a visit, Natan would sit with my mother and chat up a storm. I have no idea what they talked about. I don't know what they had in common. I didn't have that much to talk about with my mom and Ned had even less in common with her so their talks were polite but very short. Not Natan, though. He could go on for hours. Mom was very happy Linda had made such a good match. Linda and Mom were still very close but Natan talked more to my mother than Linda ever did. Ned and I didn't know Natan that well and Ned really hadn't spent much time with Linda since she lived in another state so our relationship as a foursome was not particularly close but it felt like we were on our way to becoming a decent extended family.

Little did I know those nights Natan sat up talking to Mom would come back to bite me later.

Chapter Five: The First Death

So, Linda and I were both happily married. My mother fished her fondest wish. Well, almost. What she really wanted was to have grandchildren. Ned and I were really too young for that. (Well, at least we thought so.) And, Linda hadn't yet been married that long.

The other thing Mom always wanted was to move to Florida. She had lived there for a short time when I was a toddler and I guess she always liked it. Plus, her health wasn't great and the cold weather really trapped her inside. Because of her diabetes, she had lived most of her life according to some very strict rules, which, it turns out, probably served to shorten her life. They definitely made her existence more miserable than it had to be. She was told to avoid exercise. She ate a Spartan diet with little in the way of fiber or nutrients as most of her diet consisted of meat, eggs and white flour. She shot insulin every day. All of this served to weaken her to the point where she had four heart attacks before she was 55. Her desire to move to Florida for the winter was the culmination of a life of very little fun and she was trying to remedy that with this warm weather move.

Since I had never had a healthy mom, I accepted her illness as normal for a mom. While she had always taken impeccable care of us, as she aged and got sicker the tables turned and I took care of her from time to time. When I was 16, I came downstairs into the living room one day and found Mom sitting on the sofa with a frightened expression on her face clutching her hand to her heart. She wasn't saying anything. I panicked immediately as I had in the past when I'd found Mom in any sort of abnormal way. Once I found her passed out on the bathroom floor and I was sure she'd had a heart attack but it was only a low potassium level that caused her to faint. Then there was the time she walked to the doctor's office around the corner and was gone for way too long a time. I got worried so I went looking for her and found her face down on the sidewalk, bleeding from the forehead. I was sure a heart attack had caused her fall. But, it turned out she had tripped over a bump in the sidewalk and had been too weak to get up. The point is heart attacks always loomed over her head and in my mind. Whenever

I was away overnight I worried she'd die while I was out. Some nights that worry kept me awake all night.

But, on this day on our living room couch Mom had actually suffered a massive heart attack. After spending the month or so in the hospital that was protocol then for heart attack patients, she came home. My sister had already moved to New York. My dad had to work. Since it was summer and I was off from school, the care and feeding of Mom fell to me. I loved it. I'd make her breakfast, either Farina or hard-boiled eggs and rye toast and we'd talk or read the newspaper. At lunchtime, I'd invent soups for her to try. And, when I say, "invent," I mean I'd open a can of Campbell's soup and add stuff to it to make it more interesting. She reacted as if it were gourmet fare the day I put chopped spinach into her mushroom soup. That was her favorite.

We'd spend the afternoon watching the soap operas together. This was something Mom and I shared that no one else in the family enjoyed. We didn't have much in common. I loved her dearly but she didn't really "get" me most of the time. But, oh, how we bonded over the soaps, *The Edge of Night*, *The Guiding Light*, *The Secret Storm*, *Love of Life* and especially *As the World Turns*. Because we didn't have much to share about our personal lives (I didn't want to share mine with her and she really didn't have much in hers to share with me), we wouldn't have had anything to talk about had it not been for the ATWT soap story line about Bob and Kim. As it turns out, those characters and actors both outlived my mother.

My mom was a little embarrassed about watching the soaps instead of going out and living a life. But, because she wasn't well and she didn't drive, she really didn't get out much. The soaps were her link to the outside world, although she didn't like to admit it. In fact, she was horrified one year when a friend of hers gave her a gift subscription to the magazine "Soap Opera Digest." Watching these shows was a guilty secret pleasure we shared. It might have been the main thing we shared. It might even have been the only thing. Remembering my time with my mother watching the soaps and eating that soup makes me happy. As bizarre and pathetic as this might sound, those days were among the best Mom and I shared.

Mom did get better after that heart attack, though. So, by the time she was 60 and maybe figuring her days were numbered, she decided she really wanted to move to Florida. Jerry Seinfeld used to joke that if you were Jewish and over 60, a bus would come to your house and pick you up, you'd change into white clothing (men would be forced to wear white belts and matching shoes) and you'd be whisked away to Florida whether you wanted to go or not. Well, my mother would have chartered that bus. She wanted to go, white clothes and all. She began working on my dad and after a few years she wore him down. He didn't want to retire and he didn't particularly want to move to Florida. I know for sure he didn't want to spend money on another home or apartment. He might not have minded the idea of Florida but I'm sure the thought of keeping up two homes, as northern "snowbirds" did, was not something he relished.

But, come December '77, off they went to Florida. Their plan was to spend three months there to decide if they liked it enough to make a more permanent move. Ned was teaching and I was in law school, so we had a week off for Christmas break. We planned to drive to Florida with friends and camp for a few days in the Keys before meeting up with my parents and Linda and Natan in Miami Beach for a family vacation. It was to be the first one for the six of us. We were going to meet in Miami Beach on Friday but I didn't know exactly where my parents were so on Thursday I called for directions.

"Come right away," Dad said, "Mom's in intensive care. She had a heart attack on Tuesday."

Linda and Natan had already left New York on their drive to Florida. Since this was before the advent of cell phones, they also didn't know about Mom and could not be reached.

Ned and I arrived at the hospital later that same day. Mom was hooked up to a variety of machines including a ventilator with a tube taped into her mouth. She couldn't speak as a result of that but she was awake and aware when we got there. She held my hand. She patted my hand, as if to tell me she was okay and I shouldn't worry. It didn't help. I was more than worried. I was panicked and despondent. She was going to die and there was nothing anyone could do. This was the moment I had worried about my whole life. I was unspeakably sad.

Back then we didn't know as much about death as we've learned since. I didn't think to say anything of any depth. I didn't tell her goodbye in any way. I'm sure I said, "I love you," but I also probably just said, "You're going to get better," rather than describe how much I loved her and what she had meant to me. If I could pick a few moments to relive, I'd choose to have just five minutes with my mom to tell her how I felt about her and what a wonderful mom she was. She wasn't perfect, (nor was I a perfect daughter, not by a long shot) but she did the most important thing a mom can do – she loved unconditionally and honestly.

Friday morning came. Linda and Nat got there before noon in time to see Mom still conscious. Intensive care had just four visiting opportunities each day at 10, 2, 4 and 6. Each of those was 15 minutes with only two people at a time allowed into the cubicle. But, we stayed at the hospital in the waiting room right outside of Intensive Care because the doctors told us Mom was dying and could expire at any moment. We were afraid to leave. But, after the 4:00 visit we were drained and exhausted. My dad was especially fatigued, as he had been sitting there for most of the last four days by himself. It had clearly taken a toll on him. I suggested we go back to Mom and Dad's apartment and try to sleep for a few hours. I was worried about my father. Linda agreed we all needed the rest and going back to the apartment was a good idea. It was only minutes from the hospital. The nurses assured us they'd call if Mom's condition changed.

But Natan said, "No, Linda, you can't go. It's going to be *Shabbos* (the Sabbath) soon and we're not allowed to drive so we won't be able to get back to the hospital in an emergency."

Linda said, "I know but Jewish law states you can break a law (like the one ruling out driving on the Sabbath) in an emergency. Dad needs to rest. I think this will be okay."

Natan insisted, "No, the law says you can break a rule only if breaking the rule will save a life. If they call and say your mother is dying and you want to see her before she dies, your coming back here won't save her so you can't drive. You won't be able to get back here."

My father didn't want to go to the apartment if Linda couldn't go too so we all stayed at the hospital.

The next day was New Year's Eve. We welcomed in 1978 while waiting for Mom to die. Ned had left because he had to go home to Philadelphia so he could go to work that week. We didn't know how long Mom would hang on and it didn't make sense for him to stay not knowing how long it might be.

So, Dad, Linda, Natan and I stood vigil. It was excruciating. One night, CBS News was airing a special called something like, "Heart Attack in America." As it came on, I turned off the TV in the waiting room or maybe I changed the channel, I don't exactly remember. Our family was the only group there so it was easy to control the TV.

I said, "I can't watch this."

Natan got up and turned it back on and said, "I want to watch this."

I said, I'm sure not in an unemotional tone, "My mother is in there dying of a heart attack. I can't watch 'Heart Attack in America.'"

He said, "I'm watching the program."

At that point I started yelling at him that she wasn't *his* mother and he didn't get to call the shots.

Natan responded angrily, "If you don't want to watch it, leave the waiting room."

"I should leave the waiting room?" I shouted. "Are you crazy? My mother is dying here. You leave the room."

The argument went downhill from there until Dad quietly asked us to stop. We did. Dad, did not however, turn on the heart attack show because either he didn't want to watch it, or he didn't want me to have to see it when I obviously felt so strongly about not seeing it. My sister never said a word.

Mom died that night. None of us was in the room with her. She died alone.

The next few months I was profoundly sad. My mother had died. My dad was alone. I dropped out of law school and decided to go back to teaching. My life was in turmoil.

A few months later, it was Passover, one of the Jewish holidays we always celebrated at my parents' home with my aunts and uncle. This year, though, Linda wanted us to come to her apartment in New York for the special dinner called the "Seder." That involves the ritual telling of the Passover story and the Jews' escape from slavery in Egypt. I wanted to do whatever would make my father happy so I asked him and he said yes we should go to New York. It meant my relatives in Baltimore who often joined us for holidays would not be there but at least my dad's single sister, Aunt Essie, would come because she lived in New York.

Dad asked Linda to invite Aunt Essie to the Seder. Linda flatly refused. She said Aunt Essie was an annoying guest because she complained a lot about the length of the storytelling ceremony and she was in a hurry to eat. While that's true, the service is long and pretty much no one (except Linda and Nat) likes it all that much, and it is annoying to listen to Essie whine, but the fact is families have to put up with that crap. The long service, the whining, it's all part of the holiday festivities. Linda should just have bucked up and invited our aunt.

Dad called me next because he was upset about his conversation with Linda. He was not a confrontational guy, and not at all comfortable with the role of demanding parent. But he really wanted his sister to come to the Seder. Not only because he wanted to see her but also because he knew she'd be alone otherwise and inviting her was the right thing to do. Since Dad never expressed this kind of dismay, I figured I'd better step in and explain things more clearly to Linda, who was not getting it. I phoned her and said Dad really wanted his sister there. I suggested she should let him have his way because his wife, her mother, had just died and this was the first holiday without her. Linda stood her ground. I got angry and frustrated. I called her "selfish" and she put her husband Natan on the phone.

"How dare you call my wife selfish?" he exclaimed. "You of all people. Many nights your mother and I sat up talking about you. She told me time after time how embarrassed she was because you had grown up to be such a selfish bitch."

Prior to that exact moment, I don't believe I had ever been speechless. But, his words hung in the air echoing in my ears and I couldn't form a response. My mom had never said anything like that to me. If she was unhappy with the person I turned out to be I was in the dark about it. And, while I found it hard, if not impossible to believe she would say that to Natan and not to me, there was a small part of me that wondered.

That wonder didn't quell my anger, shock, or horror, though. Even if it were true, what kind of man would say this to someone whose mom had died just two months earlier? What kind of mean and dark-hearted person was my sister married to? And, why did he hate me? I didn't want to upset my dad but I had to know if this could be true. So, I called him and amidst hysterical crying told him what Natan had said.

"Dad," I said, sobbing, "Did Mom think I was selfish? Did she ever say I embarrassed her? Or that she was ashamed of me? If she did, please tell me. I need to know."

"He's crazy," my dad replied. "Don't pay any attention to him."

I took my father at his word. I didn't feel the need to press further. His reaction was so immediate and definitive. It was as if Dad didn't even want to dignify such insanity with a more detailed response. I felt better and decided to move on with my life. But, those words do haunt me, even today.

We went to Linda's for Passover. Aunt Essie wasn't invited.

My dad was upset but in having to choose between his daughter and his sister, he had no choice. As a father he practiced unconditional love. I can't fault him for unconditional love but I believe a parent can love unconditionally and still be honest with a child. If my father had told my sister he loved her but was disappointed in her choice to leave my aunt alone on the holiday, it might have resulted in an argument, but in the end isn't it also possible Linda would have respected his opinion enough not to leave my aunt out the next time? If my dad had been able to articulate his true feelings while assuring my sister he could simultaneously love her and not like her choice, perhaps the communication in our family could have been better.

As it was, I'm not sure Linda ever understood how much her refusal to invite my aunt hurt my father. Although he did ask her to do it, he never told her how he felt about her actions. His desire to avoid conflict trumped his desire to be with his sister on the holiday. My father saw conflict as destructive to a family unit, as something to be avoided at all costs. He didn't understand conflicts are a natural part of any relationship. Strong relationships are often forged in the fire of conflict. Parents must teach their children conflicts will happen, they can be handled, and the result is often a tighter bond with greater understanding of the family members.

I think if my dad had told my sister she hurt my aunt and therefore, hurt him, Linda might have understood. He could have taken that opportunity to talk to her about how much family meant to him. He could have given Linda the opportunity to acknowledge she had made a mistake and maybe she would have apologized. In strong families, there are wounds and there is healing. Kids need to be raised knowing mistakes don't break a bond, they just allow for learning and healing. Wounds kept secret don't heal. They need air. And honesty. We had neither and it got worse. It is precisely this kind of behavior that leads ultimately to the bad post-parental death behavior that is so troublesome. Families like mine that communicate poorly or not at all are doomed to do very poorly dealing with death.

Chapter Six: Change at Jamaica

When I was a child I came across a book called "Change At Jamaica." One might think it was about trains because, in New York, to get to certain places by train, you had to take one line, get off at the Jamaica stop and change trains to a different line. I didn't read the book, and have no idea what it was about or who wrote it but I'm pretty sure, if memory serves, it wasn't about taking a train anywhere. It may not have been about anything having to do with Jamaica, NY, but in the middle of the book there was a page that said **JAMAICA** in large, bold letters. At that point, the reader was to turn the book over and start reading from the other side. I've always imagined the story in that book changed abruptly at that point, too, and a whole other story started after the flipping of the book.

Such is the case here.

Right around the time my mom died, a whole other storyline of family dysfunction erupted and took prominence in my life.

Consider this page **JAMAICA**. We will switch to a new train of thought, a new family story. This is the dysfunction junction. All aboard for an even more twisted and bizarre tale of family soap opera.

In the fall of 1977, just a few months before my mother died, I started law school after having taught for four years. I had always planned to be a lawyer and was just teaching so I could work for a few years to earn some money before going on to grad school. I liked law school and didn't think it was that hard during that first semester, although I actually had to study. I couldn't just fake my way through it as I had during all of high school and much of college. So, as finals approached I had some trepidation. Okay, truth be told, I was actually worried about taking those exams. I had heard they were really hard. And, the identities were anonymous so I couldn't even count on the professors being charmed sufficiently by me so they'd give me "benefit of the doubt" grades. In high school I was the frequent recipient of the "gentleman's B." In the classes where I didn't excel, otherwise known as anything math- or science-related, I would sometimes get Cs or even

Ds on exams. But, I was a good kid. I was nice, I was well-behaved, hell, I was just likeable. So, teachers would feel kindly toward me at report card time and they'd ignore my actual average and give me a B even if I didn't earn it. Hence my high school rank of 13th in a class of 850.

Having succeeded in school up to this point through a combination of luck and a modicum of ability mixed with a *lot* of likeability, I was understandably worried about these law school exams. I wasn't sure my holy trinity was enough to bring good grades. I was anxious. Plus, I had also missed teaching and began to have some doubts as to whether practicing law was going to be as satisfying as teaching. But, I wanted to do well on my finals and thus be able to choose my future accordingly. In other words, I may not have been sure about being a lawyer but I didn't want to flunk out.

That December 24th, Ned's dad, my father-in-law Jack, was going to turn 60. My sister-in-law, Anne and her husband Stuart were going to have his big birthday party in their home, but it was an event co-hosted by the whole family, me and Ned, Ned's younger sister Nan and younger brother Ted, and Ned's mom Bernice.

Anne was the consummate hostess and an incredibly talented domestic goddess-type person. She cooked, she sewed, she baked, she decorated, and she did it all flawlessly. She is a perfectionist and nothing less is acceptable. We knew we'd be given assignments for the party and we knew we'd be expected to perform them exactly as Anne dictated.

My last final exam was scheduled for Friday, late in the day. The party was Saturday night. My brother-in-law Stuart was a lawyer. He and Anne had been married while he attended law school so she knew just how intense those finals were going to be, especially since it was my first semester. Undaunted by that, and knowing there would be hell to pay in Ned's family if I used finals as an excuse not to contribute mightily to the party, I said to Anne, "Just tell me whatever it is you need me to do for the party and I'll do it." I figured whatever it was I could do it on Saturday after my tests were over. Also, before we knew about the party, Ned and I had planned that Christmas week trip to Florida, but we said we'd leave after the party and we'd stay at their house until it was all cleaned up so as not to leave a mess for Anne and

Stuart to handle alone. Ned has always been a dependable and reliable person. He wasn't about to let our plans to take a vacation override his responsibility to his family. If there was a party for their dad, Ned was going to be sure to help as best he could.

My assignment was this – bake two cakes and come over early Saturday to help set up. No problem. I figured I'd get up early, bake the cakes and then go over to help set up in the afternoon. Then I could come home, pack for the trip, and shower and change for the party. Ned was told to make a memory book for his Dad. He was not assigned to set-up detail, except for carrying in some chairs, which he could do by arriving early for the party.

I baked the cakes as planned. I was sure they would taste fine but they certainly weren't the works of art I knew Anne's cakes would be. I arrived at Anne's house at the appointed "set-up" time. My mother-in-law was already there, as were Anne and Nan. We worked throughout the afternoon. But upon arriving, I noticed something decidedly strange in Anne's demeanor. She seemed angry about something. She wasn't speaking to me; she hadn't even said hello. My mother-in-law chatted amiably and told me what to do but Anne never really said anything directly to me. I didn't know Anne all that well and had seen her moodiness before but not quite like this. I didn't feel comfortable asking her what she was mad about and thought maybe I was imagining something because my mother-in-law seemed not to notice anything amiss. And, I really hadn't done anything Anne could be angry about. I hadn't had any interaction with her that could have gone amok.

Ned and I arrived at the party later that day. Anne was clearly annoyed and not speaking to either of us. We stayed until 3 AM so we could clean every bit of party detritus before leaving on our trip, which, being young, we did right then in the middle of the night. Since we were driving to Florida with friends, it was no big deal since we could take turns driving and sleeping in the car.

It was at the end of that trip that my mother died. We brought her body home for the funeral. At Jewish funerals, it is customary for attendees to come up front where the family is sitting in the first pew. Attendees file by and extend condolences to the mourners. Anne was at the service but I thought she wasn't because on that day I never saw her. She didn't come up front to say anything to me, my dad, my sister, or even to her own brother, who was mourning the death of his mother-in-law. I mistakenly believed for a long time Anne hadn't attended my mother's funeral and only found out by looking at the guest book much later. But finding out she had attended didn't change the fact that my mom had just died, I was only 24 years old, I was devastated, and my sister-in-law couldn't bring herself to give me a hug or to express any condolence.

I never found out why.

A few months after Mom's funeral, Anne was still not speaking to me or to Ned. This caused a painful rift in my marriage and I wasn't having that great a year to begin with. After my mother's death I dropped out of law school. I realized practicing law was not my calling, but teaching was. I decided to return to the job I had always loved but it wasn't going to be easy to get back into the school system.

When Ned couldn't take the pain of the family dysfunction anymore, "for the sake of our family," he asked me to apologize to Anne for whatever I did that pissed her off. I didn't respond politely or nicely. At some level I understood he was counting on me to appreciate how much his family meant to him and for that reason, to put aside my pride and just give Anne what she wanted: an apology. From his point of view, if I loved him, I'd do this for him because it was of paramount importance, as it would mend his family's rift. I felt Ned was asking too much. I believed if he loved me, he would stand beside me while I was drowning. It felt like a contest between his sister and me. From my vantage point he was choosing his sister's side just when I needed him most. Ned left our home and we separated for a few days because he was so angry with me for being inflexible and not doing what he asked me to do. I guess he felt I didn't love him enough and I guess I felt similarly. I couldn't bring myself to apologize for an infraction I couldn't even identify. And, perhaps more important, I couldn't bring myself to bow down to Anne, someone who had hurt me so deeply and so recently by ignoring me when my mother died.

After Ned left I was feeling even more adrift because I was sad, I was lost, and I was alone. I didn't want my marriage to be over. I rethought

Ned's plea about the apology to Anne. Reviewing how serious Ned was about that apology request, enough to leave our home, and how much it pained him to have his family torn apart, I surrendered. It went against my grain. It felt like the wrong thing to do. I didn't think placating an unreasonable person was the right way to handle her manipulation of us. But I decided his sister's insane behavior shouldn't and couldn't be the catalyst for my divorce. Plus, I was just too weary and disheartened overall to put up much of a fight.

So I phoned the bitch. Well, that's what I was thinking as I dialed the phone, but really, I was conciliatory. No really, I was.

"I don't know what I did that made you so angry," I explained, "but whatever it is, I am sorry."

I figured she'd tell me what it was she was mad about and we could talk about it and work it out. I asked what I had done but Anne just skirted the issue and said something about being in pain, both emotionally and physically. She had sprained an ankle, or broken her foot, I don't remember which, but she was injured in some way. I thought I could talk sincerely then about how much I was suffering after my mom's death.

"Well, I understand pain but in order to know how much pain I was in when my mom died, you'd have to have broken every bone in your body. I don't think you understand how much my mom's death hurt me," I said, choking up as the words spilled out quietly.

While she supposedly forgave me and that conversation seemed to end whatever our mysterious "fight" was about, I heard years later that just after that conversation she called her mother, my mother-in-law Bernice, to tell her what I had said:

"Debby said she hoped I break every bone in my body," she reported to her mother.

But, as far as I knew at that time, things were okay after my apology. I wouldn't say I felt warm toward Anne. I continued to get the feeling she was either still angry about something or she just plain didn't like me. It's difficult to articulate what she did that made me feel this way.

She was so subtle in her treatment of me. Two illustrations might reveal how she made me feel.

Once, Anne, Bernice, and I were cooking together for a family dinner. Anne handed me a huge bag of a few pounds of shrimp and instructed me to peel and devein them. Keep in mind I grew up in a kosher home so my experience with shellfish was sorely limited. While I no longer observed the rules of keeping kosher and I ate shellfish, I had never peeled or surgically removed a vein from a shrimp. Okay, I knew they had shells, they're shellfish after all, but I had never seen one and I had no idea they had veins. Needless to say, I didn't know how to handle this task expediently. I figured out how to remove the shell; it peeled right off. I asked how to get the vein out and Anne said simply, "Use a small knife."

So, I got to work on that big bag of crustaceans, clumsily stabbing each one in the back and trying to extract the slimy black line that, I learned while I was doing it, contained the little guy's last bowel movement. This took me a while. I'm not sure how long it actually was but it felt like hours as Anne got exasperated and continually said things like, "Why is that taking so long?" and "Debby, are you done yet?" That scene would likely have left my mind years ago and been dismissed except for this. For years following that day, Anne would "joke" from time to time by comparing other slow things to how long it took me to accomplish the deveining. I can take a joke. I can be self deprecating. But her "jokes" felt insulting and hurtful. The way she said it did not feel like good-natured humor.

Another time I had spent the night at a friend's house. When I gathered my stuff to go home, I inadvertently left behind a bra. The next time I was supposed to see that friend was when she and her husband, me, Ned, Anne, and Stuart were supposed to see a movie together. We were going to meet my friends at the movie theater. My friend, also named Debbie, removed the bra from her handbag and handed it to me. I put it in my handbag. As you can see, there is nothing notable about that story. But, apparently Anne thought there was because for the many years following the "traumatic" scene she witnessed, whenever my friend Debbie's name would come up in conversation, Anne would say something like, "Uch, you mean that girl who brought your bra to the movies?" And, then she'd go on to explain to anyone else present how my completely classless friend had gauchely embarrassed Anne by whipping out underwear in public.

It wasn't just me Anne would find ways to belittle. When Anne and her second husband Dick were dating, they hosted a party at Anne's house. She said we could bring some friends so we brought a few close friends with us. Ned had recently sprained his ankle and needed to walk with crutches. When not walking he needed to keep his foot raised because it was pretty swollen. Upon arriving at the party, he wanted to be more comfortable and elevate the swollen foot. He took off his shoe and I can't remember exactly why but I think he was sitting on the ground (the party was outside) and to be seated more comfortably; he took his wallet from his back pocket and tucked it inside his shoe. When he got up to walk around a bit, the wallet remained in the shoe. Upon his return to his seat, he found his wallet was gone. We looked everywhere but it soon became apparent someone had stolen it. We told Anne but we didn't accuse anyone because there were about 30 guests, many of whom we did not know and we would have had no way of knowing who took it. Her answer was immediate.

"None of my friends stole your wallet," she announced defensively. "I'm sure it was one of your friends." She then named the friend she accused. And, again, for many years to come, she would refer to how sure she was that one of our friends had been shady enough to steal Ned's wallet.

These are trivial stories I know, but they felt meaningful in that Anne didn't let things go when it came to us. She didn't repeat any good stories about us; it was just these few she found compelling. But, these nuanced relationship descriptors aside, life as we knew it continued to pass uneventfully, family function-wise -- for a few years anyway. It was just enough to lull me into a false sense of security, so what happened later was not something I saw coming.

Chapter Seven: The Sublime and the Subliminal

On March 30, 1981, our daughter Alexis was born. We were full of joy and love and all kinds of fabulous emotions.

I was also scared to death. I hadn't had much interest in babies prior to that day. I had never actually held one or changed a diaper. Seriously, I was a baby virgin of the highest order. But, at some point, come to think of it, it was probably April 1, 1981, they actually sent us home from the hospital with the baby, thinking we were parents now and we'd know what we were doing. Happy April Fools Day, go forth and parent this child. Good luck with that.

My dad came over. He was probably one of the only people on the planet who knew less about babies than I did. Yes, he'd raised two daughters and no, I don't think he ever changed a diaper either. Which, it turned out, was not a record he intended to break. Although he babysat my kids for ten years, throughout the baby-hood of each one, he never once changed a diaper. He bought every diaper they ever wore, but changed nary a one. But, I ask you parents out there, which would you rather have? I was happy with the diaper-buying Grandpop. Hey, those things are expensive!

My mother-in-law came over too and proceeded to chase me around the house trying to get me to take off my bathrobe so she could wash it. She was seriously in need of an assignment. But, that didn't last long because Anne came over soon as well. She didn't come to help or to coo at the baby, however, as we soon discovered.

My friend Patti drove down from New York bearing two of my favorite things – lasagna and cookies. So there we all were, enjoying what was a day full of… well… joy. Patti and I were upstairs with the baby at some point, while my mother-in-law and Anne were downstairs in the kitchen, talking. Patti went down to get us a drink of water and came back empty-handed with sort of a quizzical, stricken look on her face.

"What's going on?" I asked.

"I'm not sure," she said, "but I didn't feel comfortable going into the kitchen."

"Why?"

"Well, your mother-in-law and sister-in-law are in there crying and talking."

"What about?" I asked.

"I have no idea but it seems intense and personal so I couldn't go in."

Not being too psyched about drinking out of the bathroom faucet, I figured I better go find out what was going on so I went downstairs. But, when I got to the kitchen door, I too heard what was going on inside. It seems Anne and her husband Stuart were splitting up and Anne was sharing this news with her mother in my kitchen. But, they stopped talking when I walked in so I felt really uncomfortable and got the hell out of the kitchen. Which was a bummer because besides being thirsty, I was also hungry. But, I figured if they didn't tell me what they were talking about (which they didn't, they just turned and looked at me with facial expressions telegraphing that I was intruding), I wasn't welcome to say anything or even to be in the same room.

We all hid upstairs for a while until Anne left. She lives right around the corner. My mother-in-law filled us in about what was going on and she left, too. She was quite shaken by the whole thing and didn't seem like she was in the mood to share in our continuous joy. I completely understand how hard it must have been for her to learn about her daughter's heartbreak while seeing her son's great joy.

I didn't think much about it at the time. But years later when I reflected on the timing of this breaking news story, it did give me pause. As I said, Alexis was born at the end of March. Anne and Stuart, it turned out, had been having marital problems for months. No one knew. The family had dinner together most Sunday nights at Jack and Bernice's house. Not everyone attended every Sunday but the weekly dinners were a regular happening. But even during the months before Alexis was born, nothing seemed amiss. I recall one Sunday night dinner that did have an odd aspect to it. Stuart announced at dinner he had a present for Anne. He handed their 6-year-old daughter Beth a box and told her to give it to Mommy. She did and Anne opened the box to find a diamond engagement ring, noticeably bigger than the one Stuart had given her the first time around. Anne's reaction was decidedly understated. While she did seem surprised, she didn't seem happy. She acknowledged the ring was pretty but didn't get up and walk across the room to give her husband a kiss or to say thanks in any sort of intimate way. She made a sarcastic joke about it being unromantic to have this sort of gift handed to you by your daughter in front of everyone. I dismissed that as a harmless joke resulting from Anne's obvious discomfort at being given this personal gift in such a public forum.

We found out later Anne and Stuart had split up, not right before the day we brought Alexis home from the hospital, as it appeared, but a few weeks before. I can't imagine why Anne would wait until our big day to tell her mother her bad news. And, if it had to be that day, why wouldn't she just have asked her mom to come to her house where they could speak in private?

The next few months were filled with highs and lows. Our time with our new baby was mostly ecstasy. Ned and I were nervous parents but really having a great deal of fun, too, despite being beyond tired. Ned was teaching but he'd rush home at the end of the school day to be able to spend every possible waking minute with his wife and baby girl. But, Anne would come over frequently and spend hours talking about her separation. She was more angry than sad and the conversations were extremely draining and exhausting. We wanted to help, though, so we listened and listened and listened. Regardless of the time of day, or how tired we already were, or what else we had to do, or what the baby was up to, we gave Anne our full attention and support. She said over and over her marriage to Stuart wasn't fun or romantic anymore. She said he wasn't exciting enough and their life together was dull and not what she wanted. Stuart was so predictable. He'd work and come home, eat the dinner she cooked, they'd put the kids to bed and then Stuart would sit on the couch, watch TV, and on the dot of 9:00, he'd eat a bowl of ice cream. Then he'd go to bed. On the weekends, if he had any free time, he liked to play tennis but that was about it for activities that interested him. Anne said she wanted to do things like ride a motorcycle, go dancing, and maybe even smoke some pot. Those were all things she missed by marrying young and dull, I guess.

Stuart would come over to our house a lot on weekends because he'd pick up his kids and either he'd have no idea where to take them so he'd bring them over, or he'd come by himself to talk about how sad he was. He said Willie Nelson's song, "You Were Always On My Mind" pretty much summed up how he felt about Anne. He was sorry he hadn't been more fun or attentive during his marriage but he had concentrated on working hard and earning significant money. He thought providing for his family made him a good husband and father.

Anne started going to bars right after her marriage broke up and she was meeting guys and dating a bit. She met one guy whom she liked a lot right away, sometime in the first few weeks of the separation. She was 34, had two kids, and was recently separated from her husband. But she told this guy she was 28, single, and living with her parents. When he asked her out on a date, she gave him our address and told him to pick her up there. She instructed us to hide upstairs so when he came he wouldn't figure out we weren't her parents and this wasn't her parents' house. We obliged. We were trying to be supportive, although we thought some of what she was doing was crazy. Ned has a strong moral core. His siblings know that very well. I knew he did not approve of Anne's behavior at this point but he worked hard not to let her see his disapproval.

Anne and Stuart dated each other a bit during the time they were also dating others. They went to some kind of counseling. Throughout these months, Anne constantly urged, begged, and even commanded Ned to "be her lifeline" to Stuart. She asked Ned to keep in constant touch with him, to be his friend and confidant, and to spend as much time with him as possible. When Stuart moved into an apartment, he got his furniture from my father-in-law Jack, who owned a furniture store. Anne asked Ned if he would do her a favor and help Stuart move from the temporary apartment he was in to his more permanent home. She indicated she wanted information about what was going on in Stuart's life. I suppose having information gives a person some power but I'm not sure how she thought that might be useful at that point.

Ned complied for a couple of reasons. First, he liked Stuart. Stuart had been his brother-in-law for 15 years. Secondly, he felt sorry for him. While Anne seemed to be happier after the separation, Stuart seemed to be getting progressively sadder.

Two years went by. Anne was living with her new boyfriend, Dick. He was the guy who picked her up at our house. Stuart was living with his new girlfriend, Carol. We were friendly with them, but as time went by we saw less of all of them.

Anne and Dick were doing what people in new relationships do, I suppose. And, since Dick was nine years younger than Anne and only 25, I guess when she was with him, she didn't want to be around us old married people with babies. We didn't see much of them at all. On weekends, she'd park her kids with her parents, or they'd be spending the night at their dad's and she and Dick would do what young dating couples did, I suppose.

Stuart and Carol settled into a married-type of life as they also raised Carol's son. They invited us over quite a bit and our get-togethers felt like real family. Anne and Stuart still interacted with each other because they had kids and money in common. Well, they had kids and money to argue about, anyway. Stuart made a lot of money. Anne wanted her fair share. How much that fair share amounted to was the cause of a lot of consternation.

Since Anne didn't need our emotional support as much as she had at the beginning of her separation, we really had no idea how bad things between Anne and Stuart had gotten, until one very strange summer day. Anne showed up at our house with our nephew, her 7-year-old son Rob in tow.

"Hide Rob in your backyard," she said, as if this were a totally normal request. And, she turned to leave, in an apparent hurry.

"I don't want Stuart to know where he is," she added, like that was enough of an explanation.

"I'll be back soon," she said, and got back into her car and drove off.

Later we got the scoop. Stuart had been sending a check for child support each month. But, this being July, their daughter Beth was away at camp. Stuart had paid for camp, so he figured he was justified in subtracting a portion of the child support that month. Thus the check he sent was less than usual by $500. Since Stuart was on his way to pick up Rob for a visit, Anne planned to hide Rob at our house and when Stuart got to her house, she was going to tell him he couldn't have Rob until he gave her the rest of that month's money. I have no idea what she told Rob who was expecting to go with Daddy that day. I'm guessing she came up with this idea just about the same time Stuart was due to arrive and that's why she was in such a big hurry when she dumped Rob at our house.

Shortly, Anne returned for her son and we never heard how it all worked out. But, it did give us an insight into a few things:

Money was a big part of this divorce.

These people would play dirty.

While Stuart would use money as a weapon, Anne would use people, especially her kids. I knew she was merciless when it came to what she would say about Stuart in front of their kids. Since the day we learned about the split, we had heard Anne say very nasty things about Stuart, not necessarily to her kids but to us and to friends and family right in front of her son and daughter. I never saw an instance of Anne trying to protect her kids from the vile nature of her commentary or from the details of the divorce discord. It made me uncomfortable to be in the same room as Beth and Rob when some of the issues were discussed. By contrast, when we were with Stuart he never once trashed Anne when his children were within earshot. I can't say it never happened but I can say I never witnessed it.

But, as I said, we saw less and less of them. We worked hard to stay neutral in this divorce. For one thing, we cared about both Anne and Stuart and also there were kids involved. Ned and I believe even in the nastiest divorces, if you have kids you have a responsibility to treat each other with a modicum of respect. You owe it to your kids not to destroy their lives or their self-respect, or their respect or love for both parents. Kids need their parents, even if the parents detest each other.

And, even though we saw less of all of them, Anne continued to push Ned to stay close to Stuart, which to some extent, he did. Ned and Stuart had become friends and, even more important, Anne had stopped involving us with anything having to do with her kids. On weekends she'd spend time with Dick and the only times we saw our niece and nephew were when they were with Stuart and Carol. We wanted Alexis to know her cousins so we put our family energies into that relationship.

A few months after the "Hide Rob" affair, an innocent Halloween party turned into a very scary affair, indeed. Stuart and Carol invited us and also Ned's brother Ted and his wife Kelly to a Halloween party. We all accepted the invitation.

Anne showed up at our door the day before the party.

"You're not allowed to go to Stuart's party," she ordered. "I don't like the way he treats me. I've decided you can't see him anymore. You need to cut him off now. Tell him that you won't come to the party and you won't see him ever again."

Ned said, "I'm your brother and I want to support you as best I can but this isn't reasonable. All this time you've asked me to stay close to Stuart. Now, all of a sudden, you decide that doesn't work for you anymore and I have to cut him off? I'm sorry, that doesn't feel right. I'm not going to do that."

"Well," Anne countered, "if you go to Stuart's party, I'll never speak to you again."

She didn't go into much detail about why she unilaterally decided Ned and Stuart's relationship should end. She didn't describe how our party attendance would adversely affect her other than to say she just didn't want us there. She said something about wanting to ruin Stuart's party, too.

"He isn't giving me enough money," she explained further, "and he treats me disrespectfully. You can't associate with someone who does that to me."

Ned repeated he didn't think it was right, respectful to him, or fair for Anne to make this demand. He said she had spent more than two years insisting he stay close to Stuart and "be her lifeline" and he had done so. He said his relationship with Stuart didn't mean he didn't support Anne. She was his sister and he loved her and would continue to support her to the extent he could. But, Ned explained that in the time since Anne and Stuart had separated, at Anne's insistence he and Stuart had become pretty good friends. Because of the kids they had also maintained a familial relationship. He repeated his plea that for the sake of her children, Beth and Rob, everyone in Anne's family should work at remaining civil to Stuart. As Beth and Rob's uncle, Ned believed he and Stuart could and should be friends or at least they should be respectful and warm in their dealings with each other. Being rude and not showing up at the party was unnecessary, petty, and didn't facilitate the maintenance of respect.

Ned explained he had already accepted the party invitation and didn't feel right not showing up. He also said he didn't think Anne had the right to demand he jump through her hoop about whom he could or couldn't see socially. He encouraged her to consider the benefit to her children if she too maintained a civil relationship with Stuart.

Anne was having none of it. She didn't respond to any of Ned's logical points. She simply repeated if Ned and I went to the party she would cut him out of her life entirely and forever. She also asked her brother Ted not to go, but he told us she didn't threaten to cut him off if he went.

Ned and I discussed the options. Ned felt Anne's request was unreasonable, her thinking was flawed in terms of the family unit, and it was wrong to enable her to act this way by submitting to her threat.

All four of us – Ned and I and Ted and Kelly -- went to the party.

Anne said she was really angry with Ned. She did not say she was angry with Ted, though. We assumed her anger toward Ned would abate over time. We couldn't have been more wrong.

Chapter Eight: Grandpop

One Friday night about 13 years after my mother died, I sat in my parents' kitchen mindlessly spinning around on a lime green swivel chair. Those 30-year-old chairs matched the psychedelic floral wallpaper. In the 60s swivel chairs were the hottest thing in kitchen furniture. I'm not sure why anyone ever thought revolving quickly went well with eating, but I must admit I loved those chairs. Every Friday night that comforting rotation would spin me backward through time to my childhood for just a few minutes. It was one of the best parts of our weekly dinners with Dad.

As always, I could smell my dad's approach before I could see him. The sweet smell of barbecue twisted in the air with the smoky scent of cigar. My father walked up the steps from his den to his kitchen carrying a plate of slightly burnt, barbecued, kosher chicken. He was sporting an undershirt tucked into his belted pants. The pants were hiked up high on his short trunk. He had the ever-present partially chewed, mostly burned out cigar stub sticking out of the right side of his mouth. His undershirt had once been white; his pants were formerly black. But now, after numerous repeated wearings, and slightly fewer repeated washings, the white shirt was not so white, and the black pants were not so black. In fact, his shirt and pants were now virtually the same shade of gray.

Dad was breathing heavily, wheezing loudly enough to be heard from where I sat in the kitchen, several feet away. He reached the top of the steps, paused to catch his breath and coughed a croupy sounding series of croaks.

"Dad," I said as I rocked gently from side to side, "you don't sound so good. Are you feeling okay?"

"Yeah," he answered in a huskier-than-usual voice, "I mowed the lawn today and I probably breathed in some grass. It's no big deal. Don't worry."

Seven weeks later, he would be dead and my sister would be out of my life for good.

But that Friday night I did what Sid told me to do – I didn't worry. I took him at his word, as I had all of my life. If my father told me not to worry, I didn't worry. I didn't have to. Sid would take care of whatever it was I was concerned about and all would be right with the world. So, I sat and continued to spin happily, chatting breezily about my life, my kids, my job, and all things me. That was just the way Dad liked it. He didn't like to talk about himself. I'm not even sure he was capable.

I'm not totally hard-hearted, self-centered, or narcissistic. I did, at one point say, "Okay, Dad, but call Dr. Gold in the morning and let him take a look at you. You sound like you're getting a bad cold. Maybe he can give you something." Dr. Henry Gold did double duty in our lives. He was our neighbor and family doctor. His office was in his house, just four houses down the block.

My father was a terribly stubborn 79-year-old. He never went to the doctor. He really never had to. He had rarely been sick and never hospitalized. He didn't even catch colds often. The only time he'd been very sick was just a few years earlier when he had Shingles. One day he had sprouted what looked like a burn on his face and the pain must have been excruciating because he not only saw a doctor, he took aspirin. He even admitted it was unpleasant and he'd like it to pass. It was the only time I saw my dad suffering and I too wanted it to pass quickly. After all, Dad took care of me, not the other way around. It wasn't that I didn't *want* to take care of him; it just wasn't our way.

"Okay, I will," he placated me, "I'll go over there after I finish mowing the lawn in the morning."

It was a typical Friday night at Dad's. These Friday nights were the perfect respite at the end of the workweek. We enjoyed a few hours of unconditional love without drama. My mom had started the tradition of inviting Ned to Friday night dinner before we married. After we got married, we continued to join my parents for the weekly meal. When Mom died years earlier, my dad chose to learn how to cook and continue the Friday night festivities. Later, when our children were young, dinner at Grandpop's was probably their favorite time of the week.

Grandpop was especially enamored of our three little girls. They returned the favor by being equally crazy about him. He was pretty much the only babysitter they ever encountered. Anytime we wanted to go out on the weekend, Grandpop would come over and watch the girls. He never once refused or balked in any way. If our kids got sick during the workweek, I could take them to Grandpop's house and park them in his den with a juice box and a snack. Then I could tiptoe up the steps and gently wake him and let him know one of his precious darlings was waiting downstairs. I think it made his day, as he'd get right up and go downstairs to greet his little buddy and offer her breakfast, candy, or a trip to the video store. It didn't matter that Grandpop knew next to nothing about how to talk to little kids. Here's an example of his idea of small talk.

"Do you want a shot in the arm?" Grandpop would ask in his raspy, gravelly voice.

"No, Grandpop," any one of them might answer.

"How about a sock in the eye?" he'd continue.

"No, Grandpop," they'd giggle.

"Well then how about a sandwich?" he'd ask.

From the mention of the sandwich, they'd head to the actual goal of the conversation, which was that he wanted to give them candy. Since they loved Grandpop and also loved candy, this conversation was a constant in their lives. They didn't know or understand that he had no experience with little kids. They just knew he loved them and they loved him and they felt safe and secure in his company. Alexis would talk and talk to him about whatever was on her mind. Tamra would climb up and crawl onto his lap to snuggle, having no clue that Grandpop was not a snuggler. Nor did she care, she knew how she felt, she knew how to express love, and she believed that secretly Grandpop enjoyed the embrace. Shira just hung out near him and smiled. She was quiet but she was aware what unconditional love felt like and she just wanted to be near him when she could. Some days he'd pick her up at preschool and her teacher said Shira would smile from ear to ear as she saw his white car in the pickup line.

After dinner that night we sat on the small cement patio in the backyard. Ned and I sat side-by-side on the loveseat. It was old but comfortable because, although the furniture was wrought iron, it had luxurious cushions. They were quite worn, but certainly not to the point where my Dad would throw them away. Virtually nothing in my father's world got thrown away. He'd use almost anything until it pretty much vaporized. Those cushions were only 30 years old. In Grandpop's world there was plenty of life left in those things.

The spring night felt more like summer. It was sultry and warm. I leaned back, closed my eyes, and breathed in the spicy, green smell of that freshly cut grass. Dad walked around the yard, cigar stub still protruding from the right side of his mouth (yes, the same stub from earlier, it had been parked in an ash tray during dinner), replenishing supplies in his many homemade bird feeders. He fed the birds a combination of store-bought seed mixed with bits of fats and meat from that night's chicken dinner. I would've thought birds would consider it "fowl play" to eat one of their own, but apparently they didn't mind, because lots of them flocked around as soon as Sid filled the feeders.

My dad had always had a thing for all animals, but especially birds. My mother never wanted any pets. She insisted, and I suspect correctly, ultimately she'd end up being the caretaker of any family pet so she pretty much banned anything with fur or feathers. Since Mom had always been frail and sick, she wasn't able to take on the care, feeding, and especially walking, a dog required. My sister and I were permitted to have finned friends, so we often had tropical fish tanks or turtles. Dad had to find other ways to commune with animals. At the dog food factory where he worked, he kept a rotating supply of German Shepherds as guard dogs. They were always named King and Queenie and they were essentially Dad's pets. At home, he fed birds. Particularly one bird -- one very peculiar and perhaps magical bird.

Years before that Friday night dinner, in the early spring my parents began to notice a black crow in their yard night after night. They believed it was the same bird coming each evening. It didn't have any distinguishing marks. What it had was a peculiar personality. Seriously, this bird had a unique character the likes of which my parents, avid bird watchers, had never seen.

When I say my parents were avid bird watchers, I don't mean they studied birds and charted what they saw. I don't mean they owned a copy of the Audubon Guide and looked up the varying types of birds that frequented the yard. Nor did they look at anything through binoculars. I mean they *watched* birds. In cold weather, they'd watch them from the kitchen window that overlooked the backyard. In warm weather they'd sit in the backyard and observe their little friends. They loved this activity, perhaps because they didn't talk much and this gave them something to do so they wouldn't have to actually communicate with each other. There were always birds around because my father never missed a day of feeding them.

He had all manner of bird feeders. Some were made out of scraps of wood he rescued from a neighbor's trash and fashioned into something with a shelf .The shelf would serve as a landing spot for the birds and also as a serving tray for the bits of stuff my dad would place there for avian appetites.

Since Dad made dog food for a living, he knew quite a bit about what animals eat. Dad knew dogs were mostly carnivores, so the dog food he developed had little in the way of fillers. He believed some vegetables and grains were healthy for dogs, but canines truly needed meat to be at their best. He figured birds required a mostly seed and nut diet, but a bit of chicken skin thrown in seemed to attract the minions so that's what he fed them. I suppose he was right, as my parents' yard was a regular hangout for the hungry feathered crowd. I don't know why the expression to "eat like a bird" means to eat only a little. These guys ate like elephants. (Assuming elephants will eat everything in sight.)

That brings us to the crow who came to stay. Day after day, well actually, it was evening after evening; this bird would show up and eat everything that was put in front of him, also behind him, next to him and anywhere near him. I think it was a he. That bird acted very macho. My parents and I loved that bird's antics. My sister never seemed interested in or fascinated by him the way we were. But the three of us were totally into it.

The crow was punctual. My dad came home from work at 6 and had his dinner. By 6:30, he'd step out the back door, light a cigar, and make the bird-feeding rounds. This crow would show up about 6:25 and wait by the door. I believe he wanted to make sure he got first crack at the food. Guess he knew what pigs birds really are.

So, one night, Sid got home a bit late from work. He ate dinner on a delayed schedule and was therefore a tad behind in getting out to feed the birds. At about 6:40, my mom was sitting at the kitchen table, reading the newspaper, as she did every night. A tapping sound on the window right behind her startled her because the kitchen window was two stories off the ground. She jumped a bit and turned around. Imagine her surprise and bewilderment when Mom found herself face to beak with the crow standing on the windowsill tapping on the window with a penny in his beak.

I swear it's true. I have the somewhat grainy snapshot I took to prove it. The bird must have picked up a penny with his beak and used it to tap on the window as if to say, "Hey, it's 6:40 already. Where the heck is Sidney with my dinner?"

After that my parents had a nightly date with the crow. They completely loved this bird, especially my dad. Then even stranger things started happening. One morning when my dad left for work in his Wedgewood blue boat-sized Chrysler Newport, he thought he saw the crow in the backyard, but it was early and he figured he was mistaken. Before he could check it out the bird flew away. But, the next morning when he walked out the front door to get into the Wedgewood blue boat-sized Chrysler Newport, the crow was perched on the end of the hood like a feathered and funky hood ornament. And, that wasn't even the weirdest part. If my dad were even slightly prone to hyperbole, I probably wouldn't have believed this story. But, my dad was incapable of guile, even the smallest bit to make a story better than it was. Nope. If he said the bird rode on the hood, you could take that story to the bank.

He didn't take it to the bank, or even all the way to work. The bird flew off the hood when Sidney reached the turn around the corner. This went on for several weeks as spring streamed into summer. Then one day, no crow. Several days went by without the crow's visit. My parents worried about their feathered friend. But, just when they thought he was gone for good, he was back.

Minus one foot.

He had a bit of a stump where his left foot used to be. Guess he'd visited somewhere or someone who didn't like him as much as we did. We figured he spent a few days recuperating, and once he was back on his feet, (that is to say… foot), he returned to his former glory days. And, then he was gone again. No note. No fond goodbye, just gone. My parents never saw their crow buddy again.

The summer continued. Sometime in August my dad was reading the newspaper in the backyard when he exclaimed, "Well, ain't that something!" The Local section had an article about a crow appearing nightly in a neighborhood not too far away. The bird flew in, he ate, and he rode on the handlebars of the kids' bikes.

He had only one foot.

On warm nights like that Friday night, as we sat outside I think both Dad and I secretly hoped the crow would hop up again. We relaxed and watched our three daughters play. Our storybook little girls all had a good time taking turns squirting each other with the hose. Our Friday nights at Grandpop's house were like a deep sigh you let out to relax your entire body. Stresses melted away as we all nestled into Dad's capable and loving embrace. Of course, it was a metaphoric embrace. Dad never actually hugged anyone and definitely didn't kiss people either. It didn't matter. On nights like this particular Friday night we just enjoyed life in pseudo-suburbia (because he actually lived within the city limits), somewhat simple and idyllic.

Chapter Nine: The Second Death

The dust up between Linda and me that began just after my mother died lasted a few years until I gave birth to my first daughter. When Alexis was born, Linda was in Israel working on her Ph.D., so Natan came by himself to the hospital to see the baby. He seemed genuinely touched by her birth. He gave her a tiny gold bracelet.

Natan worked as a salesman for an importer of 18-karat gold. I had been teaching but after Alexis' birth I wanted to stay at home but couldn't afford not to work. Natan came up with an idea to help me. He suggested he could supply me with gold chains and bracelets I could sell privately at home parties or to individuals. He said he'd charge me "cost" for the items and I could mark them up modestly and make a profit. Thus, my little company, "The Gold Rush" was born. I was happy to have the work and was touched Natan would reach out to help me in that way. We ran the operation in this way – I'd order a few pieces from him, he'd let me know what I owed, and I'd send a check. Then, I'd sell the pieces for a fair price and we'd continue.

This went on for a while and it ran smoothly. At some point we had some sort of disagreement and Natan blew up at me. He said I had ripped him off for $23 by shorting him on one of my checks. I said I certainly would not have done that on purpose and given the fact I had been sending him hundreds of dollars, why would I deny him $23? He wasn't budging and he was mad. I sent him the $23 but his anger was relentless. The next thing I knew, my sister wasn't speaking to me -- again. She wouldn't take my calls. She didn't come visit my dad very often, maybe twice a year, but when she did, she wouldn't see my family or me. This put my dad in a very difficult position. When he knew my sister was coming, he just didn't mention it. He didn't keep it a secret: he just didn't make a big deal about the visit. We respected what we figured were his wishes and really didn't want to see people who didn't want to see us so we didn't visit Dad when they were there.

Four years after Alexis was born, my sister gave birth to her son, Isaac. I wrote her a conciliatory letter and she called and invited me to the *bris*. (Circumcision ceremony) Dad and I drove to New York together to attend. The other attendees were mostly family members on Natan's side. He had two aunts in Brooklyn and quite a few cousins with whom he was close. Linda didn't invite anyone else from our family, no Aunt Essie, no cousins, no one she was related to. There were a few of Linda and Natan's friends there, too. Virtually every person there said the same thing when I introduced myself.

"Hi," I said as I extended my hand (only to the women because extremely Orthodox Jewish men won't touch women who aren't their wives), "I'm Debby, I'm Linda's sister. It's nice to meet you."

"Oh. I didn't know Linda had a sister," they'd answer with a puzzled facial expression.

These were people who knew her for years. They were people who were in her husband's family and therefore her family. They thought she was an only child. She had never mentioned my family or me. We simply didn't exist. I felt like an outcast. I couldn't wait to get out of there.

My dad was pretty excited about having a grandson, though. I was happy for him so I didn't talk about how weird the *bris* party had been for me. Over the next few weeks, though, when I called my sister in trying to keep extending the olive branch and build a better relationship with her, I detected a brisk coolness on the other end of the line.

And for reasons I'm not completely clear on, the "feud" that started the year my mother died was reborn. Within a few months of her son's birth, my sister stopped speaking to me altogether. I had written her what I thought was a heartfelt and sweet second letter after the *bris*. I thought I wrote about my dreams of raising our children together bringing us closer as sisters. I didn't keep a copy of the letter so I can't be sure of my exact wording but that's what I meant, anyway. Something in the letter offended my sister. Maybe the fact I openly acknowledged we hadn't been close was too much truth for her to handle. Anyway, whatever the reason, she decided to cut me out of her life for a while.

A couple of years without speaking went by. Linda, Natan and their son Isaac would drive to Philly a few times a year to visit my dad but, again, we didn't go to his house then because we knew they didn't want to see us. We did, however, hear a lot about the baby from my dad.

"Oh, that Isaac is some baby. He's talking a blue streak."

"Isaac is some baby. He's already walking up steps."

"He's speaking two languages."

"He reads the New York Times."

Yes, folks, clearly Charlotte the spider was no longer weaving the words "Some Pig" into "Charlotte's Web." She was now weaving, "Some Baby."

We found it kind of amusing and yet a tad nauseating. I guess I was quick to be sarcastic about the way my dad referred to my nephew because I was annoyed with my sister and resentful of her rejection of me. But, my sister's visits -- although infrequent--seemed to make my dad happy so I didn't let on to him his waxing poetic about his one and only grandson was amusing and annoying. It certainly didn't detract from the attention Grandpop lavished on my girls. He continued to be their only babysitter. Every Friday night we'd have dinner at his home and on Saturday nights Dad would babysit so we could go out for the evening without our kids.

My girls loved staying with him for lots of reasons. First, being kids with the acute instincts that kids have, they felt his unconditional love and it just warmed them. Second, and perhaps more important, Grandpop was completely unfamiliar with the word "no" when it came to his sweet grandbabies. Whatever they wanted to do, from putting on endless "shows" (in which they'd loudly display their complete lack of singing or dancing talents to a rapt audience of one), to polishing their nails with hot pink polish while sitting on the living room sofa (yes, we did have to flip the cushions and if you take a peek at the underside of our couch, you'll see the big swath of pink), the answer was always the same – yes.

Our girls may not have been "Some Baby," but he was certainly "Some Grandpop."

My dad chose to stay neutral in the dysfunction between my sister and me. I'm sure it wasn't easy for him but it seemed like an okay choice at the time because after a couple of years, Linda decided to reconcile with me. We didn't have a big talk about it and never went over the whys or wherefores of our estrangement. She just quietly came back into my life. She started by asking my dad to invite us over when her family was coming for a visit and the interactions grew a bit from there. We never discussed the previous rift. We just pretended it never happened. Not that there's anything wrong with that. But then again, maybe there is. Perhaps if we had a good talk about our feelings, if we had worked at communicating about what had gone wrong, it wouldn't have gone so much more wrong after my dad died. But our pretending nothing had happened worked at the time so we went with it.

From then on we went to my dad's house whenever her family came to visit. Our children played together. We attended each other's kids' birthday parties. We weren't particularly close but it was nice for a while and I believed our relationship had the potential to improve over time. One summer day, Linda's family spent an entire day and evening with us. That included spending the day at our township swimming pool so the kids could be together and have some fun and then they were having dinner at my house for the first time ever. We don't keep kosher as they do but Linda trusted me for the first time, since I do know the kosher restrictions, to plan and execute a meal she could eat. We bought kosher prepared foods and made foods we knew were acceptable and we used paper plates and plastic utensils. It was a good start toward having a more normal family relationship.

But then, within the next year or so, I went to my dad's house for dinner and it was *that* Friday night, it was the weekend of Mother's Day in May 1991…. the one that began with the slightly burnt kosher chicken and ended with my father dying.

Between the dinner and the death, here's what happened. The morning after that chicken dinner, my phone rang. My dad had walked around the corner to visit his doctor, just as I had asked him to do. He returned home and called me to say Dr. Gold said he needed a chest x-ray and he should head over to Rolling Hill Hospital. Uncharacteristic for my dad, he was asking me to come pick him up and drive him to the hospital. I was about 39 years old, I had been driving for almost 23 years and up until that moment, my dad had never let me drive him anywhere.

I flew over to pick him up and within the hour my dad was having an X-ray and I was in the waiting room. After the X-ray Dad walked into the waiting room. Without making eye contact but instead staring directly down at the floor, he said, "They're putting me in the hospital." The technician who did the X-ray had cavalierly told him, "Your lung collapsed. It could be pneumonia or maybe lung cancer. The doctor will be in to update you."

About 30 minutes later, I sat on the bed in Sid's hospital room. He looked so small and vulnerable in that hospital gown, tucked into that sterile-looking bed. He had never been in a hospital before and I must admit, it freaked *me* out so I can't imagine how he felt.

Dr. Henry Gold, our neighbor and family doctor of 30 years, came into the room holding the clipboard that had my father's chart under his arm. In my head I'm chanting in prayer, "Let it be pneumonia, let it be pneumonia, please God let it be pneumonia."

Given that Sid had smoked cigarettes from age ten to about age 50 and then smoked cigars from about age 55 to his current 79, and hadn't opened a window during much of the last 20 years, I thought pneumonia was the very much less likely of the two possibilities. Additionally, the look on Henry's face did not say "pneumonia" and he was not smiling. His eyes looked tired and sad. He raised the clipboard, glanced down at it, flipped a page or two of the chart and then closed it, hugged it to his chest, sighed, moved his glasses from his face to the top of his head, and looked at my dad. He took a deep breath and let it out slowly before speaking.

"Sidney," he began calmly, slowly, and without any emotion in his voice, "you have lung cancer."

Shit.

"It's bad and it's likely too far gone to do anything about. You have a number of massive tumors in your lungs. We'll do all we can to keep you comfortable."

Comfortable.

Not alive. Not cured, just comfortable.

"So, Doc, am I going to die?" Sidney asked matter-of-factly.

"I'm sorry Sid. There is nothing we can do. We will have to run a few tests and I recommend you see an oncologist. But you don't have to stay in the hospital for long. I'm sorry."

Note: In looking back I find it interesting no other tests were needed to confirm the cancer diagnosis. No biopsies, not even blood work. Just one look at the X-ray and the diagnosis was definitively determined. I don't think that could happen today. In a way it was better that way, there was no excruciating waiting period.

With that, Dr. Gold turned and as he did he looked at me with a slight, sympathetic smile. He exited, leaving my dad and me alone to process what he had said. It wasn't easy to digest. I thought I might actually throw up as I felt my stomach heave. But, I got ahold of myself and swallowed the lump in my throat so I could say some really important things to my dad.

My mom's death flashed through my mind. I remembered the years of regret I had for never having told her what she meant to me. I recalled the void of never having said goodbye and I love you properly. I wasn't about to let that happen again. I heard a death sentence and I was off and running.

"Dad," I started, and then launched into a long and endless sentence.

"I just want to tell you that although I never said anything like this, I want you to know you are the best father anyone could wish for and you have no idea what an incredible teacher you are because you've taught me so much about what really matters in life, and it's not just me, you've been a loving father to Ned too and a fabulous grandfather to my girls who think you are a truly wonderful person and we love you like no one else on earth and I never want you to doubt you are loved and appreciated and know this -- your life has mattered and you will leave a great legacy of love."

I was afraid to stop talking because I was frightened once I took a breath I wouldn't be able to go on and I so desperately wanted him to understand and absorb what his life meant to me. I knew "mushy" talk likely left him queasy and uncomfortable but I plugged on, determined to express my deepest and lifelong unspoken love.

Finally, I did stop and I looked him straight in the eye. He caught my eye for an instant and then looked away, kind of staring straight ahead, not really focusing. He took a deep breath and I waited with bated breath – literally. I leaned in closer in order to be sure I caught every meaningful syllable and every deep thought he was about to share. I knew I was about to hear the words I always felt from him but never heard. I was going to hear, "I love you, too." I just knew it. I held my breath a little and moved my head very close to his so I could savor the moment. Then I placed my head against his chest and hugged him. I just sat there in that position, head on his chest, arms around his body. I felt his chest rise and fall and heard a deep wheeze as he took in another breath. As he let it out, he spoke these words.

"Do you have a key to my safe deposit box?"

I sat up and looked him straight in the eye so I'd be ready for what came next.

"Yes, Dad, I do."

Then he stopped talking.

So, I waited, thinking he was just gathering his deep thoughts and he'd proceed with warm emotional words. But he didn't so we sat there in silence for a bit, me looking at his face, him staring straight off into space. I asked him the first thing on my mind.

"Are you afraid, Dad?"

64

"What is there to be afraid of?"

"Well, you know, afraid of what Dr. Gold said." I couldn't look into his eyes and utter the word "dying."

"Nah. There's nothing I can do about it. I can't change it. Being afraid wouldn't help."

Somehow that didn't do it for me. I was scared to death.

Chapter Ten: The Leftover Family

True to her word, after we went to Stuart's Halloween party, Anne did cut us out of her life. And she didn't stop there. She told any friends who continued to socialize with Stuart that they were banished, too. One of her close friend's husbands had died of cancer at 37 that year. The couple had been good friends with Anne and Stuart when they were married. Anne insisted she wouldn't make a condolence call if Stuart was there. She wanted her friend to call Stuart and tell him he couldn't come over. Her friend said her husband had just died and she was too upset to be worried about Anne and her divorce. Plus, Anne and Stuart had already been separated for two years and I guess the friend didn't see Anne's comfort level as her responsibility. She told Anne she was grieving and she needed to be surrounded by her friends – all of them – and if Anne didn't understand that, then so be it. Anne chastised the friend. She also suggested that while the husband had been sick they should have checked in with her boyfriend Dick who was a chiropractor. Anne insinuated Dick might have been able to save the husband by curing his cancer with chiropractic treatment. Needless to say, this all sufficed to end that friendship. Anne didn't seem to care about losing that friend and said as much. By then she was firmly ensconced in her "my way or the highway" lifestyle.

This manifested itself in a few ways. Chiropractic medicine was one of Anne's requirements for acceptance into her life. People who were close to Anne had to believe in the efficacy of the practice. They also had to allow Dick to "adjust" them regularly. Her children were "adjusted" all the time. This caused a problem with Stuart who did not believe his kids were in need of this bit of "medical" care. But, Stuart did not get his way on this because Dick did work on the kids. Anne's parents were a mixed bag of acceptance. Her mother, Bernice, accepted the concept of chiropractic and assented to being adjusted from time to time. She also agreed to buy the supplements and vitamins that Anne sold at Dick's office. Bernice was such a devoted fan that when our daughter Tamra was found to have the same condition I had as a child involving an underdeveloped ureter, Bernice suggested "Dr. Dick" could cure her. Since Tamra was already under the care of a top urologist at Children's Hospital of Philadelphia, we decided "Dr.

Dick's" attention was unnecessary and opted out. Anne's father, Jack, thought chiropractic was akin to quackery. He abstained from being adjusted. Nan and Ted did not see "Dr. Dick" professionally but my sister-in-law Kelly did once go for adjustment. Afterward she was in serious pain and never went back. On the years when Ned and I were "in" the family we also chose not to allow the "doctor" to adjust us. We were in no pain, had no back problems, and were of the mindset, "If it ain't broke, don't fix it," when it comes to our bodies. I guess Anne didn't feel too kindly toward our view because she made it clear if you respected her, you'd let Dick adjust you. Most of her friends were supportive and more willing to be adjusted than we were.

Meanwhile, Anne told her parents they also had to cut their former son-in-law loose. They weren't allowed to see him or speak with him and couldn't see their grandchildren when they were with their father. My father-in-law said once if the only way he *could* see his grandchildren was to go through Stuart, well then, he didn't have to see them at all.

As time went by, Anne got increasingly bitter and angrier about marriage. At Ted and Kelly's wedding, Anne remarked loudly enough for Kelly's mom to hear, "I give it a year." No one called her on her rudeness or tried to stop the runaway train of her bitterness. People were afraid of her. Those close to her knew she had excised us from her life. People who wanted to remain in her circle, her parents, her other siblings, her kids, and some of her friends, understood the consequences of disagreeing or disobeying Anne so they went along with whatever she asked, whether it was submitting to chiropractic adjustment or supporting the charity of her choice.

The thing is Anne could be loving and generous and fun to be around. Her perfectionism manifested itself in some great ways. Gifts from her were usually terrific, thoughtful and meaningful. For example, part of our wedding present from her was a beautiful heart-shaped, ruffled pillow she sewed using a blue and white gingham material, large checks on the pillow, tiny checks on the ruffle. She had embroidered our names and a cute boy and girl holding hands on the front. This gift illustrates a side to Anne's character that was quite nice. First, the piece was exquisitely crafted. It expressed a romantic feeling about marriage in general and our union in particular. That was all beautiful. With actions like that it's understandable why some of Anne's friends and family looked up to her and thought she was of sterling character. When she was on your side, she was able to make you feel valued. She could be attentive. She also had a good sense of humor and enjoyed fun times with relish. Her ability to be that person was part of the secret to her power. You wanted to be lavished with the kind of support and caring you knew she was capable of sharing. She began signing her correspondence, "Love and Light, Anne." People near her wanted to be showered with her "love and light."

So, when Anne ultimately decided the rest of the family should cut me, Ned, and our kids off (by then our second and third daughters, Tamra and Shira were born), her parents and siblings were somewhat willing to comply. When Anne said we shouldn't be invited to the weekly Sunday night family dinners and she would no longer attend if Ned and I were welcome too, the dinners ceased to exist. Ned and I tried to convince his mom giving up these weekly dinners was not a good idea. We suggested the dinners should continue with everyone invited. We said if Anne chose not to come, so be it. We believed despite how Anne felt the family unit should remain as intact as possible. We figured that if the dinners continued, eventually Anne would feel left out and she would come back into the fold. Yes, there was a rift in the family but we thought with continued work and open communication among the family members, the wound would heal.

Or not. But at least the rest of the family would stay together in the face of this adversity. But, my mother-in-law couldn't or wouldn't stand up to Anne in that way. Anne wanted these dinners to end; she wanted my mother-in-law to believe that Ned's disloyal treatment of her was the monster that destroyed the family. She didn't see herself as responsible for the family's undoing, she saw Ned as wholly responsible. And, my mother-in-law, never having been the strongest person, and certainly not where Anne was concerned, relented. She didn't even put up a fight. She just stopped inviting us to those weekly gatherings. We felt quite shut out and unimportant. Ned was hurt that Anne's demand seemed to count for more than his request for reasonableness. Ned felt keeping the family unit together was of paramount importance. He saw Anne's demand for the dinners to cease as destructive to the family unit. If two family members disagree, do you just destroy the family or let it be destroyed? He couldn't understand why his parents would opt for the choice that would tear the family apart rather than attempt to mend the rift. He felt unheard by his parents, who mattered to him a great deal.

We were invited to dinner at Jack and Bernice's every once in a while. It would be just our family of five and a random distant cousin or friend of Jack's and Bernice's. My in-laws never told us in advance who would be there. We would just be surprised when we arrived. It was often someone we didn't know. As a result, those dinners were somewhat uncomfortable and a bit awkward. If there was a new person or people at the dinner, it somewhat limited the conversations to topics of common knowledge or small talk. The inability to talk about anything of substance on a regular basis enhanced the shallowness of our relationship with Ned's parents.

After the weekly dinners were eliminated, Anne's next attack was on holiday celebrations. Since the family couldn't, by Anne's decree, be together as a complete unit that pretty much ended holidays spent together as a family. For one thing, Ted and Kelly moved to California so they were no longer local. Ned's younger sister Nan was a single woman and would go wherever her parents went. My in-laws chose to spend every holiday with Anne, despite invitations from us. Eventually we stopped inviting them. Sometimes, if Anne and her family were out of town, my in-laws would come to us or invite us to their home for a holiday. But, never--not once--when they *could* spend a holiday with her, would they *choose* to spend it with us.

Anne and Dick got married one year on Valentine's Day. We had heard from Bernice they had a wedding planned for March 1 so when we heard from a friend who worked in the local courthouse that Anne and Dick had been married there on Valentine's Day, we were surprised. We knew there was a Judge Goodheart at the county court who made a big deal of marrying couples on Valentine's Day. It made the local news each year. I guess Anne and Dick thought a ceremony on that day would be ultra romantic. So, the next time we saw my mother-in-law, after we learned about the wedding, we congratulated Bernice on her daughter's nuptials. Mom had no idea what we were talking about so we told her our friend had seen Anne and Dicks names on Judge Goodheart's record of the Valentine's Day weddings at the courthouse. Bernice basically accused us of lying to make Anne look bad because she believed Anne would never do such a thing – marry in private without telling her parents or inviting them to attend. That is, however, exactly what Anne did do, despite having a wedding on March 1 anyway. When we told Ned's mom about the courthouse wedding and she said no such thing had occurred, we suggested she ask Anne. Mom said she would never ask Anne if the story about the Valentine's Day wedding was true. She said she was so sure it wasn't true she didn't have to ask. I suspected she knew it was true and didn't want Anne to be angered by the question.

Stuart and Carol got married too. Beth and Rob shifted back and forth between homes and parents.

Years went by. We were civil for the most part with Ned's parents and Ted, Kelly, and Nan. The occasional dinners continued. Sometimes Nan would be there but we rarely saw her independent of those occasions. Ted and Kelly and their sons visited Pennsylvania every few years so we saw them then and once or twice we went to California to visit but we weren't close.

When we were with Jack and Bernice it felt like we were playacting a family rather than actually being one. Every so often, something bad would flare up and cause disruption in our pretense of family. Once Bernice was babysitting for our girls. When we went to pick them up, we discovered Bernice had taken our girls to visit Anne. We were pretty angry about it. After Anne stopped the family dinners, we didn't see her at all. Years went by without our girls seeing her as she had chosen to opt out of their lives when she opted out of ours. If Bernice arranged visits for our daughters and Anne that would have been quite bizarre for our little girls. Why make them uncomfortable by subjecting them to a visit with an "aunt" whom they didn't really know? They knew she existed and they knew she was angry with us and wouldn't speak to us. That was sufficient information for kids of their ages.

We had an incident involving Anne and our girls that had pretty much cemented our belief that seeing their aunt was not a good thing for them. One year Bernice and Jack decided to throw themselves a big anniversary party/vow renewal ceremony. Alexis, Tamra and Shira were still quite young, perhaps about 6, 4 and 3. The party was in a restaurant and there were about 50 people there. While we saw Anne and Dick there, they were sitting with a table of their friends who had been invited. We did not have friends who were invited so we sat at a table in the corner of the room, mostly by ourselves, which was fine because we'd be able to have a great deal more fun that way. Our kids were running around, all dressed up and having a pretty good time playing at this "fancy" affair, a rare special event for them. At one point I turned and was quite shocked (read: horrified) to see Anne down the hall of the restaurant where she sat on a sofa and posed for a photo with our daughters sitting next to her and on her lap while her husband Dick took the picture. I hadn't seen Anne approach my girls and ask them to come with her. By the time I saw what she was up to they were already being photographed. It wasn't the photographing of them that annoyed me. It was her brazen belief she had the right to interact with my kids without me there and without my permission. Also, I did not trust her. I had no idea what she might say to my kids. I had heard her say such harsh things about Stuart to her own children I worried about the nasty things she would say to my kids about me and Ned. I didn't want that to happen. The only way to prevent it was to make sure they were never alone with her. I walked over and told Anne in no uncertain terms she was never to approach my daughters again.

"Leave my daughters alone," I said quietly but in no way nicely. "Don't even think about talking to them. They hardly know who you are. They don't need to be confused. You are not allowed to take their picture or to speak to them unless I'm with them. Better yet, just stay away from them."

"Oh, grow up, Debby," was Anne's snappy retort.

As we walked away, the girls proceeded to jabber about their "adventure." Alexis, Tamra, and Shira said Anne had asked them to come with her to take the picture. They said they weren't all sure who she was and they didn't want to go with her. Alexis knew who Anne was so she didn't fear physical harm from her but Tamra and Shira were unsure. They were more than a little scared of Anne (Who wouldn't be?). The only thing Alexis knew about her aunt was she was mad at her mommy and daddy. Tamra and Shira thought Anne was a witch as she was dressed head to toe in black. Part of her outfit, the high neck and sleeves and legs were black lace and truth be told, it all looked strangely sinister. The idea of being with someone who didn't like their Mommy and Daddy made Alexis uncomfortable. But she was a good little girl and didn't want to disrespect an elder so when Anne said, "Oh you look so pretty, come with me I want to take a picture of you," they went along. But, when they heard Anne spit out "Grow up, Debby," they knew this was a person who was angry at their mommy so then they were worried we might be angry with them for cooperating with her. We assured them they had done nothing wrong. I admitted I was angry with Anne for making them uncomfortable but said I was not at all angry with them.

Bernice had heard from Anne I wouldn't let her take a picture of the girls. In fact, Anne told Bernice I stopped her from taking that picture and all she wanted was a nice photo of her nieces because she didn't get to see them. Anne told her mother I had yelled at her, embarrassed her, and stopped her from getting the photo she innocently wanted as a remembrance of the nieces she was not allowed to see. I found that hard to believe. Here was a woman who was opting out of my kids' lives. Why would she really want a photo of them? I had no evidence Anne cared about my children at all. But, I kept that to myself and explained to Bernice that while it was true I had angry words with Anne and I didn't want her around my kids, I had not stopped the picture taking because it had happened before I got over there. Bernice argued Anne said there was no picture and I must be lying about the photo being taken. A few weeks later, though, I saw a new, framed photo in Bernice's living room. It was the picture of Anne and my daughters, taken at the party. I pointed out to Bernice the photo I supposedly wouldn't allow to be taken was, at that very moment, in her living room. I clearly had not lied about that incident but Anne actually had. Whoops. Bernice had no response.

So, Bernice knew for sure we didn't want our daughters to go to Anne's house. But soon after that when Anne heard Bernice was babysitting our girls, she asked her mother to bring them over. As always, Bernice couldn't say no to Anne. When we picked the girls up they had mini pumpkins they were very excited about. We asked them where they got those cute things. They looked at each other and hesitated a bit before telling us Aunt Anne had given them the pumpkins when they visited her earlier that day. Mimi (what they called Bernice) had not used the word "lie" but she did tell our daughters the visit with Anne should be their "little secret" known only to Anne, Mimi, and the girls.

We were angry with Bernice and we told her so. Her response was Anne was their aunt and wanted to see them. She said she didn't see how that could harm the girls. We said she knew we didn't want our kids subjected to Anne and Bernice just shrugged that off. We told her there were not to be any more visits with Anne for our kids. We felt it was too confusing. We asked the girls if they liked visiting Anne and they said they did not. They had uncomfortable feelings while they were there and they found Dick downright creepy.

Another time after a visit with her grandmother, in the car on the ride home six- or seven-year-old Alexis asked us, "What's an affair?"

"What's that honey?" we asked, somewhat incredulously. "Where did you hear that word?"

"Mimi said Uncle Stuart had an affair and that's why he and Aunt Anne got divorced," Alexis replied.

"Maybe you misunderstood Mimi," we answered, knowing full well Alexis was simply repeating exactly what she heard but being caught off guard and taken aback we were just looking for a way out of this uncomfortable yet infuriating moment.

"Uncle Stuart and Aunt Anne got a divorce because they weren't happy together and didn't love each other anymore," we explained.

With a few moments for it to sink in, being taken aback morphed into being stunned. What kind of grandmother would share that sort of information with three little girls? We dropped the girls off at my Dad's house and turned the car around and made a beeline back to Bernice's house.

We told her what Alexis had asked us and explained if she could not refrain from having these kinds of conversations with our little girls then maybe it would be best if she not be left alone with them. Bernice was quick to throw sweet little Alexis under the bus and replied she had said no such thing to Alexis. She said we must have been the ones to tell Alexis about Stuart's affair. Or perhaps Alexis overheard us talking about it. Well, we didn't know about any affair so clearly we hadn't been discussing it. Anne had never mentioned to us anything about anyone having an affair. She had always said she was the one who wanted out of the marriage because she wasn't happy, Stuart wasn't exciting, etc.

Bernice responded, in that case, if it wasn't us she heard it from Alexis probably made the whole thing up. But, Alexis was not a child prone to flights of fancy of that nature. She was very specific in her question. She recounted exactly what Mimi had said to her. My mother-in-law had simply been caught in bad behavior. She lied to get out of it.

We let it go, though. We weren't ready to keep our kids from their grandmother. That was not what we wanted for our daughters. Our family may have been somewhat flawed but we wanted our kids to have relationships with their grandparents.

Things would ebb and flow a bit during the next few years, family-wise. We had to see Anne again at a family event when my father-in-law turned 70. It was another big party at a restaurant with about 60 or so people in attendance. Much like at the earlier anniversary party, one whole table of attendees was Anne's friends. While a few years earlier at the anniversary party we thought the presence of Anne's friends at her parents' party was odd, at this party we realized Jack and Bernice had developed fairly intimate relationships with Anne's close friends. Here's how we figured that out.

Claudia, one of Anne's nearest and dearest, got up to make a speech about her beloved Jack. As a "gift" to him, she told the following baseball themed joke because he loved the game so much.

A couple is at a baseball game. The woman leans over and says to her husband, "You kiss me between the strikes and I'll kiss you between the balls."

Ned and I, knowing Jack to be extremely prudish, were shocked. Jack didn't curse, he didn't tell off color jokes; we had never once heard one. Ned said he could only remember his dad using the F word once in his life. Jack, while he loved to entertain, did not do blue humor. So what was happening here? Did Anne's friends know Jack better than we did or was this one woman just too crude for words? Side note: a few years after that party, Anne cut Claudia out of her life when Claudia didn't want to get involved in something Anne wanted her to participate in.

Sometime during that party Anne told Ned her life was perfect except for her bad relationship with Ned. She said if he swore never to talk to Stuart again, she'd take Ned back into her life. (Cue the quote from Michael Corleone in "The Godfather" here, "Just when I thought I was out, they pull me back in.") She also suggested perhaps their relationship didn't need to include me (if only it were that easy for me to never see this lunatic again), but she never said why she detested me so much. We shouldn't have been surprised. Anne had not kept it a secret she didn't like me. Despite our lovely wedding gift from her, she hadn't really ever been that interested in us as a couple.

Anne's dislike of me may have started with my bridal shower and may have been partially my fault. You be the judge. When Ned and I got engaged, we planned to be married six weeks later. In 1974, as a wannbe hippie, I was concerned about being too materialistic. I did not want a bridal shower and I suspected my friend Eileen would throw one for me because she had a bridal shower that summer and she loved that sort of thing. You can't really tell a person not to throw you a party because what if they're not planning to? Awkward! So, I did the next best thing. I told Ned to see to it no one planned a shower for me. The thing is our friends were all young like we were, some were unemployed, and none had any money to spare. I knew they'd get us wedding gifts in six weeks; I didn't want them obligated to get two gifts for the same occasion in the same month or so. Since a shower was going to be mostly for my friends, I wanted to stop it before it got started.

Unbeknownst to me, Anne wanted to throw me a shower. I didn't think about her being the one to arrange a shower for me when I asked Ned to nip any shower in the bud. I knew my sister would never arrange such a thing and Eileen was the only friend I had who loved those events so she was the only one I thought might plan one. Anne was not on my shower radar. I hardly knew her as she had been living in Alabama until just before Ned and I got married. But she was planning a shower and when he found out, Ned, as I had asked him to, told his sister I didn't want it. She didn't go ahead with it but she was mad…. at me, I guess, for unknowingly rejecting her act of kindness. Maybe, once Ned explained my value system and the reason why I didn't want this event, she may have felt alienated from me because I had a different set of values than she did. Adding insult to injury, Eileen was undeterred and insisted on hosting a very small shower with fewer than 10 people, despite my objections via Ned. I didn't find out about Anne's aborted shower until after Eileen's shower was over. The shower wasn't any fun and had a decidedly frosty feel to it. I guess Anne was annoyed and in retrospect who could blame her for that? From her point of view, I had rejected her overture but accepted Eileen's. Apparently I wasn't the only one who found the party "frosty." My sister was there but wore her winter coat buttoned up to the neck the whole time. And, even odder, it wasn't the least bit cold outside on that September afternoon in Philadelphia.

Even though we explained to Anne I didn't know about the shower debacle, I guess that shower thing planted the seed of dislike for me in Anne's head. That might have resulted in her not being nice to Ned and me as a couple, either. We were never invited to her house just the two of us. While her kids called Anne's friends "Aunt" and "Uncle" we were just Ned and Debby. About two years after we married, Anne and Stuart bought a beautiful home in the suburbs. They had been living in her parents' small row home, the house Ned grew up in. That house was paid off and Ned's parents had moved out of it to a larger home when Anne and her family moved back from Alabama. But, the house was small and in the city so Anne didn't stay long. When she bought her new suburban house, Ned's parents generously offered us the option to move in to the old family home. Since it was paid off, we would pay only the taxes on the house, making it a dream come true for us affordability-wise because it was less than half of the rent we paid on our apartment and money was tight.

Anne told us her settlement date so we could give notice to our landlord about when we'd vacate our apartment. When the date was set we told the landlord we'd be moving out at the end of the month. Days before we were to move into the new house, Anne announced to Ned after closing on her house she had changed her mind about her move-in date. Although originally she wanted to move right in to her new home and fix it up while living there, she decided she didn't want to do

76

that after all. She wanted to back up the move-in date and paint the new house before moving in. Ned told her we had already given notice to our landlord; we counted on not paying another month's rent and didn't think we could stay in our apartment past the date we had given him. If she backed up the date even a few days we might not have any place to go and if we could stay we'd have to pay for another whole month because they wouldn't prorate the rent. Anne was adamant about her plan. She didn't care about our additional expense or our lack of a place to be in the interim and would not go forward with the originally chosen moving date. She wanted her house painted first. And, who was supposed to paint her new home? Yes, it was us, along with Bernice and Jack and Anne's in-laws. Did Ned and I show up to do the job even after she made us pay the additional rent? Of course we did. Ultimately, she later decided she didn't like the paint job her family had done and had it all redone professionally while she was already living there.

But, putting all past grievances aside when at that 70th birthday party Anne once again invited us back into the family, Ned consented to Anne's demand. Well, not to the part about cutting me loose, he ignored that and tried not to think about how much his sister still disliked me. But he did agree not to talk to Stuart anymore. After the party Ned told Stuart about his decision. Stuart said he understood and we should do what we felt was right for our family.

So, we were back in the family unit for a while. Those Sunday family dinners were somewhat reinstated and we did start to spend holidays together. Anne, Dick and her kids even had dinner at our house once. My girls said they felt a little weird about it because they hardly knew these people who were supposed to be family. They weren't comfortable with them. I understood but I figured their discomfort would ease with time. I figured maybe Anne would prove to be a better aunt than she was a sister-in-law. I wasn't so sure about Dick though. He was kind of a doofus but I didn't know him well at all so I figured I'd give him a chance. Once Tamra and Shira, then about eight and six years old, were playing with walkie-talkies when Dick and Anne were at our house. Tamra was outside and Shira was inside, each with a walkie-talkie. They were jabbering back and forth in their inimitable high squeaky voices. Imagine Tamra's surprise when out of the walkie-talkie comes a man's deep, throaty voice saying repeatedly, "I love you, I love you." Tamra looked closely at the walkie-talkie and asked tentatively, "Shira?"

My girls were open to being won over but they hardly knew this guy, having only met him a handful of times. Dick pretty much lost them at "I love you."

But, a few months went by with no noticeable horrors in the family.

At some point that year, Anne and her 15-year-old daughter Beth had a falling out. Beth ran out of the house and ran to our house as we lived only a few blocks away. Beth said she had a fight with her mother and didn't want to go home. After that Beth ended up living full time with Stuart and Carol. Anne refused to speak to her daughter. This went on for three years. Although we were familiar with Anne's habit of cutting off people she couldn't control, we couldn't believe she would do that to her own daughter. We'd talk to Anne about the rift once in a while but she would just say Beth would have to come to her. She did not ever intend to reach out to Beth, she'd say.

So, since we weren't allowed to talk to Stuart, and Beth was then living with him, we also didn't see our niece Beth. Nor did her grandparents, Ned's parents, although they may have spoken to her on the phone, I'm not sure.

Beth was a troubled teen. She had bounced around in schools, unable to succeed anywhere. She had few friends, if any. So, when her 16th birthday rolled around, Stuart was not sure what to do. Sweet Sixteen parties were popular but how was he going to throw one for a girl with no friends? Even her mother would not attend.

We hadn't spoken to Stuart for six months, as Ned had promised Anne. But, Stuart was in a bind with Beth's 16th birthday. So when he called and told us he needed us to come to Beth's birthday party, we were compelled to listen. He explained he asked Beth what she wanted to do for her birthday and she said the only thing she wanted was dinner in a restaurant with her immediate family (Stuart, Carol and their sons), Stuart's parents, and us, her aunt and uncle and her three little cousins. It was scheduled for that weekend. Stuart had been hesitant to call, he knew about Ned's promise not to see him and wanted to respect it, but this was for his little girl and he wanted to make her happy.

We said we'd be happy to attend. We couldn't check with Anne because she was away on vacation. That Saturday we attended the rather sad event. The day after the birthday we heard from Ned's mom Anne was back in town; she already knew about the dinner (I guess Rob told her) and she was furious. Ned was disgusted with his sister and her reaction. But, I thought Anne just didn't fully understand the circumstances. I believed if I explained to her, face-to-face, mother-to-mother, exactly what happened, she'd understand. Yes, I understand that given the history of Anne, my believing she'd understand and forgive our transgression after listening to reason makes me somewhat delusional. I see that now but back then I was the eternal optimist. So was Ned, if you think about it. Otherwise why would anyone have repeatedly tried to make this family interaction work against all odds?

But, over the years, that was what Ned and I always did. We persisted in our belief if we were true to our core values of fairness and honesty and reason, eventually people would come around to understanding our choices. It was the reason why we'd always accept the invitation each time we were asked to rejoin the family. In retrospect I understand our believing that after being shot down so many times makes no sense. Rational thinking aside, we wanted to be part of a loving family, we wanted that for our kids and I guess if it took a little delusional thinking to get us there, so be it.

So, I walked over to Anne's house. She wouldn't even let me in. After answering the door and seeing me, she stepped outside and closed the door behind her. We stepped away from the house and walked down her front lawn as if she didn't even want me close to her home. As we stood out on the front lawn, I told her about Stuart's plea and about Beth's request and total lack of friends to invite to her party. I explained this was not a social event for Stuart and us, it was a favor we did for our niece who was also her daughter. I said we were unable to tell her before we went because she was away but now that she knew how it came to pass, I was sure she'd understand. I figured the sadness of her daughter's life would touch her heart and soften her resolve.

I gave Anne's heart too much credit.

Her reply blew me away. She said, "No. I most certainly do not understand. You had dinner with the devil. It doesn't matter why. I told you not to see him."

She never even acknowledged her daughter's needs or wants. She turned and walked back into her house.

We were out of the family once again. Was it annoying and yet also a relief of sorts? Absolutely. When we were "in" the family we were often waiting for the other shoe to drop. We were not comfortable at family events anyway and when we were able to be just the five of us at holidays and events, we really had so much more fun.

Which is not to say we never saw our in-laws. They'd invite us over from time to time, just not when Anne was there. Once they invited us over for the second night of the Passover holiday. The table was quite big. The two leaves that were rarely used were both in the table making room for about 15 people to fit around that table even though our group was only half that size. That was curious.

When, my mother-in-law began serving the food, we noticed something a bit odd. She was serving from bowls of food that had already been in the refrigerator. Usually, with casseroles and things like that, she'd put the baking dish on the table. Not this time. This time each item was already cut or sliced and on a platter. Then dawned the light. These were not foods she had cooked that day. These were foods that had been cooked the day before when Jack and Bernice had Anne and her family and various other people to dinner for the first night of the holiday. We were getting the leftovers Anne's group had not eaten.

It wasn't the leftovers that annoyed me. I am not averse to serving leftovers to guests. It was the concept of being Ned's parents' second choice being rubbed into our noses so obviously and yet so secretly. Had Bernice been more above board about it, maybe even saying the food was what she served last night, I think it might have alleviated the annoyance. It was the secretive nature of the way the leftovers were presented as food she made expressly for us. I understand it sounds petty to be complaining about how the food was served but it felt bad even though I can't exactly articulate why.

That wasn't the only time we clearly played second fiddle to Anne. Once, Ned's aunt Ruth was visiting from California. We stopped by Ned's parents house to see her. We were turned away at the door by Ned's mom. She said she was expecting Anne soon and we weren't welcome to stay. We could come back later, but we couldn't stay then. Aunt Ruth looked kind of horrified to see Bernice turning her own children and grandchildren away but we left quietly. If we were going to visit with Aunt Ruth, we'd have to accept a slot of visitation Anne didn't want. Ruth later told us she didn't agree with the way Bernice was dealing with Anne's demands on her mother and Ruth thought the way Bernice was doing things had facilitated the destruction of her family.

Chapter Eleven: The Best Gift Sid Ever Gave Me

With the diagnosis of lung cancer and the terminal prognosis, so began the last chapter of my father's life. When I heard the news from Dr. Gold, I needed to call my sister but I knew she wouldn't answer the phone because it was Saturday. I waited until nightfall and the end of the Sabbath to call Linda and tell her about Dad. We talked about how to move forward and what to do for Sid. Dr. Gold said Sid could leave the hospital right away as there really wasn't anything much they could do for him.

I asked my dad where he wanted to go when he was released from the hospital. I invited him to move in with us so we could take care of him. Linda also invited him to move in with her in her apartment in Manhattan. Sid chose to stay with me. He didn't give any reasons but it made sense because our house was bigger and we were closer to his home should he need anything. I knew, or at least guessed, he felt closer to my family than to Linda's but I never said a word about that.

We left the hospital and I drove Sid to his house to pick up some things. When we pulled up to his house, the house I had grown up in, he started listing some things I should go in and get. I said, "Okay, wait until we get into the house and then tell me."

"I'm not going in," he replied, and continued listing what he wanted me to bring out.

"What do you mean you're not going in?" I asked, confused.

"I don't want to. You can just get me what I need," he explained without actually explaining anything at all.

He wanted some clothes and the coin collection he kept hidden under the basement steps. That was all. He sat in the car while I retrieved the items he asked for. He never returned to his house or saw his home again.

In order to find a good oncologist, I asked around. My friend Dennis, an oncologist himself but too far away to treat my dad, said if Sid were his father, he'd take him to his friend and colleague, Dr. Cornfield. I was going to call Dennis's guy but Linda wanted Sid to see a doctor at the Fox Chase Cancer Center, a noted facility in our area. She got the name of a particular physician. I phoned for an appointment. They said there would be a 6-week wait to see that doctor. Dennis said he could get Sid in to see Dr. Cornfield right away the next day. I didn't think Sid could wait 6 weeks so I checked with Sid about what he wanted to do and he opted for Dennis's recommended doctor.

We went to the doctor's appointment, my father, Linda, and I. Dr. Cornfield calmly explained due to the size and location of Sid's lung tumors, there was nothing they could do in terms of treatment to prolong his life. He said Sid was too far along in the cancer for chemo to help. He did recommend radiation in an attempt to shrink the tumors so it would be easier to breathe and Sid would be more comfortable for whatever time he had left.

Sid asked, "So, Doc, how much time do I have?"

I had heard doctors rarely disclose a number but apparently Dr. Cornfield did not share that philosophy because he did offer a number.

"Three to six months."

After we left the office and returned home Linda flipped out because the doctor I had chosen had been so frank and candid. She did not at all appreciate the doctor informing Sid he only had a few months to live. She didn't believe Sid needed to know the amount of time he had left. She felt knowing was too upsetting. Interestingly, but not surprisingly, Sid did not seem upset by the number. Once Dr. Gold had told him his case was terminal, I think he just wanted to get it over with. I believe he was pretty much ready to go as soon as he got that news.

But Linda was angry. And, she was angry with me, maybe because the doctor I picked had shared the bad news. In order to placate her, I said I would try to get Sid in to see the doctor she had chosen too, the one with the six-week wait. Both Linda and Natan seemed annoyed with me but I wasn't sure why. I detected something amok in their demeanor but I chalked it up to their grief about Sid's condition.

Turns out, since Sid needed radiation and no other treatment, the doctor Linda wanted Sid to see agreed to see him right away because Sid's radiation treatments were going to be at the Fox Chase Cancer Center where that doctor was on staff. Although his prognosis for Sid was no different than Dr. Cornfield's in that he agreed Sid's case was terminal and he was not a candidate for chemo, he refused to put a number on it when Sid asked him how much time he had left. He simply explained he rarely gave patients an exact number or a time limit because no one could be sure. His suggestion was simply for Sid to get his "affairs in order."

We made arrangements for the radiation treatments and began making the daily trip. On the first day, during the drive back to my house Sid spoke and surprised me with this tidbit.

"I'd like to die in your house."

Gee thanks, Dad. Okay, I didn't say that, but I was thinking it. DIE IN MY HOUSE!!!??

I really had no idea how I was going to handle that. But I knew the correct answer and that's what I said.

"Of course, Dad. Whatever you want."

"I don't want to die in a hospital," he added. He did not elaborate. And, come to think of it, after you tell someone you want to die in his or her house, what else can you say? Sorry?

I'm sure he was thinking about the way my mother died and wanted no parts of that. I agreed. Just before Sid's diagnosis our friends Jerry and Robin had cared for Jerry's mom until she died of cancer in their home. I told them how brave I thought they were and I didn't know how they handled it. I said I was absolutely incapable of dealing with that. Well, now I was dealing with that. And I was not prepared.

The next few weeks were an odd combination of surreal and beautiful and, yes, even fun in a very strange way. I loved having Dad in the house. My daughters, then 10, 8 and 6 had a ball with him. They watched TV together. He taught them how to play the card game "Casino" (They loved the rule about the "good 2" and the "good 10."). They snuggled up with books to read to him. He showed them the coins in his collection and they examined them under a magnifying glass we had just given him for Father's Day. It was quite blissful. I was sorry I hadn't asked my dad to move in with us years earlier when we could have had more time. I knew he would never have agreed as he was a man who valued his privacy but that didn't stop me from wishing things had been different. It's only when we're out of time we realize we didn't make good use of the time we did have, I suppose.

And, then there were the deep thoughts and conversations we shared. One afternoon, at Sid's invitation, Ned sat beside him on the couch. Sid gave Ned his diamond and ruby pinky ring. It had belonged to Sid's long-dead brother Dave. Sid loved Dave and this ring was likely my father's most treasured family heirloom. Not that the ring was all that valuable. I'm sure it wasn't. The stones were small, the setting, a belt buckle, was not very ornate. Overall, it was a man's simple pinky ring. But I knew how much it meant to my father and I was so touched he wanted Ned to have it. Sid didn't say much when he gave him the ring, just something like "Here, I want you to have this," as he handed Ned the ring. Ned was deeply moved. He loved my father so much that more words weren't necessary.

(As a side note, a few years later my Aunt Essie also gave Ned a ring that was a family heirloom in my father's family. When she leaned over the table at the Jewish deli she chose for her 80th birthday lunch, she too handed Ned a man's ring and said, "Here, I want you to have this. It was my father's signet ring." Again, Ned responded with how moved he was by her gesture. She replied, "Yeah, my father was a real whoremaster." My father's family had a real way with words.)

After Ned accepted my father's ring, Sid breathed deeply, leaned in and said to Ned, "You know the lawn mower in my garage, the one with the stain on the concrete under it?" (Because there were at least two mowers in the garage.) Sid spoke slowly and deliberately, as if about to impart some long-held secret. Ned thought Sid was going to describe a secret cache of something buried beneath that lawn mower under the garage floor.

Ned leaned in to make sure he didn't miss any important details.

"Yes, Dad, I know the one you mean."

"Good. Throw it out," Sid instructed.

My family members…they really know how to communicate. So much for deep thoughts.

The other thing Sid wanted desperately to do during this time period while the weeks of radiation ticked by was to take care of his bank Certificates of Deposit. He had quite a few which were maturing during those couple of weeks but on three different days. He wanted to go to the bank and make sure the paperwork was in order so they'd all roll over. It involved about three trips to the bank, one as each CD matured. I drove him each time he had to go. The last CD was due to mature on June 27.

Meanwhile we tried to make the most of each day. Sid was quiet and calm and said he was not in any pain. He spent almost the whole time downstairs in my house. He went upstairs only to shower occasionally. He sat in the den, where we had put a bed for him so he didn't have to go up steps every day. The powder room is also in the den so he had his own bathroom. He'd also walk into the living room but he'd never go in the kitchen which was just steps away. Once, he said he'd tell me how to make his recipe for stuffed cabbage but instead of coming into the kitchen, he'd call instructions in from the living room.

"FILL A LARGE POT WITH WATER."

Check.

"NEXT, BOIL THE WATER."

Check

86

"PUT IN THE WHOLE HEAD OF CABBAGE. LOWER IT IN SLOWLY SO YOU DON'T SPLASH THE BOILING WATER ON YOURSELF WHEN YOU PUT IT IN THERE."

Check and check. And so it went until stuffed cabbage was ready to be served just the way he liked it.

This was pretty weird, his refusal to enter the kitchen, even for my dad who was odd in quite a few ways. I have no idea what was going on in his head. It was as if he felt the need to shrink his world down to just two rooms, in preparation for the ultimate shrinking his world was headed for. I didn't understand why, nor could I believe he never wanted to see his own house again, but I think making his world smaller made it easier for him to say goodbye. Or maybe he just didn't want any goodbyes. I don't know.

I dealt with this situation the way I deal with lots of things I know nothing about – I read. I read a Stephen Levine book about caring for the dying. It was helpful. One thing jumped out at me. It said when someone is close to death you sometimes have to give the dying person permission to let go. I tucked that away in the recesses of my mind.

Linda, Natan, and Isaac would come from New York on Sunday afternoons to visit Dad. They would tell us what time to expect them but they were often late. I guess it didn't matter but it was somewhat frustrating. One Sunday I had to attend a work-related party. It was an all-day affair for employees and their kids. I suppose I could have skipped it but I did feel an obligation to attend as it was at my boss's house and I knew it was a big deal to him. I didn't want to leave my dad alone for too long, though. So, I spoke to Linda that morning to explain about the party. She said she'd get to my house by noon.

I knew Sid would be okay for a short while alone so we left home around 11:30. When we got home at 4:00, Sid was physically fine but he was alone and upset. Linda and Natan never showed up and hadn't called. Sid had called their apartment but there was no answer. He was really concerned. It was long before the advent of cell phones so there was no other way to reach them. He worried they had some kind of accident.

Shortly thereafter, around 4:30, they arrived with no explanation other than they got a "late start." We were furious. Yes, Dad was okay but he hadn't eaten anything since breakfast (because he wouldn't go into the kitchen) and it seemed cruel to have made him worry like that.

So, I was not too nice about it and told Linda how annoyed I was. Ned went one step further. He told them they were welcome to visit any time and as often as they wanted but from then on they must call and tell when they were coming and they had to show up when they said they would. He said the only way they could visit was to agree to follow those two rules. Although he hadn't checked with me first, I supported what Ned said. It seemed the best way to protect Sid from being upset like that again.

Linda and Nat were pissed and they let us know. Plus, they went on to say they were annoyed about the doctor we chose and about the abrupt way he told Sid he was going to die soon. They blamed me for how upsetting that was because I had chosen that doctor. A lot of anger was unleashed. It wasn't a pretty afternoon.

But, the days passed and the next Sunday they visited again. I was in the kitchen preparing lunch when I heard Linda ask Sid for his pinky ring. He told her he had given it to Ned but he had another ring he wanted to give to Natan. Linda was insistent the pinky ring had to come to her family. After all, she pointed out, she had the only boy in the family.

"Well," Sid explained, "I gave that ring to Ned." He went into no further detail about how he decided who got what.

Linda was upset and angry. She said she had a son and she thought Isaac should have gotten Dad's ring. Sid didn't respond with much detail other than to repeat he gave that ring to Ned. He didn't elaborate about why he chose to give his most cherished possession to someone other than her husband or son. After a lifetime of dividing everything equally so he showed no favoritism, Sid had chosen a favorite. Linda was really angry and she said so. Sid tried to make it up to her. He said he had my mother's engagement ring and wedding band and he wanted Linda to choose which one she wanted and he'd give me the other. I suppose he figured if he gave her first dibs on the rings that had been my mother's greatest treasures, and I had to take the other by default, that would make my sister feel better. Linda chose the engagement ring but it didn't seem to make her any happier.

The next week was the last week in June. The radiation treatments wrapped up. Then, on Thursday, June 27th, I took Sid to FirstTrust bank so he could deal with the paperwork on his last maturing CD.

The next day was Friday, June 28. A hospice nurse, Debbie, visited our home to get Sid set up with their program. She said beginning on Monday an aide would come daily to help him bathe and dress and a nurse would come twice a week to check him. Sid didn't seem to be listening. He told the old joke:

"A doctor gave a man six months to live. The man couldn't pay his bill so the doctor gave him another six months."

He then seemed to fade away and stared blankly ahead. I wasn't sure if he even heard any of Debbie's description of what was to come in the weeks ahead. She told us he appeared to be near the end, with maybe only a couple of weeks to go. I was quite shocked as it had only been a few weeks since the doctor told us Sid had a couple of months to live. Debbie said when the end appeared to be imminent or when he died we were to call her and definitely not call 911 because they would take him to a hospital to die, the one thing Sid stated emphatically he did not want.

Debbie described the immediate future for Sid. She listed what he could expect to experience as the cancer advanced.

- Delirium
- Incontinence
- Significant Pain

Debbie said the pain would be treated with morphine so Sid wouldn't have to suffer. She warned the incontinence would require diapers and looked pointedly at me as if to inform me gently I would be the one in charge of that. She said some other things, too, but I think I checked out at diapers. I couldn't tell at what point she lost Sid because he didn't let on if he was hearing any of it.

Meanwhile, the doctor had prescribed the sleeping pill Halcyon for Sid. The bottle was on the table next to his bed. If I had Sid's prognosis I'd just want to take the whole bottle. I didn't say that to my dad but if he wanted to do that, I wouldn't have blamed him.

He never took any of the pills.

That night, we watched the movie "Avalon" together. Like many Barry Levinson films, it was set in Baltimore. Since my dad had grown up there, I thought he'd enjoy it and I think he did. He pointed out the places he was familiar with and was excited to see the Liberty Theater he remembered fondly.

The next day – Saturday, June 29-- Aunt Essie drove down from New York to visit her brother. Sid didn't say much at all. She asked him how he liked the movie and he said, "It was okay."

Those were the last lucid words he ever spoke.

Later that afternoon after my aunt left, Sid fell into a dreamlike state. His eyes were open but he was definitely not fully awake. He was lying in bed.

At one point, he said, "I'm worried."

I had never heard him say that before—ever. So, I asked him what was worrying him.

He said, "I'm worried about moving to Philadelphia."

Since that move had taken place in 1963 and it was now 1991, I felt comfortable assuring him he need not worry.

"You don't have to worry about that anymore, Dad. We moved and we were all just fine. The factory did really well. We all had good lives."

Next, he said, "It's a big job."

90

"What is, Dad?"

But, he didn't tell me what he was referring to.

A few moments later he sat up, opened his eyes wider and said, "Why don't they teach others what they know?"

"Who, Dad?" I asked.

He didn't answer. Those were the last words of his life. He lay back down. Upon closer inspection of the expression on his face I discovered he wasn't talking to me. His eyes were open and he was looking at and talking to someone, but it surely wasn't me.

It blew me away because Sid just didn't speak like that. He NEVER asked "why" about anything. He took all of life at face value, as it came to him. He was by no means a philosopher and as far as I knew, he had never been a seeker of deeper meanings or truths. Sid could have coined the phrase "It is what it is." He did not embrace nuance. I had written a eulogy a few weeks before at the urging of a friend who suggested it's easier to write the eulogy before the eruption of the volcano of emotion that comes after the death. Ironically, given those last words he spoke, the theme of my eulogy was about what an inspirational teacher my dad was, despite never having finished high school.

The day wore on. That night Sid slept fitfully. He kept sitting up or standing up and Ned and I worried he would fall over and get hurt so we took turns staying up and sitting with him. In the middle of the night I recalled what I read in the Levine book about caring for the dying and giving them permission to accept death so I held his hand and gently stroked the top of his head as a parent would do with a sick child and said over and over, "Let go, Dad. It's okay to let go." Sid held on.

The next morning, Sunday morning, June 30, I left the den to head into the kitchen to make a pot of coffee. Tamra, then eight years old, padded downstairs in her nightgown. Her first stop was the den to peek in to check on Grandpop, as she did every morning.

She came into the kitchen to tell us what she noticed.

"Grandpop is very quiet," Tamra reported in her sweet, soft voice.

Ned and I knew what that meant.

Chapter Twelve: Incredible InEdibles

Ned and I walked swiftly back into the den to check on Sid. He seemed comfortable after struggling so much to breathe. We realized this serenity was death. I think it's possible Sid had heard everything hospice nurse Debbie had predicted about his future. He heard excruciating pain, incontinence, diapers, etc. and I think he decided that wasn't going to work for him. Plus, his last CD had matured so his affairs were in order. He checked out before anything horrible (well, besides dying) came to pass.

I don't think it's a coincidence he died as soon as I left the room. I believe he didn't want to upset me by having me witness his last breath. He may have heard me say, "It's okay to let go," but he had no intention of doing so with me watching. Always my protector -- literally until the end.

Death didn't look so bad. I thought I saw a slight smile on his face. I hugged my father for the last time and said goodbye. I thought I'd feel sadder than I did. What I felt was relief. My father looked far better off than he had a few hours earlier when he was struggling to breathe. He looked peaceful and that was all I wished for him. His ceasing to live felt natural, it felt somehow logical as the next step along his journey, and honestly, I sensed I was witnessing something beautiful and poignant.

As she instructed me to do, my first call was to Debbie the hospice nurse who said she'd be right over. Then, I had to call my sister. It being Sunday, Linda was due to visit later that day. I was glad I caught her before she left.

"Linda, I'm sorry to tell you this but Dad had a really hard night and he just stopped breathing. He's gone. The hospice nurse is on her way."

Linda immediately started yelling at me frantically, "Call 911! Call 911!"

I calmly explained Sid was dead and there was no need for 911. I said Debbie had instructed me not to call 911 and she was already on her way. There was nothing else to be done right now. Linda continued to insist I call 911-- the exact thing the nurse had told us not to do if we wanted to fulfill Sid's wishes.

"No," I replied calmly as I explained, "I'm not going to call 911. The hospice nurse told me not to. She's coming right over to take good care of him. It's okay, really it is."

"Dad was having a lot of trouble breathing but now it's over. He's peaceful. He doesn't have to suffer anymore. If you could see him right now, you'd understand this was his time to go and he's better off."

As she often did when I stymied her, Linda put Natan on the phone and he proceeded to scream at me.

"What do you mean he's dead? What did he die from? What's wrong with you Debby? Why aren't you listening to me? Why aren't you calling 911? DO SOMETHING! "

I was starting to get frustrated and upset. "Look. He's dead. I can't *do* anything. What did he die from? What do you think he died from? He was hit by a bus."

Okay, I got sarcastic. I couldn't help it. It felt like they were accusing me of either letting him die or killing him in some way or of not taking care of him the best way possible. I couldn't take it. I may have overreacted. Just a tad.

I handed Sid the phone. "Dad, Tell them you're dead. They're driving me crazy."

As always, Sid remained neutral.

And, yes, I know that was not a rational move on my part. I believe I get a pass, though, because, after all, my father had just died. I was entitled to a small blip in rational behavior.

Later that day, we made funeral arrangements. Linda wanted an orthodox Jewish burial and although Sid had not been a religious man, I knew he wouldn't have objected to giving Linda what she wanted so I agreed to all of it. She wanted a particular rabbi she knew to officiate and, again, I agreed. I figured all of these rites of passage were more important to her than they were to me, so it was easiest to go along to get along. A few weeks earlier I asked Dad what he wanted at his funeral. Was there anything he wanted anyone to say or to read? Was there anyone in particular he'd like us to notify? Was there any music he wanted played? Did he want to choose pallbearers?

He shrugged his shoulders and answered, "What do I care? I'm not going to be there."

So, I knew it would be okay with him if we let Linda call all the shots.

But there was one thing I couldn't go along with. It was the location of *shiva*. It is a Jewish post-death ritual for the immediate family of the deceased to "sit *shiva*" for seven days. During that time, friends and relatives come for a condolence call and there are some services, too. It is customary to "sit" in the home of the deceased. But, that wasn't going to work for me because there was an incredible heat wave in Philadelphia that week. It was nearly 100 degrees and Sid's central air conditioning system was broken beyond repair. He hadn't lived there for the last seven weeks so we hadn't arranged to have it replaced and couldn't possibly do it in time for *shiva*. I checked with my sister's rabbi to ask if it would be okay to sit *shiva* in my home. He said while it's traditional to sit in the home of the deceased, it was 100 degrees and it would be perfectly fine to sit in my home, given the circumstances. He said that's what *he* would do if it had been his family.

I told Linda what her rabbi had said but she refused the change of venue. She said she was going to sit *shiva* at Sid's. I said the house was dirty and disgusting. No one had lived there for two months and it hadn't been that clean to begin with. (Twenty years of smoking cigars without ever opening a window takes a toll on everything.) It was hot as hell, it stank, there was no food; I pretty much begged her to come to my house but she insisted I could do what I wanted, but she'd be at Sid's.

The next day was the funeral. I eulogized my father and talked about those last words he spoke asking, "Why can't they teach others what they know?" I said his words were an exquisite choice for his finale because, in fact, he had taught my family and me so well what he knew best. He taught us what mattered most in life was the way you treated other people. He taught us by example about the value of forgiveness and generosity. (I am still working on learning forgiveness. My father would likely not be too happy with my growth on that one. But I am a work in progress.) One time Ned was going through a difficult time in his life at the hands of some people who were treating him very cruelly. Sid said there were two kinds of people in the world, those who got walked on and those who did the walking. It's your decision, he explained, which kind you preferred to be. Sid said he'd rather get walked on. While there are gray areas in that sort of thing, it says a lot about Sid's character that he never wanted to be the person who would intentionally hurt others. He'd rather take the pain himself and protect others. What a legacy he left.

That is what I spoke about in his eulogy, his character, both peculiar and spectacular. I talked about how my friends in high school used to say if Sid grunted in their direction they figured he liked them because if he didn't like them he just didn't talk at all. I told about how my father and I weren't that close and rarely spoke about anything of substance until after my Mom's death. After her death everything changed for my father and me. The man who didn't know how to boil water started cooking in order to continue the Friday night dinners with Ned and me and later, our kids. The man who rarely if ever played a game with his daughters was suddenly letting his granddaughters put pink polish on his nails. His manner of grandparenting, I explained, taught me how to be a better parent as I witnessed the power of unconditional love. Just after my mother died the Friday night dinners with my dad had felt at first like an awkward obligation but over the years those visits evolved, much like our father-daughter relationship, into times of love and respect and never obligation.

Linda didn't speak at the funeral but she did write something for the rabbi to read. Her eulogy was a bit about Sid but it focused for the most part on how proud he was of his grandson Isaac, who could "read the New York Times at age three." He was after all, "Some baby."

After the service, lots of people comforted me with sentiments about how wonderful I was for taking care of my dad at the end. They

96

lavished praise on me for the "gift" I had given my dad with that care. But I knew what they didn't know. They were confused. I hadn't given my father a gift in taking him into my home to die. He had given me the greatest gift of all. He allowed me to help him for the first time in my life. He allowed me to give back just the tiniest portion of what he had spent a lifetime giving me. It didn't even the score, not by a long shot, but letting me take care of him went a long way toward making me feel like a "mensch," (Yiddish word for good person) in my father's eyes. It was one of the kindest things Sid ever did for me. It was like being able to pay back part of a lifelong debt. It's hard to explain what that meant.

Mourners returned to my house. We sat *shiva* for three days, not the traditional seven. Not being a religious person, nor was Sid, I felt that three days were sufficient. But, I knew Linda would sit for seven days. Since I also knew there was no food at Sid's house, either for her family or for any guests who might stop by, (not that she has any friends or family in Philadelphia, another reason why I thought she should have "sat" at my house, so she wouldn't be alone) I had a vegetable and fruit arrangement delivered. Made by a company called, "Incredible Edibles," it was fruit and vegetables cut and arranged to look like flowers. Since Linda and family were strictly kosher, I wanted to send food I was sure they could eat so I stuck with produce, which didn't have to pass any "kosher" regulations.

On day four, I went to my dad's house to "sit" with Linda, Nat, and Isaac for a bit. When I got there, the house was as hot as hell and so were they. In other words, they were clearly angry and annoyed with me. But, there were some neighbors there so we didn't have a chance to discuss it. I walked up the steps into the dining room to check on the food. I figured I could run out and get more food if I assessed what was needed. There sat the "Incredible Edible" arrangement I had sent. It was now four days old, still in the plastic wrapping, and quite rotten. The fruits and vegetables had turned to a slimy, drooping mess. I guess the combination of the heat and the plastic wrapping had done it in. I asked Linda what was going on and why she hadn't eaten or even opened what I had sent.

"Natan didn't like the way it was addressed," she answered, as if that made sense.

"What do you mean?" I asked, completely perplexed.

"The card. You addressed the card to me and you didn't include my husband or son," she explained.

I was dumbfounded. I had only one thought when ordering the food and that was to have it delivered to the right address in time for them to have something to eat. There was no deep meaning in the name I gave them for the order. I had no idea anyone would notice or care about the name on the envelope. I intended no malice. And if she didn't want to eat anything from me, why didn't she at least open it for her guests? I did wonder, though, if my sister had no intention of eating it or offering it to guests, why did she leave it there for me to see? Why didn't she just throw it away?

We left shortly thereafter. When I left, I told my sister to take anything she wanted from the house and not to worry about leaving me any particular things. I suggested she take the color TV because I knew she didn't have one. Beyond that, if there was anything she wanted, she should take it, I said, and I left. I was executor of my father's will. The job of cleaning out and selling his home would fall to me. I didn't know when my sister would be back so I figured she might as well take anything she wanted with her. It was a start, at least, to the monumental task of disposing of my parents' lifetime collection of possessions.

At that moment I had no idea about just how monumental that task would prove to be or that I would lose my sister in the process.

Chapter Thirteen: A Rabbi and A Lawyer Walk Into A Bar...

At this point in the story, if you know you are the executor of someone's estate, you may want to rethink that plan and ask the person who picked you to choose someone else. It is not always a pretty job.

I had to clean out my father's house and sell it. I kept getting hung up looking at those family pictures. As a child I loved going over them with my mother. But now that both my parents were gone, those photos were even more compelling. Suddenly I found myself looking at them anew and developing questions about who was in them and what people were doing and thinking at the time. But, there was no longer anyone to ask. That photo which I never saw before of a group of people in Russian garb and one of the woman has a large X scratched onto her chest? I'm never going to know who they are or why she is branded in that way. Who were those "kids" in a pyramid formation with my then teenage Mom on the top? I know they were her friends when she was young but now I want to know their names and where they were when this "Kodak Moment" took place. Was the guy she has her arm around a boyfriend before my Dad? Did she have any boyfriends before my father? I never asked and now I have these photos generating a flood of forever unanswered questions.

I guess that's part of what happens when parents die. The finality of knowing you can never see that person again has an unpredictable impact. You become obsessed with looking at pictures and trying to memorize and practically inhale every detail so that each becomes a part of you, so ingrained you actually feel you now have a piece of that person within you. You stare at the pictures trying to see the parts of the photo that are just out of range, around the corners, in the next partially-visible room. I look at the snapshots and I try to hear the voices of my mother and father. I strain to recall the touch of their hands, the feel of my arms around them. I see photos of my Mom in that turquoise beaded evening gown and I can feel the crepe texture of her eyelids as I dusted on blue eye shadow because she was no good at applying makeup. I wonder what Mom or Dad would say if they could comment on the turns my life has taken.

It's not that I needed or necessarily wanted my sister's help in cleaning out the house and getting it ready to be put on the market. It was a big job (maybe the one Sid referred to on his death bed) but I knew I could do it with Ned's help. My problem was that Linda's belongings were in the house and I didn't know what to do with those. Linda never responded on that last day of *shiva*, when I told her to feel free to take anything she wanted from the house. But the next time I was at my father's house nothing appeared to be gone.

Several weeks passed after Dad's death so I started calling my sister to ask when she'd be coming home and what she wanted from the house. She wasn't terribly friendly but she did say she wanted a sofa and my parents' bedroom set. I said that was fine. She had keys to the house so she could easily come and get whatever she wanted.

More weeks went by and I didn't hear from her. She didn't take anything from my parents' house as far as I could tell. Months started to pass and I didn't hear from her. I would phone and she wouldn't answer. She didn't return any calls or respond to any messages. I left several messages saying as the months were passing it was necessary to start cleaning the house out and put it up for sale. I didn't hear anything from her.

In the interim, I decided I wanted to keep my parents' house so I found out what it was worth and I offered my sister half of that amount in order to buy out her half. In the interest of fairness I said if she wanted the house, she could do the same – pay me half and buy me out. I didn't think she'd want the house but I figured if I made the same offer for her to purchase the house she'd know I was suggesting a reasonable price. I didn't hear from her but I did get a letter from a lawyer saying he was now representing my sister in the matter of my "father's estate" and from now on, I should communicate with him and not contact her directly. I had no idea why my sister needed a lawyer since my dad had divided everything down to the penny, 50% for me, 50% for her. But, I conveyed the offer about the house to her lawyer and also said he needed to tell my sister if she wanted anything from the house, she had to come and get it.

More months went by and nothing seemed to be missing from the house. But, I did notice something odd. The mailman threw the mail that was still being delivered to my dad's house into the mail slot that emptied into the foyer. Normally when I opened the front door, the mail was there on the floor, having piled up behind the door. But, at some point I noticed the mail wasn't right next to the door. It was in a pile moved further away from the door. Plus, some of the mail looked as if someone had rifled through it. It was strange and I wondered if Linda had been in the house. There wasn't anything wrong with that but it was pretty weird because nothing seemed to be gone. I wondered why she would come in and not take anything. She still didn't return calls or answer letters I sent so the mystery remained unsolved.

After my dad had been dead about eight months, I got a letter from a new lawyer my sister had retained. He was an interesting choice: my family's former rabbi. Yes, retired Rabbi Arnold Friedman, the one from our synagogue in Philadelphia had gone back to school to become a lawyer. This was the rabbi from the synagogue my family attended, the rabbi who had officiated at my Bat Mitzvah and at my mother's funeral. He had known us for 30 years and now he was suing me. I wasn't sure for what as his letter didn't state exactly what the "case" was about. But, it alluded to the fact that my sister was accusing me of taking things that belonged to her. (Also known as stealing.) At that point I *had* taken some things from my parents' house but I had told her lawyer if there was something she really wanted and I had already taken it, she should just let me know and I'd give it to her.

I phoned the rabbi to tell him how disturbing it was to have him be the attorney who accused me of stealing from my sister. I said when I was a Bat Mitzvah at 13 years of age I had a certain moral code that kept me from stealing and I still lived by that code. I explained it would hurt to have anyone accuse me of stealing from my sister but it was even more painful to have it be our own rabbi! I told him I thought it rather despicable he'd take this case.

Rabbi Friedman said he didn't take the case just because he wanted to practice law. He said he thought perhaps he could help mend the rift and he wasn't actually accusing anyone of anything. Well, that was news to me since the letter I got from him was only about suing me; it in no way suggested any mending of any sort. But, potential mending was okay with me so when the rabbi suggested we all meet at my dad's house to talk, I agreed. A few weeks later, on an incredibly frigid February night, Rabbi Friedman, Ned and I, and Linda and Natan all rendezvoused at my dad's house. I hadn't been there for a few weeks and when I walked in I noticed it was exceptionally frosty in the house despite the fact I had kept the heat on so the pipes wouldn't freeze.

We sat in the kitchen on those lime green, swivel chairs, surrounded by the 60s psychedelic floral wallpaper. The rabbi swiveled to look at my sister and then swiveled back to look at me.

"Well, girls, what is the real problem?" he asked. For a moment there I was 13 again and standing in front of the rabbi feeling a bit intimidated as if I had misbehaved at synagogue. But then I remembered I was an adult and I had done nothing wrong.

I shrugged my shoulders and said, "Honestly, Rabbi (or perhaps I should have said, Honestly, Lawyer) I have no idea." We both looked at my sister as if to ask, "So, Linda, what *is* the real problem?" She turned her head away and looked at Natan. She didn't speak.

After a moment or two (or what seemed like an eternity of silence) Rabbi Friedman asked me why I took my sister's things from the house. (Way not to accuse someone, Rabbi.) So I told him the story... how my dad had died last June and I'd been charged with taking care of things and I had to start cleaning out the house to sell it. My sister had communicated though her previous lawyer she didn't want to keep the house but was not willing to sell it to me either so it had to be sold.

"But, Rabbi, I haven't gotten rid of anything in the house yet," I explained. "My sister's things are still here just where she left them in the basement. I've been asking her for months to come and take what she wants so we can sell the house. I can't understand why she won't do that. And, seriously, I can't understand why we're here." I swiveled toward Linda and looked directly into her eyes.

"Why are you mad at me? What did I do?"

My sister opened her mouth to speak, but Natan placed his hand firmly on Linda's forearm and said icily, "Don't talk to her." She closed her mouth, leaned back in the chair and swiveled away. It was freezing in the house and we were all shivering, especially Linda (A woman seriously lacking in the layer of body fat that keeps one warm.). At one point, she whispered something to her husband about being cold and Natan scolded her, "Why didn't you dress warmer? You knew the heater was broken!" I wondered how she knew the heater was broken. I didn't know that and I was here pretty often.

Totally ignoring my answer to the Rabbi about not having discarded my sister's belongings, Natan continued to insist I had gotten rid of Linda's very valuable things, including the "priceless" pages of notes and tapes of interviews with Menachem Begin from her doctoral thesis for the Ph. D in Middle Eastern politics she earned at Columbia University. I repeated I had touched none of her things; they were all still in the basement, just where Linda had left them. Natan continued to insist her "priceless and irreplaceable" things were gone. I said, "Why don't we go downstairs so you can see everything is still there?"

Natan ignored me. It was as if I hadn't spoken at all. Then the rabbi/lawyer suggested we go down to the basement so Natan could see where everything was. What a good idea. Why didn't I think of that?

We did go downstairs, despite the fact Natan clearly didn't want to. I opened the basement door, flipped on the light, and started down those old wooden steps as I had done so many times before with my father. The basement had always been a place of joy and delight. My dad had turned that cold unfinished room into a small warehouse of interesting things. At our Friday night dinners I'd follow Dad down the steps and I'd always feel the slight lift of anticipation. I'd stand in front of the pink antique cupboard he used for shelving and Dad would load my arms with supplies. From canned goods, to diapers, to spice racks (yes, we once needed an engagement gift for a friend and sure enough, Sid had one waiting in the basement), to juice, and much more. Each week we went home with a bounty of necessities my father had bought for us. I was overwhelmed with the sense my father was watching me descend the steps and shaking his head in dismay at this scene.

Once we got to the bottom of the basement steps, with all of Linda's boxes and assorted crap staring us in the face, Natan stopped insisting

Linda's things were gone. Oddly, he didn't seem happy or relieved to see these priceless items of paramount importance. We went back upstairs. Natan reluctantly reported the items were in the basement. It became apparent that nothing good was going to come of this get-together.

Finally, the meeting ended with no resolution. I got the feeling the light had just dawned on Rabbi Friedman. He must have realized his client didn't have much of a case so he needed to wrap things up before he wasted any more time. He muttered something about the need for us to keep the lines of communication open as he got up to leave. As we walked out of the house my sister took a quick detour upstairs to her old room and walked out clutching her childhood scrapbook in her arms.

We stepped outside into the frigid night air. Linda and Natan got into the maroon Chrysler Caravan minivan Ned and I had given them a few years earlier when we bought a new car. As they pulled away from the curb I started to cry. The rabbi--or maybe it was the lawyer, it's hard to tell the difference-- asked why I was so upset and I pretty much flipped out on him.

"Why am I upset? Well, let's see, I'm standing outside of my childhood home, both of my parents are dead and I've just left a meeting where my sister won't speak to me and won't tell me why, but she does have our family's rabbi (or lawyer) accusing me of stealing from her. Why do *you* think I'm upset?"

"Plus, she just drove off in a car which I gave her!" Not sure why I thought that was relevant but I guess I just didn't want the rabbi to think I was a bad guy.

The rabbi sent me one more letter a few weeks later. It said he would no longer be representing my sister. It didn't say why. But, fear not, she retained a third lawyer. Not a rabbi, this time, just a garden-variety attorney as far as I knew.

104

Chapter Fourteen: The Peoples Court

In April our lawyer sent Linda's lawyer a letter informing her she had one more month to get anything she wanted out of my parents' house. In May, about eleven months after my dad's death, we'd be emptying out the house and giving away anything left in there.

Linda took nothing. After the appointed date, we gave everything left in the house to charity. We threw away the items they wouldn't take. At some point, Linda's lawyer said my sister wanted our childhood train set and a silver tray that belonged to my grandparents. I gave her the tray but I kept the train set. It wasn't much of a train set, just a small set of tracks and five cars. Had she asked for it a few months earlier, I might have given it to her but after the way she had acted I was hurt and annoyed. Plus, my daughters had spent hours playing with that train set at Grandpop's house and I wanted them to have it. So, I said no to that request. Some days, when I think back on that, I'm sorry, and some days, I'm not.

After a few months I sold my dad's house and car and sent my sister half of the money. I did keep the 10% executrix fee allowed by law. Sometimes I regret doing that too but at the time I was in pain and maybe not feeling so charitable. I may also have been motivated by a small desire to hurt her back. I'm not sure. I didn't hear from Linda after that. I'd reach out to her either by phone or by mail. She never answered. Sometimes the letters would come back to me stamped, "Return to Sender."

Then I got a ten-page letter from lawyer number 3. He said he was instituting a lawsuit on my sister's behalf. The letter was mostly a list of the things I had gotten rid of in my parents' house, for which Linda wanted compensation. The itemization of the list was absolutely uncanny. Every item in the house was listed individually. Every piece of old and tired furniture was mentioned. At the end she summed up the value of everything at $10,000 and that is the amount for which she sued. I have no idea how they figured the value. This was before the accessibility of the Internet or Ebay. I imagine they just made up a figure or they looked through stores to get an estimate.

Here is the letter Linda sent her lawyer, a copy of which went to my lawyer. I guess after her lawyer received this missive, he drafted the official lawsuit that ultimately came to me.

Dear Lawyer #3, *(Okay, it had his name but I didn't think it was important to include his name here.)*
In preparation for our court appearance and in accordance with your request, I am listing the contents of the house including my personal affects (sic) which were removed without my consent.

<u>Personal Items</u>

1. Cartons located in the basement of research notes, transcripts and tapes of interviews with Prime Ministers and other high-ranking Israeli ministers and government officials for my Ph.D. dissertation and book. This is priceless, irreplaceable and historic material.
2. Cartons located in the basement of research material and interviews in Arabic, Hebrew and English for Master's Essay on the P.L.O. This, too, is priceless, historic and irreplaceable.
3. Two Judaica book collections
   a. One collection was boxed in the basement and contained antique, rare books in Hebrew, Yiddish and English.
   b. A second collection was located in my room. This included a six-inch thick Bible concordance, Hebrew grammar and modern Hebrew literature book, Jewish history books, books in English on Jewish holidays, several Bibles in Hebrew with commentaries, Hebrew books of the Prophets, other Hebrew scriptural writings, prayerbooks, and workbooks on teaching and understanding the Bible.

4. Two book collections in English
   a. One collection boxed in the basement included journal volumes of the <u>International Journal of Middle East Studies</u>, volumes of the journal <u>Midstream</u>, textbooks on physics, chemistry, English as a second language, health sciences, computers, and more.
   b. 1. A second collection located in my room consisting of approximately 200 paperbacks on American and world

106

history; religion; education; and light literature. Specific titles include The Making of the President by Theodore White; Commission on Race Relations in America; Bridge Over the River Drina by Tor Andre; Gideon's Trumpet by Anthony Lewis; Early Philosophy by Henry Frankfort; The Sumerians by Samuel Kramer; and numerous Agatha Christie and Dorothy Sayers titles. (Several of the mystery titles were actually on a shelf in the adjacent smaller room.) 2. Numerous hardback books on English literature; Spanish literature, American literature; Arabic language; Middle East history; politics, and religion; Specific volumes include Genghis Kahn, Early Church Fathers; Arabic dictionary; The Source by James Michener; yearbooks of the World Book Encyclopedia; Outline of History: a two-volume anthology of English literature; two volumes of Spanish literature; a book by Henry Kissinger; Also on the bookshelf were junior and senior high school and college yearbooks.

5. Copy of Ph.D. dissertation located in my room.
6. Lionel electric train set *
7. My bedroom furniture: white French provincial set included twin beds with headboards and footboards; night table and lamp; desk with lamp; desk chair; two dressers; three hutches with shelves and closets; custom made bedspreads and drapes; mirrored dresser tray.
8. Personal letters located in my desk and closet including one signed by John F. Kennedy and other miscellaneous memorabilia.
9. Collection of newspapers and news clips of the Temple University News on which I was a reporter and editor, located in my desk. There are irreplaceable.
10. Personal and family photographs including wedding album, located in my room.
11. Movies of my wedding, located in my room.
12. Royal typewriter (manual, standard with cover), located in my room.
13. Violin and case and music stand, located in my room.
14. Wedding and engagement gifts and other new household items, located in set place in basement, including:

Embroidered tablecloths and napkins from Israel
Planters
Wooden salad bowl set
Ceramic cookie jar
Hamburger maker
Crystal glassware
Ceramic plates
Tea sets
Set of service for six of new brown and orange stoneware
dishes
Candlesticks

15. Two bicycles located in garage; one Schwinn English racer and
    one regular woman's bike. *
16. Two jewelry boxes located in my room.

It goes without saying I intended to take the personal items, but those
noted with an asterisk indicate those that I had specified several times
in writing and verbally, particularly in a meeting with my sister and our
respective attorneys in February 1992.

Contents of the House
Items marked with an asterisk indicate items I had specified in writing
and verbally that I wanted.

1. * Furniture in master bedroom: Mediterranean style set
    including two beds with connecting headboard; armoire; large
    double dresser with two mirrors; large wrought iron lamp
    * dresser tray
    * valet chair
    * lounge chair
    custom made bedspread and drapes

2. Living room furniture and furnishings
    * 96 inch blue brocade custom made sofa in brand-new mint
    condition
    * two brass and glass coffee tables
    two red club chairs
    one white wood frame chair (I salvaged this from thrift shop)
    one wood end table

one curio case containing china figurines, candy dishes,
decanter of liquor
one round glass table with wooden base
one hanging lamp
one oriental style lamp
one blue tone cabinet and mirror with candelabra style lamp
silver decorative bible

3. Dining room furnishings
   Breakfront
   Dining table with six chairs
   Brass and glass serving chart
   Crystal chandelier
   The breakfront contained:
   China
   Set of crystal glasses with sizes for water, wine, liquor
   Walnut wood salad set: extra large bowl, smaller bowls, serving
   pieces
   Large red glass plate
   Wooden leaf candy dish
   Silver plated candy dish
   Ceramic mugs
   Salt and pepper shaker sets
   Steak serving set
   Corn serving pieces
   Americana including Marilyn Monroe tray and novelty items
   Coasters
   Silver-trimmed drinking glasses

   Serving cart contained:
   Twin chafing dishes
   Copper tray and holders with glasses for tea

4. * Silver tray
5. * Silver wine goblets
6. Two sets of candlesticks
7. Electric menorah and menorah with candles
8. Kitchen table and four padded swivel chairs and beige stepstool
   chair
9. Furnishings for den

At date of death two beige sofas were located in the den; one striped wood frame foam cushion sofa was located upstairs in a smaller bedroom; a second identical wood-frame sofa was in the basement
Two backless padded seats
Two orange upholstered chairs located elsewhere in house at date of death
Two credenzas
Corner table
End table
One long dark wood shelf and three smaller shelves
Bookends
White hanging lamp
Red area carpet
Cabinet style record player
Egyptian wall hanging

10. Antique bureau with drop-leaf table located in small room upstairs
11. Antique armoire in garage
12. Two color televisions and stands
13. One large color television with walnut cabinet frame
14. VCR and tapes
15. Toaster Oven
16. Microwave oven
17. Deep Freezer
18. Two closets
19. Approx. five sets of dishes located in kitchen and basement
20. Polaroid camera
21. Professional home repair tools and hardware including electric drills and saw, wrenches, hammers and soldering tools
22. Liquor

This is the list to the best of my recollection at present. Unfortunately, I cannot remember more specific titles of my large personal library and papers.

Just a reminder that this letter covers only the contents of the house and also at issue besides the house itself are:

1. A car, estimated by my sister to be worth $4900 which I had strongly indicated I wanted and which she has sold.
2. A coin collection
3. A NOW account in FirstTrust Bank. As I explained in an earlier letter, this account contained approximately $3961 at date of death. My father used this account for his living expenses, and therefore, each month interest from two CDs one in my name and one in my sister's name was deposited into this account. Before he died, my father put my sister's name on this account for her to pay any outstanding bills. I am contesting this account. The interest from the CDs continued to be automatically deposited in this account. When I made the banker aware of this situation, he retroactively put the amounts from the July-November 1991 into my CD account. However, my sister argued that the June amount should remain in the NOW account, and the banker did not give me June's interest on my CD. Further, my sister regarded this account as hers personally. She wrote a check to cash for $3000 and has charged the estate for bills which should have been covered by this account.
4. A Social Security check.

Hope you had a pleasant summer and vacation. Looking forward to seeing you on the 13th when hopefully this matter will finally be resolved.

Sincerely,
Linda Schwartz

There are so many interesting and yet humorous things about this list. This was not something anyone could have done in a day or two. This was months of tedious work, documenting every item and every piece of crap in my parents' split-level, three-bedroom home. And then. OH MY GOD, I figured it out. This was what my sister was doing in the year after my dad died. Instead of taking what she wanted from Dad's house, she took inventory! She was driving down to Philadelphia on Sundays (being religious she can't drive on Saturdays) and going through every room in the house writing down everything she saw. She had to have been planning the whole time to wait until I sold the house and everything was gone so she could mount this lawsuit.

I was speechless for only the second time in my life. But I was only speechless because I wasn't sure where to begin my reactions to this masterwork. Mint condition furniture? It was 30 years old, having lived all that time with a heavy smoker who never opened a window. Her wedding photos and movies? She had gotten married in about 1977, it was now 1993, shouldn't she have had them in her possession by now? Not that I blamed her for that. If I had married Natan I'd want no visual reminders either. Did she really include the plastic corncob holders? Yes, she did. Priceless paperwork? Really? Is my sister a renowned expert whose work is worth untold millions? Not exactly, she's a mostly unemployed person with a degree. Plus, if your possessions were priceless would you abandon them in a vacant house? I wouldn't. The bikes she noted as #15 made me laugh out loud. I won one of them in a contest at a local shoe store when I was about seven. I have the photo of the host of the morning show giving me the bike to prove it. That "Schwinn English Racer" as she described it-- as though adding "Schwinn" and "English Racer" to the moniker made it incredibly valuable-- was now 30 years old, rusty, and had flat tires that suffered from dry rot. Plus, I can't recall ever once seeing my sister ride a bike. My favorite part of the list had to be under Personal Items, #4, part b. in parenthesis where she notes that several of the mystery titles are on the shelf in the adjacent smaller room. The "adjacent smaller room" was the bathroom and the books she referred to were the discounted coverless paperbacks my father read while sitting on the toilet.

But even that wasn't the most ridiculous thing about the list. The existence of the list was almost too absurd to be articulately described.

I was stunned and wondered what my sister would say when she went to court. She had almost a year to take whatever she wanted from the house. She took nothing and then sued me for everything. Logic would dictate the first question a judge would ask is, "Why didn't you take what you wanted while it was all still there?"

It took about two years for the case to come before a judge. I couldn't imagine what Linda would say but I knew one thing. My sister is really smart. She has that Ph.D. in political science from Columbia

University. She was going to have one hell of an interesting answer to that pertinent question and I really wanted to know what it was.

We arrived at the conference room where my sister's case would be heard and decided by a judge. We sat around the table. I was there with Ned, and our lawyer/friend Donnie on one side. The judge was at the head of the table. Linda, Natan, and Lawyer #3 were seated on the other side. Behind them sat their son Isaac, then about eight years old.

The judge turned to my sister and asked for her plaintiff side of the story. She launched into a long and disturbing account about how her parents died and she was grief-stricken. She said she was really upset after her dad passed away and losing all of her personal and precious possessions made the whole experience much more excruciating. I'm summarizing here because the actual telling of her side of the story took more than an hour. She looked like a frightened mouse as she recounted the sad tale. Linda had a habit of spitting a little bit when she was nervous and had to speak. (She'd also drool a bit when she laughed but that didn't happen in court.) I could see the tiny droplets spewing from her lips. She seemed frail and was shaking almost imperceptibly but I could see it happening. She verbally painted a picture of a mean, avaricious, and nasty sister who exhibited callous disregard for Linda's tender emotions and fragile state. She said losing everything she cared about was akin to having everything one loves destroyed in a catastrophic fire. I thought, "Wow, this poor woman's sister IS a bitch." Then I remembered that bitch was me. But, man, Linda really was a pitiful character and I felt sorry for her.

The judge then turned to me and asked for my side of the story. I recounted my tale a lot more quickly, literally in just a few minutes. I said I was also upset about losing my dad but he had left me a job to do which was to take care of his home and possessions and I had to do that expediently and responsibly. I explained how many times I had reached out to my sister via phone and mail and how she refused to reply or to cooperate. I said I tried time and again to give her what she wanted (minus the train set) and she just refused to take anything. I said it became apparent she had gone into my dad's house many times during the year after his death but never took anything she supposedly wanted so badly. I explained that although I had spent a great deal of time pondering the question, I had no idea why she didn't just take the things she wanted. My eyes filled with tears as I spoke. That surprised me because I thought I had been able to get past how much this whole episode hurt.

Next, since Ned had been the person who found the buyer for Dad's house, the judge asked him to recount how we sold the house. Ned described how we found an appraiser so we'd know what the house was worth and then found a buyer through a neighbor's referral, and finally how we negotiated a fair price and split that with my sister.

The judge asked our lawyer if he had any questions for my sister. He said he did. He proceeded to ask her why she didn't take the items within the year after my dad's death.

"Well," Linda said, "we really couldn't get down there often enough to take the things we wanted because my son can't miss school during the week and our religion forbids us from driving on Saturdays."

"You mean that son over there, the one who's sitting here on a Wednesday?" our lawyer countered. I thought this was one of the most spectacular questions ever asked by an attorney at law. It was all I could do to stop myself from applauding and shouting, "Well played, Donnie, well played!"

"Yes," Linda replied with some confusion on her face. I guess she couldn't think of a more clever answer.

The judge appeared to be running out of patience at that point, because he asked the next question.

"Well, Ms. Schwartz," he began slowly and then speeded up for this next part, "if you wanted these things why didn't you take them?"

I had waited years to hear this answer. I held my breath. I leaned forward so I wouldn't miss a word or a nuance. There was money riding on this as my friends had taken bets on the answer. Okay, that wasn't true but predicting what my sister might say had been a fun party game for a few years among my closest friends. When I went back to my friends with the big reveal I wanted to be able to repeat exactly what she said.

114

"I didn't know what the hurry was," my brilliant sister began.

We all waited for the rest of the explanation. A moment or two of silence passed. One by one we each came to the same realization and as we did each of us leaned back in our chair. There was no "rest of the explanation." She was done. That was her complete answer to the giant question.

That was it. Several years of waiting, years of speculating what she might say because we all knew she'd be asked that question. I was stunned. Really? She didn't understand the hurry? That was her answer? It boggled my mind.

I suppose the judge was caught off guard too because after a moment of silence he leaned against the back of his chair and then quickly leaned forward again and swept his pile of papers into his arms as he responded abruptly and stood up.

"Okay," the judge replied, "you'll receive my decision in the mail."

With that he left the room along with the lawyers. Ned left the room to make a phone call. Natan left with Isaac to go to the bathroom. My sister and I were alone for the first time in years. I walked around the table to Linda's side of the room. I reached out to her and rested my hand gently on her arm.

"Linda," I said, "I don't know why you are so angry with me but if you ever feel like you can tell me, I'd really like to know. I love you and I'm always going to be your sister." It was hard to speak without crying. I did sigh audibly mid sentence to steel myself through the rest of the painful message but I was determined to get the words out quickly because I wasn't sure how long she'd stand there.

She looked at me blankly, coldly, and with no visible emotion. She said not one word. She didn't move; she blinked a few times like Bambi in the headlights and just stood there frozen in silence.

At that moment, Natan came back into the room, looked at me with a repugnant, icy stare, abruptly pushed my hand off my sister's arm as if I were a bee he was swatting away from his bee-allergic wife, placed his arm on the small of Linda's back, turned her away from my gaze and guided my sister out the door. She never said another word. She didn't even turn around to look at me.

I never saw her again.

I found out later that a few days after the hearing my sister wrote a follow-up letter to the judge who heard our case. My guess is that on the way home Natan wouldn't shut up about all the things she had done wrong at the hearing. I had heard him berate her many times before about the way she comported herself. I could almost hear him listing all of the things she should have said to the judge.

Dear Judge Powell,
I want to express my deepest gratitude to you for all of your time and patience, allowing me to express myself in the hearing on the estate of my father on Dec. 22. I am writing to beg your indulgence in permitting me to add to the record.

In recalling my testimony, I find that three points may not have been clear. I did not immediately remove items from the house after my father died because I did not know the contents of the will nor that my sister was executrix, and only after numerous requests did I receive a copy of the will from Donnie Goldstein. I thought that the will might designate items of the estate such as the car and various contents of the house to specific individuals. I was under the impression that I was therefore not permitted to disturb any contents.

In contrast to my lack of information, my sister knew the contents of the will and that she was executrix from the time the will was written in 1984 because Mr. Goldstein is her good, personal friend. In fact, he and his wife witnessed the will.

With the delay in conveying the will, Mr. Goldstein established a pattern of not disclosing to me necessary information. He never properly informed me of bank accounts in my name. Mr. Arnold Friedman, my first attorney, repeatedly complained in writing to Mr. Goldstein about the lack of information and particularly in a letter of

116

January 2, 1992, Mr. Friedman complained to Mr. Goldstein about Mr. Goldstein's providing numerous unorganized pieces of paper, many representing closed accounts. All the information I had about bank affairs, I obtained myself by visiting the banks according to a record my father had given me in 1988. Until this day, I do not know if my information is complete.

I also want to clarify my testimony about why it was so difficult for me to arrange time to remove items from the house sooner. My husband and I are Sabbath observers; we do not travel or otherwise work on the Sabbath. Therefore we could not take care of this moving on a Saturday. Our child attended school on Sunday, and therefore Sundays were also problematic. We never came to Philadelphia expressly to visit the house. We came either to attend to affairs at the banks searching for information we never received from Mr. Goldstein or to visit the cemetery in memory of my mother or father. We would stop only briefly at the house before rushing back to New York, which is a four hour round trip, to pick up our son from school. In addition, I had a new job where I was on probation, and weekdays were difficult. Furthermore it was a distressing time for us, for my husband's younger brother was diagnosed with terminal cancer. We were occupied with attempts to find him medical treatment. He died after a few months. Given these difficult circumstances, the fact that my belongings had always been secure in the house, plus the fact that the house was not advertised for sale, I did not feel pressed to make extraordinary efforts to remove items before the summer of 1992 when my son would be finished with school and I would have more time.

Once again, thank you for permitting me to speak so freely last Wednesday, and I beg your further indulgence in adding this letter to the record. With best wishes for the New Year.

Sincerely,
Linda Schwartz

Ten months after the hearing we did receive the judge's decision in the mail. He found I was not guilty of any wrongdoing and I did not owe my sister any money. The judge concluded I did not have a fiduciary responsibility to protect my sister's "irreplaceable belongings" and in fact, she had not proved those items to have any value. He said my responsibility as executrix was to empty and sell my father's home exactly as I had and my sister couldn't use "her deceased father's home as a warehouse for an indefinite period of time." He also said he didn't believe her when she claimed she had not received written notice about when we would be emptying the house for the final time.

In the years following the hearing I called Linda a few times but she'd answer and hang up. One time she actually said, "I'm not hanging up but it's not a good time for me to talk." Then she did hang up. I only phoned one more time on 9/11 when I wanted to hear her voice so I'd know she was okay. She lives in Manhattan and I was worried. I got her answering machine. I didn't leave a message.

I got news about my sister once a year. Linda kept in touch with my parents' friend, Frieda. Over the years Linda and Natan developed a close friendship with her. Ironically, when we were children and my parents would take us to visit Frieda and her husband Marty, Linda always balked. They weren't Jewish and they weren't kosher and they lived by the beach on Long Island. When we visited, they'd host clambakes. While I loved those slimy guys coated with ketchup, my increasingly religious sister was horrified we were eating a forbidden food. At some point Linda demanded that my parents tell their friends clambakes were unacceptable for us. They did and the clambakes halted abruptly. So, I was surprised that while my sister cut out of her life other friends and all relatives of my parents, she worked at building a stronger relationship with Frieda. She visited her every summer for a few weeks. Frieda became a substitute parent for Linda and surrogate grandmother for Isaac. While I wasn't close with Frieda, we did exchange Christmas cards. Each year her card would come with a letter updating me about my sister's life. She knew I cared about Linda and I was interested in knowing how she was.

From time to time Frieda would remind me she was sworn to secrecy; my sister had made her promise never to tell me anything about her life. So, whether times were bad or good for Linda, I had to promise

118

Frieda I wouldn't contact my sister and let her know Frieda had shared any information. One year Frieda told me Natan was very sick with an "undisclosed" illness and was not expected to survive. He did survive and to my knowledge he is still alive. I never found out what the illness was. Frieda shared that Isaac was embarrassed about where he lived because at some point the apartment building my sister had lived in for 40 years became an old age home but Natan refused to vacate because the building was rent-controlled and he didn't want to give that up. Apparently, the management tried everything to get them to leave. They withheld utilities; they refused to deliver mail (yes, both of those are illegal), they wouldn't repair things that broke even when the apartment flooded. There was an article about the battle in the newspaper at some point. So, despite not being over 60 and having a young son, Linda and Nat lived in an old age home. Isaac told Frieda in confidence his living situation and his parents were embarrassing and he never felt comfortable bringing friends home. Each year I learned a bit about my sister's life and was always grateful for the information. But then Frieda died and all news of my sister disappeared from my life.

I had just one more one-sided interaction with my sister. Our Aunt Essie (the one Linda refused to invite to Passover) died about 16 years after the court case. Linda had cut Essie out of her life for no apparent reason right around the time our father died. Essie had never married or had any children so I suppose she thought of Linda and me as her daughters. She didn't understand why Linda stopped talking to her. That really hurt her. Still, when Aunt Essie's health declined and she knew she wouldn't live much longer, she gave me a small antique gold and onyx ring with these instructions.

"After I'm gone, send this ring to Linda. She always loved it."

I sent the ring to Linda after Essie died. I know the package was delivered because I sent it via UPS and asked for an acknowledgment of delivery. I enclosed a note that said simply, "Aunt Essie wanted you to have this ring." Linda never responded.

A close friend asked me a tough question.

"So, Debby, after all you've gone through with your sister, if the ring had been a very valuable diamond ring, would you have sent it?"

I'd like to say "yes." I really would. I'm the heroine in this tale, right? But, I don't want to lie and I'm not sure what the truthful answer is.

Losing a parent is hard even when you are a parent yourself. When my dad died, I lost not just my only living parent, but my sister too. She isn't dead but she might as well be. It might even be easier to deal with it if she were dead instead of just voluntarily missing in action. That really sounds horrible. It's not that I wish her dead; but having to accept the fact she has no need or desire to have me in her life hurts. As time passes it hurts less and less but it is always poignant.

Chapter Fifteen: The Therapist's Couch

When my dad died, I didn't hear from Anne or her children. I didn't expect to hear from them as it was during a time when she wasn't speaking to us. But, then again, I thought it was possible the death of my parent could bring her around. Not that it had when my mother died, but I thought perhaps the years had made her wiser and more empathetic.

Not so much.

My mother-in-law, though, had changed a bit over the years and I guess she thought our relationship wasn't so great and she wanted it to be better. Or, at least that's what she said when she asked if I would go to therapy with her.

Yes, me. Not Ned, not Anne, just me. What the hell? I was going to therapy with somebody else's mother? Seriously? I mean really, somebody else's mother and I were in therapy together. Is this normal? Clearly, Bernice thought I was the cause of her family's dysfunction. But, ever the optimist, and never having been in therapy, I was kind of curious about what it would be like so I agreed. But did I mention I was in therapy with somebody else's mother? I couldn't really get over it. Driving over there (because I figured I should just meet her there in case it didn't go well, artfully avoiding a potentially awkward drive home), I actually laughed out loud.

At the first session the therapist listened while my mother-in-law filled her in on the family history. Anne, Stuart, the divorce, Ned's "betrayal" and "disloyalty," my refusal to see how "wonderful" Anne is, etc. This saga took a while to recount. I listened politely and honestly tried not to roll my eyes…. too many times. I'm not a saint. It was challenging to listen to her wax poetic about a woman I thought was truly an awful person.

The thing is my mother-in-law Bernice believed Anne to be wonderful. She had been a golden daughter, perhaps Bernice's greatest achievement. Anne was the consummate homemaker. She could make a cheese ball that looked remarkably like a fresh pineapple by meticulously placing sliced almonds on the beautifully sculpted pineapple-shaped cheese just so in order to make them mimic exactly the scales of pineapple skin. She threw lovely parties. She bought her mother terrific gifts. She was attentive and lavished dutiful, daughterly attention on her mom. Plus, Anne had a cadre of friends to whom she was generous and loving. They virtually worshipped her and told my mother-in-law as much. So, Bernice felt justified in thinking Anne was pretty much God's gift to humanity. Bernice just didn't, couldn't, and wouldn't understand why I didn't see Anne the way everyone else did. According to Bernice, everyone thought Anne was an exceptional person. If I didn't see that, my mother-in-law likely concluded, there must be something wrong with *me*, like I must be demented or crazy or intentionally ornery. Hence, the therapy, where I guess she expected the therapist would cure me of my (what she hoped was temporary) insanity. I don't just *think* these things, Bernice carefully and painstakingly described how much it hurt her that Anne was so terrific and I was incapable or unwilling to see that truth. As a result of my inability to understand Anne's fabulousness, Bernice reasoned, her family had been decimated. I was the villain in the piece for sure.

"But, the emperor has no clothes!" I screamed. But only in my head.

I told the therapist my side of the story beginning with how Ned and I initially tried hard to form loving bonds with Anne. When she first moved to Philadelphia and moved into the house her parents had just moved out of, we surprised her by wallpapering her kitchen in a cheery yellow gingham pattern. We chose it because she had given us that gingham pillow for a wedding present so we knew she liked the design. I said we wanted to be a good aunt and uncle to her kids but she never seemed interested and didn't even have the kids call us "Aunt" and "Uncle." I explained we never stopped trying to reach out to Anne but we believed it was morally right to remain neutral in her divorce. We encouraged all the people involved to treat Stuart civilly and respectfully for the sake of his and Anne's kids, and we begged my in-laws to keep up all family activities, despite Anne's refusal to attend if we were there, etc.

The therapist listened intently. After I was finished recounting history as I knew it, she turned to my mother-in-law and said she didn't understand why *I* was the one at the therapy session. Bernice looked confused by the question. After all, I was the problem, I was the crazy one, and so I was the one she invited to therapy. Didn't that make sense?

"Your problem," the therapist concluded, "is with your daughter, or maybe your son, but certainly not with your daughter-in-law. You need to bring your daughter and son in."

My mother-in-law was not happy with the therapist's conclusion. She said she'd bring my father-in-law to the next session. I guess she thought Jack could explain it better and help the therapist to see I really was the problem.

So, the next week, the three of us showed up and retold the family saga. Now I'm in therapy with somebody else's mother AND somebody else's father. My father-in-law threw in some additional "bad" details about me. I wasn't affectionate and didn't hug or kiss them enough. Not never, just not enough. In addition, I didn't phone them often. According to Jack, these negative behavior quirks of mine were the cause of the family dysfunction. In response, I explained I treated my in-laws much the same way I had treated my own parents, whom I never called much either. As for my affection level, it was true, I wasn't a huggy or kissy person with them but I wasn't with my own parents either. It wasn't a measure of how I felt about anyone. It was just the way I am; maybe it was the way I was raised by people who weren't so affectionate either.

Again the therapist explained to Jack and Bernice she didn't believe I, or my lack of affection, or dearth of phone overtures were the family's problem. She repeated her plea they come back with their daughter and their son.

The next week Ned joined the group and the cycle repeated. Now I'm in therapy with somebody else's mother and somebody else's father but at least the somebody else is there. The therapist listened to Ned's side of the story and concluded the family's dysfunction revolved around Anne.

"If you want to improve your family dynamics," the therapist explained, "you need to bring in the person who is causing the disruption. Your daughter Anne really needs to come with you in order for us to talk about this and work it all out. Without her we can't really get to the bottom of this. She is obviously running the show."

"Oh no," answered my mother-in-law dismissively, "we can't bring Anne in. She would never come and if we asked her it would make her angry. We're not going to do that."

The therapist shrugged, figuratively and literally. She said she didn't think there was much more she could do to help, although she was willing to try.

Per Jack and Bernice's wishes, we didn't go back to therapy again. They both said they thought the therapist didn't know what she was talking about. I believe Bernice may have said, "She's full of soup." Bernice never used profanity even when she thought someone was actually full of shit as she did in this scenario.

Ned and I continued to be exiled from family events. But, in our little family, the one we shared with our three sweet daughters, life was warm and loving. We were concerned our kids were being deprived of a more normal extended family life so we worked hard to insure our nuclear family was a safe and wonderful place. We talked to the girls about the family problems as best we could, appropriate to their ages. We never wanted to burden them with more than they had to bear. Experts counsel when it comes to sharing delicate information with children you let them lead and only tell them what they seem able to handle. So, we gave our daughters information and answered their questions as they arose, but tried not to dwell on it. We worked hard not to paint their grandparents or their aunts with too broad a brush of nastiness. We always hoped someday the problems would be worked out and we didn't want the girls to be unable to welcome these folks back into their lives. We also didn't want them to conclude their grandparents didn't care about them. They easily could have given how rarely they saw them.

Our daughters had the nicest relationships with each other. They played beautifully together. Arguments were rare. When they did argue, we encouraged them to work out the problems and reach compromises or apologize when necessary. We taught them never to let anger fester. We fostered this basic rule in our house: Take care of each other and value each other above all else. Your sisters are precious, we told them. We knew just how important sisters could be and we wanted to make sure they learned that lesson despite not seeing us live that way.

In some ways it felt like the five of us were alone in the world, family-wise but that was okay because together we were formidable. We had tons of fun together. We traveled in the summers, often taking the kids on extended camping trips and even one cross country jaunt that lasted about six weeks. Talk about togetherness! I declared a family theme song, and despite the requisite eye roll of the girls, I think they agreed with my choice, Jefferson Starship's "Nothing's Gonna Stop Us Now."

Let them say we're crazy.
I don't care about that.
Put your hand in my hand, baby, don't ever look back.
Let the world around us just fall apart.
Baby we can make it if we're heart to heart.
And we can build this thing together, standing strong forever, nothing's gonna stop us now.

As a result, as the years flew by, we were able to help each other through any lonely times. In fact, our girls say they never felt the least bit lonely. When other kids talked about visiting grandparents like that was a fun thing to do, our girls were confused but not morose. When other kids described their holiday dinner tables with aunts and uncles and cousins, our kids didn't feel bereft, they just knew our celebrations to be more intimate but no less fun. It also helped that the good times as a nuclear family far outnumbered the difficult times as an extended family. Our home wasn't a sad place, it wasn't a place where Ned and I sat around and continually trashed our siblings. We didn't concentrate on that. We focused on raising happy children who felt unconditional love.

One of the ways we escaped the madness was to visit coastal North Carolina where we ultimately opened a seasonal ice cream shop. It was a true "Mom and Pop" operation, staffed by our family and children of a few friends. At "Fresco," each of our daughters worked side by side in the store, even though Tamra and Shira had to stand on stools to be seen by the customers for the first season, as they were only about 12 and 13 and teeny tiny girls. Working together was awesome. If we had had a more loving relationship with our extended family I'm not sure we would have ended up living part of the year so far away but I wouldn't, nor would any of our daughters, trade our summers in North Carolina for anything. We believe the Outer Banks to be magical. Each of us has been changed for the better as a result of the time we spent there working and playing together. Alexis met her husband there. Ned and I made loving and lifelong friends. To this day, we all look forward to our family time there even though we no longer have a store.

During the next few years we continued to see Jack and Bernice sporadically. We began to see Nan regularly as she was seeing a therapist who lived in our neighborhood. She'd come over twice a week and hang out or stay for dinner. When we found out she was a hoarder and a recovering crystal meth addict with pretty severe mental illness, we stepped in to help her live a more orderly and cleaner life. We worked to clean out her place in which she had accumulated 20 cats and a horrible amount of dirt and clutter. We had to throw out her ruined furniture so we bought her new things to replace the trash we threw away. We tried to teach her basic life skills. When she turned 50 we took her to see her first Broadway show. We invited her to come out with us and be among our friends. We spent a great deal of time with her hoping we could facilitate her learning to be independent. She was difficult to deal with and she had a lot of anger directed toward her parents and toward Anne (who ignored her) but she seemed to be making some progress. We were hopeful about her chance at a happier life. She was trying to distance herself from her abusive, drug-addicted boyfriend Frank and we supported her in that effort.

Sometime during the next few years, Anne phoned Ned and said her life was perfect except for her estrangement from her brother. She invited us back into the family once again. We accepted and the family dinners, although infrequent, were resurrected.

My father-in-law was turning 80 and a big party was planned, yet again. This time Anne wanted to coordinate a performance. It's actions like this one that make so many people love Anne. She can be creative and giving. It's confusing to me but I recognize that the people who only know this side of her think those of us who don't worship her are wrong. Anne wanted the four siblings to write and perform a song parody. They chose the tune of "Rocky Mountain High," a song Jack didn't know the words to but loved to sing constantly.

The "show" performance of Jack's "Rocky Mountain High" (a funny title for a man who is a teetotaler), was a huge hit. Jack loved every minute of his party. While not all of his grandchildren were there because Ted's kids in California did not attend, Jack's four kids and five of seven grandchildren were surrounding him for all his friends to see. Our niece Beth lived in California at that time. She had been living there for about ten years since she was sent to boarding school there, but she came home for the party.

Family matters stayed quiet and calm for a few years. We were invited to Anne and Dick's house for a Thanksgiving dinner for the first time. Anne called and told me to come at 5:30. At 5:20 on Thanksgiving, Dick called. That was quite unusual; he had never phoned us before.

"Where are you?" Dick asked in a voice that sounded more annoyed than friendly.

"What do you mean?" I responded, thinking "Happy Thanksgiving" would certainly have been a nicer way for him to start the conversation.

"Anne told us dinner was at 5:30. We're leaving in a few minutes." They lived four blocks away so we could get there in about two minutes.

"Everyone's here and waiting for you," Dick said somewhat exasperatedly, "dinner was called for 5:00."

I may not be sure of a lot of things in my life but I was sure of one thing. Anne had said 5:30. But apparently she told everyone else 5:00. Now, this next part I don't know and I can only theorize. Maybe it was an innocent mistake. Maybe Anne didn't set it up so we looked rude in front of the rest of her friends and family. But, Dick's call just felt odd in tone. Because, really, shouldn't he have opened with "Happy Thanksgiving?" Or at least "Hello?"

"I'm sorry," I said. "We'll be right over."

So we went right over but when we got there, no one answered the door when we knocked so we just walked in. Nobody took our coats or greeted us. We knew Ned's mother and father, Anne's husband and kids, and Ned's sister Nan and her boyfriend. But then there was another family of four people we didn't know (turned out to be Dick's brother and family) and one other guy about Rob's age who was unfamiliar. No one introduced anyone else. They were actually too busy eating because they had clearly not waited until all the guests had arrived to begin.

It was completely unwelcoming. Considering this was our first Thanksgiving with the family in many years, you might think someone would have thought to try to extend a warm welcome. This was literally the polar opposite of warm. The guests were seated scattered around the house in different rooms. Dinner was buffet-style despite the fact Anne's formal dining room was more than big enough to seat this number of people. She had chosen not to host that kind of intimate dinner, I suppose. She served on paper plates, which the Anne of the earlier years would not only not have done, but she would have blasted as gauche anyone who would do such a thing on Thanksgiving. When one of our daughters went to sit in the small den adjoining the dining room, a room separated by an archway without a door which had the same hardwood flooring as the rest of the house, she was accosted by Anne and Dick who explained the "meditation room" was not to be entered with shoes on. I believe that was the only time that night Anne spoke to anyone in our family.

Just when we thought it could not possibly get any more bizarre or awkward, they broke out some drums and started a kind of a drum circle in the living room. Since they didn't have enough actual drums, Rob brought out some plastic containers for people to bang on. They started drumming and chanting. It sounded a bit like free form jazz. Each person sang a tune or some words but none were connected to any other person's "song." Rob interspersed some narration and commentary with the chanting.

"There's Ned on the Wheel of Life," he called out, as he handed Ned a drum. Ned tried to take part by tapping the drum and attempting to "sing" along.

"And Mimi on the plastic," he continued, as his grandmother laughed and banged wildly on a round container.

Jack, always the songbird but without the knowledge of the "songs" they were chanting wanted to participate anyway so he started singing "The Twelfth of Never," at the top of his lungs to be heard above everyone else. He then launched into "What's It All About Alfie?" This seemed to fit right in given the total strangeness of what was going on. The rest of the people continued to chant and bang so it was quite the cacophony of bizarreness. My girls and I and even Ned, although he was "playing" along, found this entire scene weird and uncomfortable. We stayed a polite amount of time after dessert. When Nan and her boyfriend left (because we didn't want to be the first), we left to visit some friends who felt more like family. Finally we felt the warm embrace and comfort of Thanksgiving.

We were back in the family, all right, but I'm not sure we belonged or really wanted to be there. Be careful what you wish for, you may get it, I suppose. Time passed, though, and relations were calm. Our nephew Rob went away to school in Colorado. Anne's kids had little to no contact with their dad, who had moved away to Arizona and remarried a third time. We didn't get together as a family often.

As time passed, our family relations remained stable. When Anne went through another difficult time because her son Rob was experiencing a major depression, we went to talk with her and to support her. Rob was far from home. His mental/emotional disturbance was serious. He appeared to be losing touch with reality. Anne told us he was eating out of dumpsters, pouring chocolate milk on his head, and telling people he was Gandhi. She said she was going to fly to Colorado and bring him home because he had burned his photo ID cards and could not board a plane by himself. We replied we thought that was good as she could then get him to a hospital or a doctor who could give him the care he so desperately needed. We said we were relieved to know he'd soon be in good hands. Imagine our surprise and dismay when Anne replied she had no intention of taking him to a hospital or to a doctor of Western medicine. Her plan was to have his "auras checked." This young man was having what appeared to be a psychotic episode and his mother was going to have his AURAS CHECKED? We weren't sure how to respond. He did come home and he lived with Anne for a while. We didn't hear much about his health for the next couple of months and she kept a pretty low profile with him in her house.

Alexis did visit Rob once. She said it was quite a strange scene in their house. Rob's relationship with his mother was strained, Alexis said, based on the fact that while she was there they were yelling at each other a great deal. Alexis thought Rob seemed to love Anne and yet to fear her. Their interactions made Alexis uncomfortable, though probably not as uncomfortable as she was when she and Rob went for a walk and he told her he saw her dead grandfather walking behind them. Guess his aura check didn't exactly solve his problem.

The next time we connected with Rob was on his 21st birthday a few months after he came home. We wanted to do something special for him. He loved and wrote poetry so we thought buying him wonderful books by beloved poets would be the perfect gift. We called Anne's house that night to find out if they would be home. She said they would be home all night; they were celebrating his birthday at home and had no plans to go out.

"Great," we said, "we'll be over in an hour with a gift for him."

We went to Barnes and Noble and chose several hardcover volumes of poetry. The gift was expensive, more than we normally would spend, but we wanted it to be worthy of this big birthday. We arrived at Anne's house when we said we would.

No one was home. We left the gift at the front door. We never heard from Anne or from Rob about the gift.

Soon after that our niece Beth moved back to Pennsylvania from California. We all attended a family dinner at our in-laws' home. It was the Jewish New Year holiday of Rosh Hashanah. It had been many years since we had all sat around their dining room table and it went okay. It was a bit awkward at first but it got easier as the night went on. Beth, Rob, Alexis, Tamra, and Shira got along well. They joked a bit and tried to get to know each other again. They really appeared eager to do so. I think they were all happy to reconnect with their cousins. That part was kind of nice, bittersweet in that they had been denied access to each other for years for no reason, but still sort of nice.

The next day, Alexis, then about 16 years old, walked over to Anne's house to visit Beth. Beth seemed happy to see her. Alexis was thrilled to have a cousin to hang out with. She told Beth to call her so they could arrange to do something together. Beth never called, so, undaunted, Alexis called and left a message but she didn't hear from her.

A few weeks later, Ned called his mom to invite his parents to Thanksgiving dinner, which was coming up soon. Ned told Bernice he'd call and invite everyone else in the family, too. We were excited about having the event at our house for the first time for the whole family.

"Dad and I can't come," his mom answered, somewhat awkwardly.

"What do you mean you can't come?"

"We're having Thanksgiving with Anne. Nan is too."

"Oh," Ned said, quite taken aback. "I haven't heard from Anne. Aren't we invited?" Ned asked, somewhat incredulous this was happening again.

"I don't think so," his mom said. "You better call and ask her why she didn't invite you. I don't want to get in the middle. I'm not going to ask her about you."

Ned chose not to call Anne. He didn't really need to know why we were out of the family yet again. It hadn't made sense any of the other times we had been exiled. He didn't expect this time was going to be any more logical. He just felt disheartened and hurt all over again. He wasn't up for beating that previously dead, reincarnated, and now re-dead horse, I guess.

At some point before Thanksgiving Ned's brother Ted talked to Anne on the phone. Living in California, he wasn't coming to Thanksgiving dinner anyway, but I guess he was curious about what was going on and why we hadn't been invited. Anne told him she didn't want us at her Thanksgiving dinner because she was offended when we had all been at our in-laws for that Rosh Hashanah dinner a few weeks earlier and our daughters didn't wash the dishes. I could understand Anne being annoyed if she thought my kids were acting a bit too much like princesses and maybe she even could have thought them a tad lazy and perhaps even spoiled except for one tiny detail. Her kids hadn't gotten up to help either. Somehow that didn't exclude *them* from being included in her Thanksgiving festivities, though. That was the only reason she ever gave for why she didn't want us at Thanksgiving. My daughters hadn't done the dishes.

Drum roll please…we were out of the family again.

That Thanksgiving night, we enjoyed the holiday with our favorite people -- the five of us. We had a blast and laughed about the comparison between this year and the last when drums and plastic ware were the entertainment. After dinner, we watched home videos of the girls when they were young. We snuggled, we laughed, and we enjoyed the trip down memory lane. It was fun to watch the home movies and be reminded of just who we were as a family. Maybe it was as a result of "us against the world" or maybe it was because we genuinely like as well as love each other. The bottom line was our lives were so much more fun than pain. We chose to focus on the interactions between the five of us. We worked hard to communicate. If there were problems, we worked them out. We were open about how we felt. Honesty ruled. Lies were never a means to an end. All of these things, I believe, grew out of learning from the mistakes all around us in our extended families. We couldn't change the people in our extended families but we could and we did work hard at making sure nothing like that happened in our nuclear unit. All in all, it was a nice evening. There was so much to be grateful for that year, as there had been every year leading up to it and every year since. But that year, at 9:30 PM, there was an unexpected knock at the door. I answered the door. Ned was in the kitchen, finishing up the last of the dishes.

There stood my in-laws, who were stopping in on their way home from Anne's. Well, not exactly on their way home. Anne lives three blocks away. After having Thanksgiving dinner at her house, Jack and Bernice decided they'd stop at our house to wish us a happy holiday. But Anne asked them to drive home a friend of hers who lived near where they lived, about 15 minutes away. Being too afraid to tell Anne they weren't going straight home, but instead were stopping at our house, my in-laws drove Anne's friend home and then turned around and drove back to see us. I was stunned and not happy to see them. I didn't want the peace and tranquility of our lovely night to come to this abrupt end. I stuttered a bit and then opened the door to let them in. I don't think I smiled or greeted them warmly. I couldn't handle the bullshit politely. They came into the living room and sat down with Alexis, Tamra, Shira, and me. Ned stayed in the kitchen.

Ned was angry and upset about the whole scene. He was fed up with years of playing second fiddle to his sister. He had invited his parents and wanted to invite his whole family to Thanksgiving. But they chose to go where we weren't welcome. He heard them come in but stayed in the kitchen. Ned is usually very polite so that sort of rude behavior was out of character for this good son. Knowing his behavior was unusual; my mother-in-law walked into the kitchen and confronted Ned about why he was being rude. That was ironic if you think about it. Bernice would never once question Anne's actions in any way but if Ned was rude, that was cause for confrontation. Ned tried to explain to his mother a bit about how their late-night, surprise Thanksgiving visit made him feel. Alexis came in to support her dad, whom she felt was under attack. She told her grandmother calmly that showing up at 9:30 on Thanksgiving, acting as if that were perfectly normal and pretending to be loving and caring parents and grandparents, was upsetting. Alexis wasn't nasty or rude or fresh. She just spoke her mind and pretty much summed up what neither Ned nor I could articulate. Tamra didn't quite understand why Alexis was speaking to her grandmother that way. It wasn't that Tam wanted them to stop over like that either; she was less hurt by it than Alexis was. Shira didn't seem to understand much about what was going on either. The age difference between my girls mattered in this situation. Alexis was the oldest. She had a better understanding about how her grandparents' behavior was hurtful. For Tamra and Shira, what their grandparents did on that holiday wasn't a big deal. They were used to not having them around; they didn't much care.

Jack and Bernice left soon after hearing from Alexis. I don't believe they ever forgave her for speaking the truth.

We settled back into a familiar family routine. We spent holidays as a quintet and they were harmonious. Ned's parents and Nan spent holidays with Anne. Our little family of five remained vigilant about our personal interactions. We traveled together in the summers and spent time in nature hiking and camping (causing all three girls to insist they'll never hike or camp again!), we went to resorts for winter holiday weeks, we even visited friends in Rome. We had fun together and we still do.

Even though Jack and Bernice stayed in the Anne camp, and Anne continued to do dutiful daughter things, the relationship between Anne and her parents began to unravel. Although we weren't around to witness the events, we'd often hear stories from Nan (who tried to stay neutral in the family mess) about things going awry. When Bernice turned 80 Anne wanted the family to make a memory book for her. Anne's plan was for each child and grandchild to create a page with pictures and anecdotes about their grandmother. She sent each participant a page of the book to complete. Of course, Ned and our children didn't get pages so the book Bernice ultimately received, ostensibly made by "all members" of her loving family was minus a few pages. As far as that book was concerned, Ned and his offspring didn't exist. I don't know how Bernice felt about the book but I do know this, she didn't keep it out on display and we've never seen it. Even when she moved years later and we helped her clean out her house and pack her belongings, that book was nowhere to be found.

One Sunday night in June 2001 Anne wanted her family to go out for dinner to celebrate some family birthdays. Jack wanted to have dinner at home with the family because his beloved 76ers basketball team was in the NBA playoffs. LA led the series 2 games to 1 and Jack did not want to miss the game that was to start at 8:30 that night. If he had to go out to dinner, he said, he wanted to be home in time to watch the game. Despite Jack's plea to eat close enough to home in order to get back in time to watch, Anne chose to take the family into Center City for dinner. Jack, who never liked going downtown anyway (It was too far to drive, hard to park, expensive, etc.), was annoyed at having to go so far away from home. I guess he worried his chances of catching the whole game were starting to evaporate. Apparently, Anne told him they'd go early enough for him to get home in time. But, once they were at the restaurant, things were going a lot slower than he hoped. He began to grumble he was worried about missing the game. Although he was muttering this under his breath, Anne was able to hear him and she flipped out. She said she was tired of hearing his selfish complaining and if he didn't like what was happening, he should leave.

So, he did. Eighty-three-year-old Jack walked out of the restaurant by himself at about 7:30 on a Sunday night in downtown Philadelphia with, as far as everyone knew, little to no cash in his pocket. Nobody, not his daughters, not his wife, not his son-in-law or his grandchildren went after him. In order to get to his house via public transportation, he'd have to take an elevated train and several buses, many of which don't run often on Sunday night. He did get home but no one knows how.

Sometime shortly after the downtown dinner debacle, Anne told her mother she thought Bernice should divorce Jack. Anne cited as a reason that Jack did not treat Bernice respectfully and she should refuse to keep taking it. Although we heard this story from Nan and thought advising your 81-year-old mother to get a divorce from the love of her life was bizarre and perhaps cruel, it didn't have much impact because Bernice didn't divorce her husband. We did hear Jack and Bernice spent several days apart, though. Either way, Jack and Bernice maintained their relationship with Anne.

When her son Rob graduated college Anne invited her parents to attend the party she was making for him but she had a list of hoops for her dad to jump through in order to earn entrance to the party. I mean she literally wrote a list of things her father could and couldn't do. He had to promise he'd abide by her rules or he wouldn't be allowed to attend the party. I don't recall what all the rules were but I remember two of the things. He had to refrain from complaining to her guests about pains in his legs, and he had to promise not to mention Germans, Nazis, or World War II. Although we didn't see that much of Jack, we didn't know what the reference to pains in his legs was about. We never heard him complaining about his legs. As to the World War II and Nazi conversation, we had heard a number of his stories about "French bastards" and some tales about how he cooked for soldiers during the war but it wasn't as if he talked about it ad nauseum. Jack was offended and upset but he wanted to attend his grandson's graduation party so he agreed to the list of conditions.

Time passed as it had before. When Jack's 84th birthday rolled around Ned and I offered to host a brunch at our house. We said we'd call and invite Anne too if Bernice and Jack wanted that. They did. Ned phoned her. He said Dad was getting on in years and wouldn't it be good to bury the hatchet and gather 'round the birthday table to wish him well?

Anne said she had a "laundry list" of conditions Ned would have to meet before she'd come to our house. This woman was clearly into lists and conditions. I felt no need to hear this woman's dirty "laundry list," but I deferred to Ned because she was, after all, his sister. Ned declined to hear her list because it seemed to him if you had a list to begin with, you probably aren't truly open to reconciliation. Jack and Bernice declined our birthday invitation and went to Anne's instead. (Shocking? Hardly. We were well used to this by that time.) When Anne carried out the birthday cake with lit candles waiting for a wish to be made, Jack wished aloud for a chance to see his whole family around a table again before he died.

Anne exploded. She told her father he'd have to leave her house immediately.

"I warned you what would happen if you ever mentioned Ned's name again," she shrieked.

While Jack hadn't actually mentioned Ned's name, because of his birthday wish about gathering his children and grandchildren, she was done with him. Jack didn't leave right away so his grandson Rob backed up his mother.

"Pop Pop, you really have to go now," Rob told his grandfather.

Jack was clearly upset (Who wouldn't be?), so Nan tried to intervene to defend her dad. Anne threw her out too. Bernice, Jack, and Nan left.

Happy Birthday indeed.

About two months after the birthday blow up Anne was diagnosed with Multiple Sclerosis. Among other things, she angrily told her parents the stress they had caused her in asking her to help mend the family had resulted in her illness. Bernice was devastated at the thought that something she did could have harmed her daughter so severely. She even called a doctor to find out if she could have given her daughter MS. The doctor assured her she was not to blame for her daughter's MS.

Anne continued to pull back from her parents and she totally cut off Nan as well. Jack and Bernice tried to see her and support her in her illness but she was definitely giving them a hard time. She did, however, continue what she had been saying for years -- that it would be good if they would "gift" money to her while they were alive instead of waiting to leave it to her after they died. It's not like they hadn't been giving her anything. They had paid for her health insurance for 18 years. They had paid for many improvements in her home. They'd given her gifts of cash. She just wanted more.

At some point after that birthday wish horror, Nan came to Ned with a concern. As a result of her mental illness and emotional problems Nan is not capable of earning or managing money. My in-laws had set up their will with Nan's inherited money to be placed into a trust in the care of a trustee. They had picked Anne to serve as trustee. Nan was not comfortable with Anne being her trustee. She knew Anne to be a vengeful person and also a control freak. Nan was never that comfortable with Anne being in charge of her money but after being ejected from her sister's home during the birthday party, Nan was even more worried because now Anne wasn't speaking to her. She was afraid she would have to kowtow to Anne for the rest of her life in order to get access to her own money after her parents were gone. She didn't want a trustee, but if she had to have one, she wanted it to be Ned.

So, Bernice made an appointment with a lawyer to see about changing that aspect of their will. The three of them, Ned, Nan, and Bernice went to see the lawyer. The lawyer went over the will with them. At some point, the lawyer looked confused. At that moment he was pointing out the provision that stated "Ted" was only being left half of what his three siblings were getting. After an awkward moment, and obvious confusion on Ned's face, they decided Ned and Nan should leave the room so the lawyer could speak privately with Bernice.

The reason for the lawyer's confusion was this. The person actually being left only half of what the others were getting was not Ted. It was Ned. (This is one of the problems with giving your children rhyming names. People get confused!) Since Ned was the man sitting in front of him, the lawyer must have been puzzled and thought maybe the names were reversed. After all, if you were so mad at one son you'd cut his inheritance in half, why would you bring that same son into the office to discuss the will? And, clearly, this "half" inheritance was news to Ned and why, the lawyer must have wondered, would you want your son to find out about this stunningly cruel stipulation in your will in this way? I also suspect once he figured out Ned was unaware of this unfair split, the attorney really didn't want to be the one to break the news to Ned he was being left far less than his siblings. That's likely why he asked Ned and Nan to leave the room so he could sort it all out.

While Ned and Nan were in the hall with Ned thinking Ted was the one being slighted, they discussed it. Nan didn't say much but Ned said he thought his parents were doing the wrong thing. Ted had gotten into some trouble with the law a few years earlier. He had been arrested and pled guilty to a fraud felony. Ned thought his parents had decided to punish their son for his mistake by cutting his inheritance. Ned had always supported Ted, despite his criminal activity. We often hired him to work for us so he could earn some money. Ned believed the family should rally around any member who was in trouble or who had made a mistake. So, Ned told Nan he didn't think cutting down Ted's inheritance was the right thing for their parents to do and they – the siblings – should do something to make sure Ted inherited the same amount the rest of them were getting. Ned thought despite any mistakes Ted may have made, everyone should be left equal shares. Otherwise, it didn't feel right, he would be uncomfortable inheriting more than one of his siblings, and most important, that wasn't a loving legacy for their parents to leave. Nan didn't voice an opinion and remained oddly silent.

But, when they came back into the office and the will's stipulations were clarified, Ned was informed *he* was the one being punished. He was the one being left half of what the siblings were getting. His mom said nothing by way of explanation. They left the office soon after the big reveal. I suspect an attorney has never been happier to see a client exit the office. And just when you thought this mother and son outing couldn't possibly get any more awkward or uncomfortable; Ned had to drive his mother and sister home. I can't imagine what that car ride was like. When he got home and told me the story, I did not react quietly or calmly.

"Tell your parents you don't want any of their money. They can shove the money up their ass. We never need to see them again."

I was officially done with these people. Unfortunately, they were Ned's parents and he wasn't willing to be done with them. I do understand, I really do. I just was so angry with them for treating Ned, and by extension his daughters and me, this way.

Within a day or so my in-laws came over. We asked them why they did what they did with their will. What they did was this – they set up an irrevocable trust leaving each of their kids 28.3% of their estate, except for Ned who was left only 15%.

At first, they admitted they had been angry about Ned's disloyalty to the family and drafted the will punitively. But quickly, I mean literally while they were standing in our family room talking to us about it, they developed a new cover story. It wasn't out of anger, they explained, it was because Ned had more money than his siblings. Well, that was highly implausible because a few years earlier Ned had left his job as an elementary principal and I left the job I had and we started our own small business. It wasn't like we were captains of industry. And how would they have known how much money we had? They never asked. They had no way of knowing how much money we had. We certainly didn't live a higher or more affluent-looking lifestyle than his sister Anne. She lived in a nicer house, she drove more expensive cars, she traveled more, and she dressed in more expensive clothing. I don't know how else one judges the amount of money in a person's bank account but if appearances counted for anything, we certainly weren't the wealthiest of their adult children. Not that it should matter anyway.

Then they said my father had left us money when he died so they figured we didn't need their money. Again, they had no way of knowing how much my dad had given me. He certainly wasn't a rich man after a career as a foreman in a dog food factory.

These were excuses. It was obvious Jack and Bernice didn't want to own up to the real reason they had written their will this way. They had been so angry about Ned's "betrayal" of Anne they set up a punishment that was going to live on in perpetuity. The way this trust worked it would pay an interest payment each year for 3 generations, so every year Ned would get a check that was half the amount his siblings got. It would serve as an annual reminder his parents had been angry and would be angry for many years after they died. They made no special arrangements for our children to get what would have been part of Ned's share, either, so our girls would be punished as well. The sins of the father…

We knew the cover story about us having more money was a lie. We knew it because they had also made Ted, Nan, and Anne promise never to tell Ned what the will said. They had all known for years how the will was structured. While Jack and Bernice didn't exactly apologize, they did say they'd see the lawyer and explore options to "fix" the will. Ned was pretty fed up with his parents. Ned's mom was in therapy again with a new therapist. She asked Ned to join her. Yay, not me this time! The therapist, Rose Farkas, was an older woman, probably about 75. My mother-in-law liked her a lot. When Ned met her, he liked her too. At their first session, after hearing from both Bernice and Ned, Rose asked Bernice this question:

"Why do you let your daughter control you?"

Bernice really had no answer for that. Rose said Ned's parents had to bring Anne into a session (sound familiar?) but again Jack and Bernice said Anne wouldn't come and they would not even ask her. Some things never change. Ned and his mom, and later his dad, continued to

140

see Rose for a while that fall. They didn't talk too much about the will but Ned assumed it had been "fixed" in some way because that is what Jack had told him. In the meantime, Anne really wasn't talking to or seeing much of her parents once she heard they were changing the details of their will and not in a way that benefited her.

Chapter Sixteen: The Third Death

During the next few months, lots of things happened. First, Ned found out Jack and Bernice had lied to him again. They had never actually "fixed" the will. This came out during a therapy session with Rose, who continued to support Ned. She said in order to make amends and try to heal the damage to Ned's relationship with his parents; the will should be altered so it was equal for all. My in-laws swore again they'd do exactly that expediently.

More and more of the background story about the "ill" will had come out over time. It turned out the will had been drawn up years before. There had been about ten meetings with financial planners and lawyers over the course of a year to draft this will. Jack, Bernice, and Anne had attended each meeting. The lawyer said he had explained time and time again that what they were doing was irrevocable and could not be changed, but Jack insisted that was exactly what he wanted. Ted (who may also have been present at one of the will planning meetings) and Nan also knew about the will during those years but all agreed it should remain a secret from Ned. So, his parents and all of his siblings had conspired against him for years. No one ever let on. They just pretended it hadn't happened.

A few years before we found out about the will and the big secret, I was speaking to my sister-in-law, Ted's wife Kelly, on the phone. She told me the family had this huge secret, which Jack had shared with her when he visited California. She said Jack had told her he was really angry with Ned because he blamed him for the destruction of the family and he planned to leave Ned half of what he was going to leave his other children. He also told Kelly everyone else in the family knew the secret but they had all conspired to keep Ned from finding out. Kelly said she told Jack what he was doing was not right but he obstinately refused to listen. Kelly suggested to Jack if he was that angry with Ned, he should tell him rather than planning to punish his son after his death when they could no longer discuss it. Kelly was divulging the secret to me because she was at the time separated from Ted and angry with him. I repeated the story to Ned but we both dismissed it as a story Kelly must have made up in anger. We didn't ask Jack, Bernice, Nan, or Ted about it. We didn't think Ned's parents would ever do such a thing. We surely didn't think the whole family would keep such an ugly secret. Wow, were we wrong on all counts.

No one said the details of the will had been Anne's idea but no one said they hadn't been either. It was clear Anne was, at the very least, instrumental in the plan. When Anne got wind of the fact the will she had helped craft was in the process of being altered, she was not happy. When she learned some of the details of the new will, including that she was no longer executrix, she wrote her parents a plaintive letter.

The letter was a quintessential sample of Anne's lifelong bullying tactics. She went into great detail about how much emotional pain Bernice and Jack had caused her. She upbraided them for being "lonely now" because they had taken her for granted. Apparently she assumed without her in their lives they'd have no one and she reveled in the thought of her elderly parents being sad and alone. She chided them for not being there for her in that year when she needed them most, without mentioning they had repeatedly tried to see her but she refused. But in the same sentence she described how "not one of the many" notes they sent offered sufficient apologies for how they hurt her.

She reminded them of the years they complained to her about Ned and berated them for choosing that man as their executor, displaying remarkable distrust and disrespect for her. She went on to describe the "one point of entry" to reconcile. By Friday of that week they had to take her to their lawyer's office and reinstate her as executrix. Failing that, she was pretty much done with them forever.

Next, she played the MS card, employing a decidedly sarcastic tone just to make it a tad more painful for them to read:

"In case you don't recall, I have **MS,** an incurable disease that requires my attention every day in order to maintain my health. Stress is the last thing that I need. Since I have removed myself from my family of origin I have not had stress and I am not interested in jeopardizing my health by exposing myself to stressful situations. Although you have done many kind things in the past, you have also caused me much trauma over the years."

Poor Anne. Her parents' occasionally wishing aloud to have their family rift healed (because that is the only offense they committed) was traumatic for her.

And then she had the gall to blame them for making her write this letter!

"Just writing this letter is upsetting as it evokes so much sadness and disappointment about the way things turned out. There is so much more that I have to express, however if you are not willing to restore your trust and respect for me by reinstating me as executrix there is no reason to proceed."

But, don't worry. It wasn't all gloom and doom. Anne wrapped up by telling them she loved them because they were her parents. But, if she didn't hear from them by Friday, things would "remain as they are." In other words, she'd continue to do what she had been doing, refusing to see them or to speak to them and excluding them from her family events with her children.

For her grand finale: "Love and light, Anne."

Ouch. My stomach heaves when I think about how any parent would feel reading that missive. Bernice and Jack had spent nearly a lifetime giving Anne everything she wanted and more. They had pretty much sacrificed their family at Anne's alter. But, when at the end of their lives they just wanted peace in the family, she destroyed them.

At the time that letter was written Jack was sick. At some point a few weeks after that letter was written, Jack was diagnosed with bladder cancer. His prognosis wasn't great. He worked at wrapping up his will as best he could. He stipulated he wanted his four children to receive equal amounts in inheritance and changed the executor of his and Bernice's will from Anne to a bank. At that point, Anne was not speaking to Ned or Nan. Jack didn't think it made sense to have her be the executor since they couldn't count on her to handle affairs fairly. She was right about one thing in her letter. They could no longer trust her. After they didn't meet her Friday deadline, Anne was furious.

144

Just about two weeks before Jack's death while he was hospitalized, Bernice had gotten home from a visit to him on a Sunday night. About 10:00 PM Anne showed up at the door. She argued with her mom for a while. She was angry about the change in the will. Anne had spent years crafting her revenge against Ned. She attended all those financial planning meetings about her parents' will to get it to be exactly as she wanted it. Not only would Ned get half of what his siblings got, because they all agreed to keep this secret, Ned wouldn't find out about it until after his parents were dead. It would be a double whammy: Ned would lose money, true, but more hurtful would be the fact he'd find out when it was too late to reconcile, that his parents had been angry for years and punished him accordingly. He'd find out that while his parents pretended to love him and his daughters, they had been working behind his back and siding with Anne throughout much of his adult life. I'm sure as Anne saw it, the moment of revelation when Ned learned the truth would be *her* greatest triumph. And, then, poof, that moment was pulled out from under her. The truth had come out. Her parents were no longer under her control. Her great moment of triumph was forever elusive. According to Kelly, when the truth about the will came out, Anne paged her brother Ted, "911." He needed to contact her immediately; there was an emergency, their secret was out, their plans were thwarted.

So, yes, Anne was mad when her father was dying and still wouldn't do her bidding. That Sunday night when she went to her mother and found *she* would no longer be controlled either, Anne was astronomically pissed off. They had a huge screaming argument. Anne demanded her mother hand over the jewelry Bernice had promised to leave Anne upon her death. Apparently, at some point earlier, Bernice, Nan, and Anne had gone through all of Bernice's jewelry to decide which pieces would go to whom. There were some pieces earmarked for Anne, some for Nan, some for Beth, and one for Rob. No one else was left any of Bernice's treasures. But that night, while her dad was literally on his deathbed and her mom was, well, not nearly close to death, Anne decided she didn't need to wait until after her mother died to get her jewels. She wanted her mother's jewelry at that exact moment.

On that night, Ned and I were eight hours away in North Carolina because it was the time of year when our ice cream store was open for business. So, while Jack was dealing with bladder cancer, we had to live in another state. That's where we were when Anne showed up at Bernice's to collect the loot she wanted. Nan was at her parents' house too; that's how we found out about Anne showing up. Nan was very upset about the fight between her mother and her sister. She was already overwrought about her dad's impending death and witnessing this fight was too hard. Nan didn't know what to do so she called us in North Carolina to tell us what was going on. She began repeating what Anne was screaming at Bernice. Nan couldn't hear Bernice's answers, but she could hear Anne loud and clear.

"I'm just standing in my authentic truths," Anne stated firmly and apparently at the top of her lungs.

Here's the backstory on that tasty morsel of total bullshit. Years before there had been a self-help guru named Debbie Ford making the scene. She was an Oprah sensation. She was a "life coach," and she offered certification for others to become "life coaches" as well. The so-called coaches weren't licensed therapists, but could be more like unlicensed charlatans, and therefore, the perfect career choice for Anne.

Anne took the Debbie Ford training and became a "life coach." People actually pay Anne for her advice and counsel. I've heard some of her clients consider her guidance essential to their well being. I've known a lot of people in my life but I can assure you I've never known anyone more poorly equipped to teach people how to run their lives than Anne. But, this "authentic truth" thing was a phrase Debbie Ford promoted. Somehow, Anne's "authentic truth" meant she needed to take immediate possession of her mother's cherished treasures. Bernice didn't want to give them up just yet. Her agreement with her daughters was she'd keep the jewelry and they would get it when she died. And, Anne's "truth" didn't stop with the jewelry. It also extended to how she felt about Ned and me.

Again, Nan couldn't hear what her mother was saying but she could hear Anne's reply.

"No, I won't be around Ned and Debby. They are forces of negative energy," Anne offered, I'm guessing in answer to her mother's request

146

that the family pull together to support Jack while he sick and perhaps dying.

Because Anne still intimidated her in a big way and was able to bully her mother, Bernice handed over the 20 or so pieces of jewelry. Well, all but the Mikimoto pearls that Jack had bought for Bernice's 75th birthday. Anne said she really wanted those too, but Bernice was either not yet ready to part with them or she didn't want Anne to have them. But, stay tuned, because those pearls will make a return appearance in this story. (As an aside, I can't believe I even know the name of those pearls. I never thought pearls and I would be on a first-name basis. Or, perhaps Mikimoto is their last name, but you get the idea.)

Anne took her mother's jewels and went home, leaving Bernice despondent. Her husband was days from death and she just suffered through a pretty ugly argument with one of the great loves of her life.

About a week or so after the jewelry bullying, we got a call from Bernice saying Jack was about to have some kind of surgery the next day. They weren't sure he would survive so if we wanted to see him, we had to come back to Philadelphia immediately. We left North Carolina at night after we closed the store and drove all night to get home in the morning before surgery. When we got to the hospital room, Jack was asleep but Anne was sitting in his room reading aloud to him from the book, "The Tao of Pooh" by Benjamin Hoff. I swear to God I'm not making this up. I am pretty sure Jack wouldn't have known Winnie the Pooh if the bear had hit him over the head with the honey jar. Nor would Jack have ever been remotely interested in any form of Eastern Religion. (Or Western religion for that matter). Jack was not a philosopher, far from it. So, this scene was just as bizarre as it might seem.

I mean her 85-year-old Jewish father is pretty close to death and she's reading him quotes like, *"Lots of people talk to animals...Not very many listen though...that's the problem."*

And

"Do you really want to be happy? You can begin by being appreciative of who you are and what you've got."

And…

"How can you get very far,
If you don't know who you are?
How can you do what you ought,
If you don't know what you've got?
And if you don't know which to do
Of all the things in front of you,
Then what you'll have when you are through
Is just a mess without a clue
Of all the best that can come true
If you know What and Which and Who."

Don't get me wrong. I am a fan of Pooh. That bear and I go way back. I am also a fan of Eastern philosophies. I'm sure Hoff's book is wonderful in the right circumstance for the right people. I'm not making fun of any of those. But, please, you gotta know your audience.

And, I did.

So, I took in the scene and leaned in very close to Anne. I mean very close. My mouth was about an inch from her nose. Keep in mind my mouth held teeth and a tongue that had not yet been brushed after driving all night to get there. Considering the impact those hours and cups of coffee might have on my breath, I leaned in close enough to kiss Anne (not that I did or would) and I said slowly and deliberately in the most threatening, breathy voice I could muster,

"Don't even think about starting trouble with me or with Ned. Don't even think about saying anything nasty to either of us or to my kids. Because if you do, you will be standing knee deep in your authentic truth that will BE STEEPED IN NEGATIVE ENERGY!"

Anne didn't flinch. She didn't blink. She just sat there, eyes on Pooh.

Meanwhile, our niece Beth, who was about 30, took our daughters aside and talked to them about how screwed up the family was. She said the dysfunction didn't have to extend to the next generation, though, and gave Alexis her cell phone number. My girls were pretty

148

happy about that, especially Alexis, who really wanted cousins and an extended family. She called Beth soon after that day but Beth didn't pick up so Alexis left a message. Beth never returned the call. I had seen Anne watching the girls talk outside the hospital. I suspect when Anne heard about Beth's plan to connect with her cousins, she either forbade her to do so or strongly discouraged it.

Near the end of Jack's illness, Anne visited her father in the hospital again. While alone in the room with him she badgered him about changing the executor of his will back to her. He began to cry. Then he relented, telling her he'd make her the executor after all. Shortly after Anne left his room we arrived at the hospital to find a very vulnerable and shaken Jack lying in the bed. He sobbed as he related to us the whole story of Anne's visit. He said he didn't want to change his executor but he had capitulated in a weak moment. He said he wasn't really going to make the change, though, and he would tell her the next time they spoke.

The next few weeks were hard for everyone. Jack was in and out of the hospital. He was either in pain or very uncomfortable. And, making matters worse, Anne wouldn't visit him in the hospital if Ned or I were there so there were a lot of awkward moments when arrangements had to be made to get us out in order to get her in.

Jack had lived through that surgery but when it became clear Jack wouldn't survive the cancer they sent him home from the hospital to die. We went there quite a bit. One day I cooked a meal and took it to my in-laws' house so everyone could have dinner. My mother-in-law was touched and a bit surprised at my thoughtfulness. Of course I pointed out it was certainly no big deal (turkey meat loaf and mashed potatoes is not exactly gourmet fare) and it was just part of what families do at times like this. She looked confused and muttered something about perhaps being wrong about me. She also admitted perhaps she hadn't been "a good mother" to me. It was the first and last time she took any responsibility for the quality of our relationship.

My father-in-law was in a hospital bed in the family room. He was, for the most part, unconscious, although he'd wake once in a while. Each day he faded away a bit more. One day we were all there, just kind of hanging out together, Ned, Nan, Ted, my mother-in-law, and me. Jack had been quite out of it and was mostly sleeping or unconscious, it's hard to say which. I had read dying people may seem unconscious but even when their eyes are closed they may be hearing what's happening around them. They can't always demonstrate they're hearing things, but they are.

So, since that 80th birthday party had been, according to Jack, the best day of his life, and since we had a video of it that also had audio, I suggested we put on the video in the room where we were all sitting, just in case Jack could actually hear it. I figured if I were dying and could hear the soundtrack of the best day of my life, that would be a pretty cool way to go. What could be better? Not only would he be able to hear the party happenings, but that song parody of "Rocky Mountain High" was also on the video so I figured he'd at least enjoy that. We put on the video of the party and a good time was had by all, except Jack who remained unconscious. But, then a fascinating thing happened. On the video there was a quick scene of Ted hopping on one foot with his other foot tucked behind his head. No, he doesn't do yoga, but, yes, he can turn himself into a human pretzel. That scene was so funny Ned let out a loud cackle/laugh. You've heard of noises so loud they can "wake the dead"? Well, this laugh was so loud it woke the almost dead. It woke Jack out of his practically unconscious state. He sat up with a start, and put on his glasses to watch the video. Then he asked for a bowl of ice cream, which he proceeded to enjoy with gusto while watching the video of his best day. We rewound it and played it again so he wouldn't have to miss a minute.

It was a remarkable scene. There was Jack truly enjoying what could have been his last moments of life, surrounded by his loved ones, eating one of his favorite foods. I thought Bernice probably wished Anne could be there so I suggested to my mother-in-law she call her and encourage her to come see her dad while he was lucid, maybe for the last time. Anne refused to come because Ned and I were there. Her mom told her Jack was awake and happy and it might not last very long. Anne was unmoved. Well, maybe she was moved, but not enough to come over to see her father and she said so. Ned and I offered to leave so Anne could come and see her dad and perhaps say goodbye. Ned didn't want to give up the limited time with his dad but he figured he'd had his turn and it might be important for Jack to see his daughter one last time.

Anne refused to come.

Jack spent a bit more time awake and happy. He didn't say much, just enjoyed the moments. Then he went back to sleep. He didn't wake up again and died peacefully soon after.

Chapter Seventeen: Father's Day

The day after Jack died it was time to plan his funeral. The rabbi (this one not a lawyer) who was to officiate at the service said he'd come over to speak to the family in order to learn enough about Jack to speak eloquently at his service. He asked to speak with everyone in the immediate family and explained everyone needed to be there in order for the rabbi to develop a well-rounded idea of Jack's life. Bernice called Anne to tell her when the rabbi was coming. Anne said she would not come. She said she didn't want to talk to the rabbi and had nothing to say about her father. She didn't want to be involved in the planning of the funeral. I'm sure Anne's disinterest hurt Ned's mother but Bernice didn't have time to dwell on that. She had to plan to bury her husband.

When the rabbi had heard enough stories about Jack to summarize his life, the talk turned to the other aspects of a funeral service. Ned's mother was adamant; she wanted specific music played. She wanted Johnny Mathis, Jack's favorite. That was easy, we could just play a CD. But, she also wanted the recording from Jack's 80th birthday party where his four children performed Jack's "Rocky Mountain High," the song he sang repeatedly. (Okay, so he never actually learned the words. That didn't stop him from singing it loudly and often.)

We had a video on a VHS tape of the "kids" singing the song but none of us knew at that time, how to turn a video into a disk or a more user-friendly recording to play at the service. But, Bernice really wanted that song to be part of her husband's send off so we arranged to bring in a portable VHS tape player to play the video during the service. Next we turned our attention to the limo service needed to drive the family to the funeral and to the cemetery. Anne had told her mother she would not ride in any limo Ned and I were riding in so Ned's mother agreed to pay to get a second limo for Anne and her family, despite there being enough room in the one she was already paying for.

The day of the funeral arrived. Ironically, it was Father's Day. We arrived at the funeral home. The director ushered us into the back room where we could have a few private moments with our dearly departed if we wished. Anne wouldn't come into the room so we had to vacate in order to give her private time.

We filed into the chapel where the service was to be held. As is traditional at Jewish services, the people lined up to pass by the front pew where the family sits. Quite a few people were lined up to speak to us. There were some family members, some friends of Jack and Bernice's, some of Anne's friends, and some of our friends. Anne has two girlfriends whom she has known for many years so we've known them for about twenty years as well. Each of them did something I've never seen before at a funeral. The two women approached the family. They gave condolences and hugs to Bernice, to Anne, and to her husband. Then, they stepped a few feet away to pass around me and Ned-- to skip over us-- and move on to give condolences to Ted and to Nan. They did not acknowledge Jack's death to me or to Ned. I don't believe I've ever seen anything quite so rude. Wait a minute! I had seen this behavior before. It was 24 years earlier when my mother died and Anne didn't acknowledge me. Apparently this rude funeral behavior is a regular thing for Anne and her cronies.

"Are you freaking kidding me? Did you actually just dis Ned at his father's funeral?" went the impassioned conversation inside my head. "Did you actually take six steps away in order to avoid offering your condolences? What kind of women are you?"

My friends Judy and Tom, who were next in line, saw this and did something that just made me want to laugh and kiss them both. They hugged Ned's mom and then gave Anne a hug as well and told her how sorry they were about her dad's passing. See, Anne, that's how you behave at a funeral.

The funeral was one Jack would have loved. He was a character, a constant performer. He pretended to be drunk at affairs just to make people laugh even though he drank nary a drop. I found his "drunk act" creepy and obnoxious but I understood his intention was to be funny. It was part and parcel of who he was to be the center of attention. So Jack would have loved that we played the video of his 80th birthday party for all the attendees to appreciate. He would have loved that three of his four children (not Anne, she declined) spoke eloquently about him. Even Ned, who surely had reason to have mixed feelings about his dad, delivered a beautiful eulogy, both tender and funny.

We returned to Jack and Bernice's home for the *shiva* after the service. Anne and her friends went there also. She and a few of her girlfriends, in particular the two rude ones, chatted amiably in the kitchen about how they love to call themselves the "*shiva* girls." I guess they meant because their behavior is so wonderfully warm and helpful at *shiva* houses. I heard them laughingly refer to themselves several times as the "*shiva* girls" and I literally had to put my tongue between my teeth to stop myself from smiling and offering politely, "Well, you ain't the funeral girls, that's for damn sure."

And, the "*shiva* girls" had to move over in that kitchen to make way for our girls. Having remembered Anne once ousted them from the family for not washing the dishes, my daughters made sure Anne saw them washing every dish during *shiva*, and most of those were paper plates!

"Comin' through," they'd chirp, as they moved through the crowd from the dining room into the kitchen holding the empty bagel platter, "gotta wash this."

But, a couple of hours later, Anne marched her contingent of "*shiva* girls" and their entourage out of the *shiva* house. They departed en masse as a group. We learned later they reconvened at Anne's house but we never knew why they had left. We sat one more day of condolence at Bernice's, but Anne did not return. We didn't see the "*shiva* girls" again either.

The day after *shiva* a very upset Bernice called Ned. Anne had come by that morning to tell her mother the funeral was the most embarrassing one she had ever witnessed. Anne said her mother should be ashamed of having been a part of this circus. (Circus was my word, not hers, but that was the gist.) Bernice had thought the service was perfect and just what Jack would have wanted. Attendees remarked about it to the family members, saying just how much Jack would have loved his send off. Some of those attendees were even on "Anne's side." One of them was actually the son of a "*shiva* girl." So, Anne's attack on her mother was devastating and shocking. Bernice had just lost her husband of almost 65 years. She was vulnerable and weak. Anne's commentary on the service was an arrow that pierced her heart. Bernice actually phoned the funeral home to ask the director if there had been anything embarrassing about her husband's service. He assured her all he saw was a lovely and loving tribute.

But I'm not sure that made Bernice feel any better. Her daughter's opinion and respect meant the world to her. Anne was perhaps the person Bernice held most dear in the world so to have Anne say something so hurtful was pain beyond belief for her mother.

Chapter Eighteen: Oh The Irony

After Jack's death Bernice was left with quite a mess to clean up. The details of their will hadn't been ironed out; they owned several properties that had to be sold. Plus, Bernice lived alone in a three-bedroom house she couldn't maintain alone. Some of the work and support fell to Ned, the only one truly capable of understanding what had to be done who also had the organizational skills to make the business run smoothly.

During the next few years, Bernice surprised the family with her steely determination to take care of the things left hanging after Jack's death. She got a new lawyer and proceeded to update her will insuring her estate be divided evenly with each of her children getting 25% of what was left after some money was given to the grandchildren and bills were paid. A year or so after Jack died, Bernice moved to a retirement facility where she essentially restarted her life. She made friends and each night a group of about nine women had dinner together. Bernice never told anyone about her family dysfunction. It was as if she just rewrote her history. She wasn't a mother who had allowed her daughter to control her and destroy her family. She wasn't a mother who had an adult daughter who refused to speak to her. She wasn't a mother who had conspired against one son, had another son who was a felon, and a daughter who was mentally disabled. She was just a mom in her eighties enjoying her golden years. That's all anyone had to know. With that backstory she could go to dinner each night and appear happy and serene. However, during the days she struggled with the truth of her life. Her oldest daughter was perpetually angry and wouldn't see her or speak with her most of the time. Anne would contact Bernice from time to time and say she was really sorry Bernice could no longer be included in her life or her children's lives but she just couldn't include her unless Bernice met her conditions. The conditions would vary but they always in some way involved changing Bernice's will.

Every so often they'd meet for lunch and Anne would unveil her current demands. Pretty much every time that would result in a fight with things left unsaid and unresolved. Months would pass without contact. Then Anne would call and the whole thing would start again.

In between calls and lunches, Anne would send flowers for Mother's Day or her mother's birthday. She always signed them, "Love and Light, Anne."

What did Anne want each time? That varied. At the beginning, just after Jack died, Anne wanted to be made executrix of Bernice's will. Unless she got that, Anne said, Bernice really couldn't be a part of her family. Bernice was unable or unwilling to comply. Anne wasn't speaking to any of her three siblings. Bernice couldn't in good conscience put Anne in a position that required fairness. She just didn't trust her to take care of the estate and of her siblings honestly or justly. For a while the executor of Bernice's will was a bank. A few years later, Bernice made Ned the executor of the will but he insisted he would not take the customary 10% of the estate fee executors can take.

Ned would hear these stories about the conditions from Bernice. The tales were always upsetting. But Ned never saw Anne, even though she still lived only blocks from our house. Unfortunately for Anne, from time to time I'd run into her at the market, the dry cleaners, the pharmacy, pretty much anywhere one might run into the average nasty bitch. (Meaning me, I guess, from Anne's point of view.) Our conversations were brief and to the point. Like the time I went to pick up some clothes at the cleaners and unbeknownst to her, I was standing right behind her in line. I knew what she could not know and that was in a minute or so when she turned around, she'd find herself nose-to-nose job (hers, not mine) with me.

"Well," I said, when the moment finally came, "isn't this an unfortunate coincidence."

Not a question, really, simply a statement of fact.

"Debby, you never change."

I took that as a compliment. She couldn't get away from me fast enough, though. That was typical of our encounters. She actually seemed frightened of me. Which was interesting because other than the time I foisted my bad breath upon her in the hospital when she was reading the Pooh book and warned her she better behave herself, I had not actually threatened her in any way. I didn't even have to speak to her to scare the crap out of her. Once I saw her standing in the supermarket line next to the one I was in. We were both near the door that led to the closest part of the parking lot. Instead of going out that door which would have required passing by where I was standing, Anne walked all the way to the opposite end of the supermarket to leave via the door on that end. Alas for her, again what I knew that she did not -- because I had noticed her car in the parking lot after I parked next to it -- was that she could walk to the farthest exit if she wanted to but when she reached her car she was going to be standing right next to me.

How did I recognize her car you might wonder? She drove a blue BMW sedan. There is certainly no shortage of those in my area. But her car is recognizable because she has a huge decal across her rear window that reads, "Life is Good." And there's a happy face for emphasis.

So I knew we were about to see each other up close and personal despite her ploy to avoid me. What I couldn't have predicted is that in her taking the long route to get to her car, she didn't account for the medial strip that ran along only a few of the lanes in the parking lot. Her car was perpendicular to the strip. I got out of the market and reached my car just in time to see her a few feet away struggling to lift her full cart over the concrete median so she could roll it to her car. I smiled and waved. I couldn't stop myself; I'm only human.

A few years after Jack's death, Anne phoned Bernice with a new request.

"I'd like the honor of planning your funeral," Anne said to her mother.

I have heard of people making some bizarre demands of their family members. I have heard about some pretty strange mother-daughter relations. But that one topped them all. *The honor of planning your funeral.* I can't even imagine how it would feel if one of my daughters said that to me.

And, there was one other thing, too. Anne wanted to be made Power of Attorney.

Bernice wasn't sure what to do. She didn't quite know what it meant to have someone plan her funeral. And, to her knowledge, she wasn't dying anytime soon so she was a tad perturbed about the thought of her funeral being planned. She also didn't know what it meant to make someone Power of Attorney. She told Anne she'd think about these things and get back to her. Bernice called Ned and told him what Anne requested about the honor of planning the funeral.

"Well, Mom, it's your funeral." You don't get to use that line in real life very often.

"Anne wants something else too. I can't remember what she called it, something with the word attorney, maybe."

"Was it Power of Attorney?"

"Oh yes, that was it."

Ned explained what it meant to give someone Power of Attorney (POA). Basically it means you give that person the power to act as your agent in all things. They have access to your bank accounts the same as if they were you. It's a distinction that must only be given to someone you trust with your life because they are going to be able to control how you live. The POA is supposed to act in the best interest of the person he or she represents but it can be a mess if that person isn't trustworthy because they can take your money and use it as they see fit. And, while it can be revoked, it requires legal action and can take some time to work out. In the meantime, you could have one hell of a mess on your hands if that person has wiped you out. Once your money is gone, there'd be no way to get it back, either.

You need a person to act as your Power of Attorney if you are no longer capable of handling your own affairs but it must be someone with impeccable ethics. (Thus far in this story, does it sound like Anne is a person with impeccable ethics?) Once Bernice understood what a Power of Attorney was she decided Anne might not be the best person for that job. Years before, she and Jack had chosen Ned to serve as Power of Attorney so she just kept it that way.

Bernice called Anne back the next day.

"Okay, Honey," Bernice began, "I thought about it. You can plan my funeral."

"What about Power of Attorney?" Anne asked.

"No, I don't think I can do that," her mother replied softly.

"Well then I don't need to hear from you again," Anne answered as she hastily hung up the phone.

Ironically, this woman who was so cruel and causing such distress in her family was lauded elsewhere for being a humanitarian. Years earlier Anne described going to a seminar for chiropractors and others in the healthcare industry. It focused on the value of getting involved in a charity. The seminar taught them it was great marketing for a chiropractor to connect with a charity and then to showcase their good work in their office. This would telegraph to their patients they were good people with charitable hearts. So, Anne did exactly that. She worked with a charity that assisted underprivileged children. While I'm sure the charity does benefit the kids who received the gifts, it also benefits Anne who has the charity pay her and her husband "rent" for its office space. But apparently the local basketball team didn't look that deeply into whom they honored for being charitable because one summer night we got a text from a friend who was at a game.

"You won't believe who was just honored as a halftime hero!"

Yes, Anne was some kind of hero. Okay, I understand it is possible for a person to be a dichotomy. Logically I know Anne can treat family poorly and still do valuable charity work. I just can't wrap my mind around someone who could sink as low as she does in her personal interactions and rise up to do nice things for strangers. Does that even her karmic score? I'm voting no but it's not for me to judge, I suppose.

Chapter Nineteen: A Separate Peace

For the next few years after Bernice was widowed, Ned found a sort of a peace with his mother. He had to accept his parents were good people, who, because they were weak and insecure, made some bad choices in parenting their adult children. In addition they didn't know much about the man Ned was. They didn't understand the essence of his character. When their children were kids, Bernice and Jack viewed each of them a certain way. That view of their kids didn't change when the kids grew up. Ned had been a shy child but in adulthood he worked on and developed the ability to communicate. He was not shy overall and in fact he became a strong leader professionally. But, his parents never saw the man he became because their view of Ned was stuck in his childhood. We heard the stories and comments repeatedly.

"Ned doesn't have moxie," Jack would say.

"When Ned was a little boy he wouldn't even give his dime to the ice cream man. Someone else always had to do it for him," his mother would relate.

While their other three children became products of their upbringing and took the sibling rivalry competition well into adulthood, Ned somehow managed to take his own path. He disengaged from the narcissistic personalities of his siblings where power and control and their parents' money mattered over all.

When they were children, their parents created an environment of fear combined with conditional love with a smattering of deception thrown in. Don't tell Dad the truth, he'll be angry and he might hit you. Mom will lie by omission to cover up indiscretions she or the children commit. That led to the realization that Mom can be manipulated to do whatever you want and Dad can be manipulated into giving you money (and affection) if you do what he wants.

Ted, Nan, and Anne took those basic concepts into adulthood. At some point, when Ned realized how destructive and unhealthy that dynamic was, he got off the merry-go-round of their conception of family and lived the life of integrity and respect he thought was right. Thus, he became the family scapegoat. Family not functioning the way they thought it should? It was Ned's fault for not falling into line the way Anne wanted him to. The ultimate punishment was in leaving him less money than the others were going to inherit along with keeping that anger a secret until after the parents were dead. That resulted in a family relationship that was for many years a sham.

I think about Jack and Bernice coming up to light a ceremonial candle on the cake at Tamra and Shira's joint Bat Mitzvah. As the honored grandparents, they got to light the flame. It's hard for me to understand how they could stand there harboring the secret about the will. I wondered if they ever thought about the dichotomy.

But, now Jack was gone, Bernice was a widow, and she needed Ned's help. So, a peace was established. While Bernice had apologized cursorily and made sure her estate was to be divided equally among her children, Ned's hurt didn't just dissipate. Bernice hadn't articulated a heartfelt regret for what she had done. She had never spoken to our daughters about it. It felt as though she didn't really take responsibility for what she had done. But, Ned moved on. I don't think he felt a deep and abiding love for his mother anymore but he did feel a responsibility to help her in her old age. She didn't really have anyone else she could depend on. I believe Ned, in part, wanted to show his mother she had been wrong about him for years. He truly was "the good son" they never believed him to be. So, he visited his mother regularly and took her to doctor's appointments when she needed help.

Since Anne had cut her mother out of her life, Bernice was not included, or as Anne once put it, Bernice was not "permitted" to be part of Anne's family events because Bernice hadn't earned her way in with her continued refusal to do whatever it was Anne wanted her to do, will-wise. In other words, although Bernice saw Anne's children Beth and Rob from time to time, per Anne's orders, Bernice was not to be included in the family events of that group. Rob and Beth could see their grandmother if they wished but they couldn't invite her to events that included Anne. Bernice did attend each of their weddings, and when they had children Bernice was allowed to see the kids on rare occasion but she was not invited to any other holidays or events Anne was attending or hosting for her family.

162

Thus, by default we pretty much got custody of Bernice and Nan at holidays. The whole dynamic had a disingenuous feeling to it. We were pretending to be a normal multi-generational family but it was always uncomfortable. Nan and Bernice were often arguing or grumbling to each other. Thus, being around them was, to put it mildly, unpleasant and awkward. None of us looked forward to holidays, least of all Ned. For my daughters, to have their grandmother in their midst after a lifetime of her ignoring them felt insincere. I think if Bernice had ever been honest enough to talk to her granddaughters about what she had done and why, they would have been willing to forgive her. But when you hurt someone and then never acknowledge it, forgiveness is elusive.

During the years after Jack died, while Bernice was mostly estranged from Anne, she sought out a therapist to help her deal with the pain. Bernice saw the therapist every few weeks. She didn't talk about their sessions but they seemed to help her. For most of the next ten years, Bernice's life was pretty calm.

Chapter Twenty: Bernice Moves On

At some point Bernice developed COPD, Chronic Obstructive Pulmonary Disease. It worsened over time and she struggled to breathe, eventually needing oxygen around the clock. During a second hospitalization for congestive heart failure in two months time, her doctor suggested palliative care. She was 93, her lung disease would not get any better with treatment and she said she didn't want to go into the hospital again. The aim of palliative care, as opposed to curative care, is that the person is kept comfortable. A person receiving palliative care is not given a boatload of drugs that may have annoying side effects and don't make her any more comfortable. Since Bernice had said she did not want to be taken to a hospital again, even if a crisis occurred, the doctor suggested she receive hospice care. That meant an aide to help her dress and bathe would visit her daily and a visiting nurse would come weekly. But, the doctor felt, since she was at risk of a crisis at any time, as she had already had two in two months, Bernice needed 24-hour care and would have to leave her independent living situation. Bernice was willing to do whatever the doctor suggested for the most part. She was insistent about not returning to the hospital.

Meetings were held with Ned, Nan, and Ted via speakerphone as he was in California. Bernice did not ask for Anne to be included because at that time Anne still wasn't speaking to any of her siblings or her mother. Bernice chose not to attend the meeting. She just wanted to be informed afterward about what her family had discussed. The doctor explained Bernice's prognosis, which was "two weeks to two months" to live. He said she was no longer safe alone and if she wanted to be enrolled in a hospice program, she'd have to have 24-hour care. She could hire private care and stay in her apartment, or she could move to the skilled nursing facility in the complex where she lived, or she could move to an inpatient hospice facility.

Ted said he thought Bernice wanted to stay in her apartment because she wouldn't want to give up her independence. Since hiring 24-hour care was prohibitively expensive, Ted suggested she didn't need that anyway. The doctor said Bernice really did need 'round-the-clock care. She was no longer safe alone and she also had a bit of dementia and was occasionally disoriented. Ted was rather insistent she should stay in her apartment. The doctor said since Bernice had indicated she didn't want to return to the hospital, if she had a crisis in her apartment, the staff in her building would call 911 and she would be taken to a hospital. The only way to avoid that was to have her enrolled in hospice. Otherwise, she could have a crisis and either be alone in her apartment and possibly not able to call for help, or she'd call for help and would be taken to a hospital.

"I'm willing to take that risk," Ted replied.

We all tried to explain to Ted that it wasn't his risk to take. His mother had said what she wanted and combined with the doctor's prognosis, there really was no option other than to move her to a skilled nursing care facility. The doctor suggested ultimately Bernice would be the one to make this decision. We returned to her room and the doctor laid out the options. He shared his estimate of how long she had to live. She chose to move to the skilled nursing facility in her complex. She was familiar with it, having stayed there a few years earlier after hip surgery. Ted called Bernice later that same day and tried to talk her into returning to her apartment as *he* insisted she wanted. He badgered her, demanding to know *why* she didn't want to be put into the hospital again. She did waver for a bit but then decided to stick to her decision to move into the nursing home.

Bernice settled into the nursing home. Since Ned was her Power of Attorney he arranged to clean out and relinquish her apartment. He figured he'd pay the rent for the upcoming month and that would give him enough time to go through Bernice's belongings and distribute them as needed. On the first night Bernice spent in the nursing home Ned and I and two of our daughters went to visit her. Before we did, though, we stopped off in Bernice's apartment to pick up some of her photos so we could take them to her room at the nursing home. We opened the door to find all the lights on and things in total disarray. Nan came quickly out of Bernice's bedroom with a furtive and somewhat guilty expression on her face. Seeing her boyfriend Frank right behind her in the bedroom for a moment I thought we had caught them in an embarrassing situation in bed. Before we could even say hello, Nan blurted out, "What are you doing here?"

That struck me as odd. Wouldn't you normally just open with "Hello?"

We explained we stopped in to get some framed photos for Bernice's room and noticed Nan and Frank had brought in a shopping cart, which was already overflowing with some of Bernice's possessions. Over the next week or so Nan, who was a hoarder, visited the apartment nightly in the wee hours and eventually took home virtually all of her mother's possessions including all furniture and jewelry and clothing and even every knickknack, toiletry, and piece of junk mail. She left behind only trash and photos of Ned, our girls and me. It saddened Ned because he knew his orderly and precise mother would not have been happy to see her life dismantled haphazardly. He wanted to handle Bernice's things with dignity; making sure things of use found good homes or were donated to charity. Bernice had specifically said she did *not* want Nan to take her furniture (Although in the will Bernice's lawyer mistakenly wrote Nan should get the furniture and Bernice hadn't caught the error and signed it.) because she knew Nan had no room in her four-room overcrowded apartment for four additional rooms of furniture and she could not take good care of anything. But Nan's hoarding Bernice's furniture and possessions turned out to be the least of the damage Nan was to cause Bernice.

Ted immediately stepped in to express his unhappiness with Bernice's choice. He opposed his mother choosing to be in the skilled nursing unit instead of in her apartment. (Risking death) He spoke at length with Ned about the situation and at one point Ted said to Ned, "I question your motives." Ned asked what he meant. The implication was Ted thought Ned had pushed his mother into hospice care because he was trying to kill her. First, Ned did not push Bernice into anything. He merely supported what he agreed was a good choice Bernice had made. Secondly, Ned was not trying to kill anyone. Ted didn't understand what hospice care was; he thought it was euthanasia. Ned explained to Ted again what hospice meant and why Bernice had chosen it.

In the skilled nursing unit Bernice was comfortable and well cared for. At some point she asked to see Beth and Rob so Alexis called them and informed about their grandmother's situation. Bernice did not ask to see Anne but we all understood that asking for Beth and Rob was Bernice's way of asking to see Anne. A few days later, having heard about her mother from her children, Anne showed up at the nursing home to visit.

When Ned and I visited just after Anne left, Bernice told us the visit with her daughter went well. They didn't argue.

"We forgot each other," Bernice told me.

"Do you mean you forgave each other?" I asked, knowing that her dementia occasionally resulted in her using the wrong word.

"Yes," she laughed a bit as she answered, appreciating the humor in her malapropism, replacing "forgave" with "forgot."

"We forgave each other."

Considering the pain her daughter had caused Bernice, Jack, and everyone in her immediate family, I kind of thought the former might have been far superior. But, I reasoned to myself, if I were dying and I had been estranged from my child for so long, I'd want the peace forgiveness brings. I don't think Anne and Bernice actually spoke about the transgressions each had made, I think they just talked civilly without arguing and that, to Bernice, was forgiveness. In a way, "we forgot each other" was a very apt description of the resolution of their dispute.

A few days later, though, at Anne's next visit, their temporary peace was disturbed. The social worker from the nursing home phoned Ned.

"I just wanted to give you a heads up. Your sisters are both visiting your mother and they just went to the nurse's desk to ask for a pen and paper. They are writing something for your mother to sign. They're talking about getting an attorney and your mother seems upset," the social worker explained.

From Bernice's previous stay in that nursing home, the social worker was familiar with the dysfunction in the family. She was aware of Anne's history and was on the lookout for Anne's visits to make sure she wasn't fighting with her mother and upsetting her. She knew Ned was concerned about his mother's mental state and if anyone put a legal document to sign in front of her, she'd likely sign it despite not fully understanding what it said. There was a strong possibility a nefarious person could take advantage of Bernice's weakened condition and get her to change any or all of the stipulations in the will she had written when she was of sound mind.

We have a friend who had lived through a painful situation when her father was dying. Her father owned a valuable piece of property jointly with his sister. Upon his death, his share was to go to his two daughters. But, his sister's husband was his lawyer. While the dad was in the hospital dying, the brother-in-law got the dying dad to sign over his share of the property to his sister, ostensibly by handing him a sheaf of papers to sign so he wouldn't notice the details of anything he was signing. That document essentially cut his beloved daughters out of his will by robbing them of his most valuable asset. When the case went to court, despite the dad's wife testifying he loved his daughters and she knew he would not have cut them out of his will, the daughters lost the case. So, this kind of dirty deal was worrying Ned as he believed Anne, Nan, and Ted capable of doing a similar thing with their vulnerable mother.

So, when the social worker reported that the sisters seemed to be planning something, Ned phoned his mother's room. She answered and immediately, in a very agitated voice, cried out, "Ned did you take the pearls? Do you have the pearls?"

"No Mom," Ned replied, "I do not have the pearls."

Yes, the Mikimoto pearls I mentioned before and promised they'd make a return appearance in this story are ba-ack.

"Ned, do you have the pearls?" his mother asked again, having failed to hear his answer.

"No Mom," he said, a bit louder this time.

"NED, DID YOU TAKE THE PEARLS?" Bernice asked again, louder and more panicked.

168

At this point, Ned is screaming at the top of his lungs because he figured out Bernice is not wearing her hearing aid and she can't hear anything he's saying.

"NO. I DON'T HAVE THE PEARLS. NAN HAS THE PEARLS. SHE HAS EVERYTHING!"

Ned tried hard to get this message across because he could hear his mother was upset and he wanted to calm her down. It's not really that easy to calm someone down when you have to scream to be heard.

Nan had already taken almost everything out of her mother's apartment; it was virtually empty. On that first day, when we thought we caught Nan in the "act," what she was most likely doing was taking all of her mother's jewelry, leaving no gemstone unturned, as it were. That's why Ned knew exactly where the pearls were. But he thought Nan was in the room with her mother, as the social worker had said a bit earlier that Nan was there, so he was confused as to why Nan didn't just tell her mother she had the pearls. Ned didn't understand why Bernice had to be so upset about these pearls if Nan was standing there and knew she had them.

"Mom, is Nan there?" Ned asked finally. "She is? Good. Put her on the phone."

"Nan, *you have* the pearls. Don't you know where they are?" Ned asked his sister.

"I'm not sure," Nan answered evasively.

"Did you look for them?" he asked, now getting annoyed.

"Well, not very hard," Nan admitted softly.

"Nan," Ned said in a completely exasperated tone, "You have the pearls. You have everything. Go home and look for them. You are making Mom upset for no reason. You have them."

Ned thought Bernice was upset because her very valuable pearls were missing. Always the dutiful son, he just wanted her to be at peace in her last days. Getting her worked up about these pearls was counterproductive to promoting peace. Then he recalled what the social worker had said about the sisters talking about writing a document and getting an attorney to come in.

"Also, what kind of document are you writing for Mom to sign?" Ned asked Nan.

I have no idea what Nan thought when Ned asked that. She answered quickly, maybe before she had a chance to wonder how he could possibly have known about them discussing planning to bring in an attorney.

"We're writing a document that says that I get the pearls."

"You don't need a document," Ned countered. "You already have the pearls."

Nan didn't respond; she just handed the phone back to her mother.

Lest you wonder what precipitated all of this brouhaha concerning these pearls, there is an explanation. We learned it about two weeks after that night when Ned was visiting his mother again. The night the social worker called Ned, it was because Anne showed up and asked her mother where the pearls were. She wanted them. Bernice claimed to have no knowledge about where they were. On a previous visit, Bernice said, Anne had been searching Bernice's room for the keys to Bernice's apartment before it had been vacated. Failing to find the keys, according to Bernice, Anne asked the security people to let her in to her mother's place and then she searched Bernice's apartment looking for the pearls. Of course, she didn't find them because the pearls were at Nan's house, where they had been the whole time.

Bernice and Nan knew where the pearls were, the necklace's whereabouts had always been known. The night Ned had phoned his mom and she was so upset about the "missing" pearls, he was just part of a play written by his mom and performed by Bernice and Nan. When Anne asked again about where those pearls were, neither Bernice nor Nan wanted to tell Anne the truth because they were afraid if Anne found out Nan had the pearls she'd be angry or she'd try to bully Nan

170

into handing them over to her. So, guessing in advance Anne might ask about the pearls again because she had always wanted them, Bernice had devised this ruse. If Anne asked about the pearls again Bernice and Nan would pretend *Ned* had taken the pearls. I guess they thought since Anne had already been angry with Ned for 30 years for his previous transgressions, what was one more? So, the plotline was decided and then Bernice and Nan played it out on the phone. No one thought to tell Ned, however.

Even at this late date in her life, Bernice didn't want to make Anne angry. Even when Bernice heard from Rob that his mother Anne didn't like his wife and was therefore cutting him, his wife, and their young son out of her life unless Rob was willing to come around without his wife, Bernice didn't want to tell Anne how awful she thought that was because she didn't want to make her angry. Even with death staring her in the face, Bernice was still intimidated by Anne. That bitch is scarier than death!

A few weeks later, one night Ned got a call from a nurse who was taking care of Bernice.

"I'm sorry to bother you so late and I know I'm overstepping some bounds here but I thought you should know what is going on in your mother's room," the nurse began.

"Your sister Nan is in there and your other sister is on the phone," she continued, "they're talking about changing the Power of Attorney. They're talking about this in front of your mother and she is upset. I went in there and told your sister to stop upsetting your mother. Then I asked to speak to the sister who was on the phone and I told her she had to stop having this conversation because it was upsetting your mother terribly."

"I looked at your mom's chart and I saw you are Power of Attorney so I thought I should call and tell you what's going on," she explained.

Ned phoned Nan immediately and asked her why she was plotting to change the Power of Attorney. She insisted she wasn't doing that and that she had not spoken to Anne. Ned persisted. Nan then admitted a bit.

"Well, we think you are withholding information about Mom," Nan said.

"Who's we?" Ned wanted to know.

"Me and Ted," Nan replied.

"What information am I withholding?" Ned asked.

"About Mom's medications," Nan answered.

"I told Ted everything I know," Ned replied, "and I would have told you too if you had asked. Mom is on heart medication, blood pressure medication, and pain medication that also helps her breathe. Now you know everything I know. But why are you and Anne scheming?"

Nan insisted she and Anne weren't plotting anything. She also added she was annoyed with Ned because, as POA, he wasn't giving *her* enough of Bernice's money. He was paying some of Nan's bills, as Bernice had been doing, though. He explained that to Nan and further explained that as a responsible POA he was supposed to be acting as Bernice had. He was supposed to be handling her finances much the same way she had handled them. He was not supposed to be giving away Bernice's money; that would not be appropriate POA behavior. Plus, Bernice's monthly expenses in the nursing home were quite high at almost $13000/month. She was likely going to need her limited cash to pay her living expenses. But, Nan pressed further. She was short of cash that month and wanted Ned to write her a check from their mother's account. Ned asked what Nan had done with the rent check (Nan lives in a two-apartment duplex her parents bought for her and the renter pays Nan each month.) she got earlier that month. Had she already gone through the $500? No, she said she just hadn't yet "gotten to the bank." (It was about the 20th of the month.) Ned told her to cash the rent check she had and use that money. He said he couldn't give her any more of Bernice's money.

But what Ned had learned from the nurse was interesting. After ten years of not speaking to each other, Ned's sisters had formed an alliance and it seemed to be against him. Each sister wanted something.

Nan wanted her mother's money and was panicked about her mother's impending death. Anne wanted to be made POA (not to mention those pearls!) and I guess she saw an opportunity to get that by convincing Nan to work with her to talk Bernice into changing her Power Of Attorney.

Ned wanted something too. He wanted to do right by his mother, despite or maybe even as a result of, all the wrong that had been done to him. His siblings, though, were making that extremely difficult. Ted came in from California and stayed for a few weeks. The last ten days of his visit he stayed at our house without incident. He went home around Christmas.

A week later a social worker called Ned and expressed concern for Bernice's well being. She asked Ned to come in to meet with her so we both went immediately. She explained that the interactions of Anne and Nan seemed to be upsetting Bernice who started crying almost every day. While she was unable to stop crying or to clearly articulate why she was weeping inconsolably, the staff deduced that the crying was connected to things Anne and Nan were doing or saying around Bernice. They could calm her down only by giving her an anti-anxiety medication. The social worker also said just after he left Pennsylvania, Ted called a few times to speak to the social worker about moving Bernice. Ted's talk about moving was also upsetting Bernice, she reported. The social worker was seeking help from Ned, because he was POA and obviously trusted by his mother, about how to speak to Anne and Nan and Ted to get them to stop doing whatever they were doing that was hurting their mother.

Ned explained a bit about the background of the family dynamic. He asked the social worker what she wanted to do. She explained her first responsibility was to protect the patient. Toward that end she talked about prohibiting the siblings from visiting or talking to their mother if necessary. Ned said he thought that action would cause his mother even more pain because despite everything, she loved her children and needed to see them. He encouraged the social worker to find another solution. She said she would send Ned's siblings a letter informing them their actions were hurting Bernice and if they wanted to continue seeing her, they would need to be much more considerate of her needs. They would have to stop harassing their mother and if they persisted, the nursing home would contact Adult Protective Services to seek an order of protection against them. The social worker felt Anne and Nan and Ted's actions were destructive. She even described Anne as "evil" based on what she had learned about her and the family history.

Before the letter could be sent out, Ned got another call from the nurse who took care of Bernice. Bernice was crying and couldn't stop. But this time she refused to take the "happy pill," as they described it to her. She said something about Nan visiting her the night before, staying until midnight and talking to her mother about why she shouldn't take the anti-depressant or morphine medication. Bernice was confused and upset but wouldn't take the medication because Nan had told her not to. Ned spoke to his mother on the phone and ultimately she agreed to take the meds. She soon felt better.

Meanwhile the social worker told Ned she decided prudently she would hold off sending the letter to Adult Protective Services, as she was wary of blowback against Ned and Bernice. But she intended to monitor the situation closely.

A few days after that, Bernice told this story to Ned. Nan and her boyfriend had come to visit one night at 9:00 PM. Bernice was already in a nightgown and in bed for the night. She was tired and wanted to sleep. Nan turned off all the lights and she and her boyfriend each got comfortable in a chair. Nan put her head back and closed her eyes. It became apparent to Bernice they intended to sleep in her room. Bernice was completely uncomfortable with this. She didn't want to sleep with people watching her. They stayed for several hours. Bernice was unable to sleep with them there so the next day she was exhausted.

"Well, Mom," Ned began, after hearing the story, "why didn't you just tell Nan they should leave because you wanted to go to sleep?"

"I didn't want to hurt her feelings."

Just how little trust must there be in that mother/daughter relationship if a simple "I'd like to go to sleep now, Honey" can hurt someone's feelings?

Ned couldn't talk to Nan about her visiting hours either because she was already annoyed with him about the money she wasn't getting. His mother had told him to ignore Nan's constantly coming to him with her hand out. Bernice didn't want Ned to continue giving money to Nan but she wouldn't say that to Nan so she kept asking.

Soon after that Ted told Ned he was coming from where he lived in California to visit their mother for a week or so. He suggested, since he and Nan wanted to move Bernice to a cheaper assisted living facility, maybe they could have a meeting with the siblings and figure out what was best for Mom. He said this despite the fact his mother told him repeatedly she was happy where she was and didn't want to move. He said this despite being told by the doctor Bernice wasn't healthy enough to live in as assisted living situation, which was designed for healthier people, not those at death's door. He said this despite the fact Ned assured him their mother was receiving excellent care in a highly rated facility. Ted insisted Bernice was paying $7000/month more than necessary and she could step down in expense and get even better care. Bernice said Ted told her he was making appointments to take her to see other places but she didn't want to visit them. She did not want to move to another facility. Ned and Ted had a huge argument about it. Ted insisted Ned step down as POA. Ted said when he came into town he'd force Ned out as POA and take the position over himself. Then he'd move his mother to another facility. Ned went to talk to his mother to find out what she really wanted. The social worker went with him so she could also ascertain what was best for her resident.

"No, I don't want to move," said Bernice when they asked her. "I don't even want to go outside."

"Well, Mom," Ned asked, "did you tell Ted that?"

"No."

"Did he tell you he was making appointments for you to see other facilities?"

"Yes."

"Well, why didn't you tell him you didn't want to go?"

"I was scared."

"Mom, do you see what you're doing here? I am fighting these people on your behalf and they think I'm doing this for myself because you are telling them something completely different. You are destroying your family because you can't be honest and tell them how you really feel. You're putting me in the middle because I'm trying to help you and you won't even help yourself."

"I'm sorry. I'm sorry," was all Bernice said.

Ned was unbelievably frustrated. Here he is arguing with his siblings trying to protect his mother from them and trying to help her get what he thought she most wanted, when in fact, the person she had to be protected from was herself. Her relationships with her other children were without any honesty or depth. She needed them to need her continually and she also needed them to "save" her continually. These were quintessential co-dependent relationships.

Ned's mother didn't really want to be honest with her children because she wanted to perpetuate the myths that she could meet their every need and they could meet hers. The lifelong cycle where they'd come to her with their hands out, with their problems to solve and she'd give them money or solve their problems without helping them to learn to handle things independently was not one she was going to let go of now. She kept some of her adult children dependent on her all of their lives. Their dependence on her kept them tethered to her and she wanted that above all. She was so afraid if she told them the truth about how she felt about certain things she'd hurt their feelings. Then they might not love her as much as they had before. She needed and wanted those constant interactions with her adult children. She wasn't about to do anything that would halt them.

The calls from the nurses about how desperately unhappy Bernice was, were constant. Ned was anxiety-ridden about how much his siblings were torturing their mother but he was unable to stop it. It was a bad situation all around. Then it got worse.

Chapter Twenty-One: Bernice's Death, Part I

A few days before Ted was to arrive for his return visit and his "takeover," a nurse phoned Ned.

"I'm sorry to tell you but your mom declined rapidly overnight."

She said while she couldn't give an exact timeline, she indicated Bernice was not likely to hang on much longer given how much trouble she was having breathing. She suggested Ned come soon to say goodbye.

Ned couldn't come that soon, though, because he was in the hospital having what he thought was a heart attack. He had announced that morning, after returning home from the gym, he felt pressure in his chest and his heart seemed to be pounding and he thought it prudent for me to rush him to a hospital, which I did -- during the blizzard that was pounding outside.

After some tense and nerve-wracking time in the ER, the doctor concluded Ned did not have a heart attack but he did think Ned was having a "coronary event." He also said Ned had very high blood pressure, 170/120. He wanted to keep him overnight for observation and perform a stress test the next morning, believing Ned would likely need a procedure involving inserting a stent into the heart.

So, that's where we were when the nurse called to tell Ned to come right away to say goodbye to Bernice. Within a few hours, Ned's test was over. They declared him to have a healthy heart and not in need of any procedure. They said he had reacted to extreme stress and anxiety and needed to find a way to reduce those. With that, we left the hospital and went directly to the nursing home to see Bernice. Not so much a stress-reducing jaunt.

A few days earlier Bernice had developed a high fever and had even more trouble breathing. The doctor ordered an antibiotic. We were confused because we thought being on hospice care meant no antibiotics would be given. We believed hospice care involved keeping a person comfortable while not trying to cure anything. Plus, when

Bernice was admitted to the nursing home she signed a document stating she did NOT want antibiotics. That was also clearly stated in her Living Will – no antibiotics. Given that Bernice was suffering and had already said she was ready and wanting to die, an infection that might end her life was almost a gift. But, the doctor prescribed Augmentin.

When we arrived Bernice looked pretty bad but she wasn't in pain and she was awake. I asked her if she was worried about anything and she said she was a bit worried about her granddaughter Beth. Beth had called earlier and told her grandmother her car had died and she and her husband didn't have enough money to replace it. I suppose Beth was just doing what Anne had raised her to do, to go to her grandmother with her hand out whenever she felt the need. So, Bernice was worried about it. I think she thought Beth was asking to inherit Bernice's car or to be given some extra money in the will to cover the cost of a new car. Bernice wanted to help her granddaughter but she wasn't sure how she could do that being ten minutes from death. I assured my mother-in-law Beth would be fine. She and her husband both work, they live in a perfectly nice home in the suburbs, and they would find a way to buy what they needed without her help. It wasn't the first time in recent years Beth had come begging to her grandmother. She had called frantically one Saturday night about five years earlier insisting she needed $48,000 immediately in order to buy a house. She needed to make a $60,000 down payment; she said and she only had $12000. If her grandmother couldn't commit to giving her the money that night, she'd lose the house. Amazingly, her grandmother turned her down and she somehow managed to buy the house anyway. Soon after that, Beth told her grandmother she had developed a paint allergy and it would cost more than normal to paint the new house so she needed $9000 to avoid allergic horror. Again, her grandmother said she didn't have that kind of money to spare and, again, amazingly, Beth somehow managed to get her house painted without going into anaphylactic shock. After that, she asked for $900 for a new vacuum to clean the house she couldn't afford to buy or to paint. Apparently, she also couldn't afford to clean it. Again, her grandmother said she didn't have $900 to spare. So, this time around, without reminding her grandmother of the many times Beth had come to her with her hand out, I simply promised Bernice Beth had resources and Bernice didn't have to worry about her buying a car.

178

Then the phone rang. Bernice asked me to answer. It was Beth.

"Put my grandmother on," she demanded.

"Okay, Beth," I began politely but with a distinct chill and a side of sarcasm, "I will put your grandmother on if she feels up to talking. But here's what you will say. 'Mimi, I love you. You have always been a wonderful grandmother.' That is all you will say. What you will not say is, 'Mimi, I don't have enough money to buy a new car.' You will not worry your grandmother with your problems on her deathbed. You will let her die in peace. She deserves that. You're a big girl, you know what I'm saying."

Beth gave me a pretty nasty answer. But I did hand the phone to Bernice and I did hear her say, "I love you too," so I assume Beth did as she was told. Then Bernice rested back on her pillow and looked pensive.

"It changed so fast," she said wistfully. "But, I want it to end. I can't wait to get out of this room. I'm ready to go. I just want to say goodbye to everyone."

We promised her she would have that chance. We told her Ted was flying in that night. That helped her to rest easier.

"I want to be buried in my beige evening gown, the one with the lace. Not the sleeveless one."

We promised her we'd get it for her. When Nan walked in a few moments later, I hugged her and quietly updated her about her mother's potential imminent demise. I suggested she take some time to say whatever she wanted in the time she had left. I said we'd leave so Nan could have private time with her mother. She began to cry and didn't respond.

Bernice asked about the replacement eyeglasses she had ordered after hers went missing.

"They're being delivered tomorrow," Ned reported.

"Oh, I'll be dead tomorrow." Then she laughed.

What a way to go.

But, she didn't go. Not that day or the next or even the next. And her life got a lot worse. Did the Augmentin prolong her life needlessly? We wondered what was the doctor's goal for Bernice? And why had he ignored her clearly expressed wish not to be given antibiotics? Was he trying to help her or to keep a $12,000+/month patient in the bed?

Bernice's ability to live longer unfortunately gave her children more time to be who they were, that is to say, crazy and cruel. Ted flew in from California and within a week or so, seeing that his mother hadn't died, he resumed talking about moving her to a facility that would be cheaper with fewer hours of nursing staff. He even arranged a meeting for Bernice's four children and Bernice's doctor who was on staff at the facility. None of the three siblings were talking to Ned at that point but he went to the meeting because he wanted to protect his mother's wishes.

The meeting didn't go well. It started in Bernice's room at 7 AM. She was barely awake. When asked if she was happy or wanted to move she said she didn't know. From there, they moved to another room and it was a blood bath. Even the doctor was afraid and at one point said, "You're not going to punch me are you, Ted?" While Anne opened with "No one is talking about moving my mother," Ted began spewing venom about how Ned was a lousy POA with questionable ethics who wasn't acting in the best interest of his mother. Ned (who thought something of this nature might occur so he came armed with documents to shut Ted up) whipped out one of Bernice's tax returns to remind Ted of the time Ted stuck his mother with a $30,000+ tax penalty bill because he had given his mother bogus tax figures to report to the IRS for a business they owned jointly. Needless to say, Ted didn't appreciate that and went ballistic on Ned. (Ned had only brought those documents to shut Ted up before he could make any trouble for their mother.) After that day, Ted frantically started calling Bernice's attorney and financial planner desperately seeking a way to remove Ned as trustee for Ted's and Nan's inheritances. Because of Ted's felony conviction, he owed the government almost half a million

180

dollars in fines. If he inherited money the government could take it so any money left to him in his mother's will was going into trust for him. Nan was too incompetent to handle money so her inheritance was going into trust for her. Ned's mother had chosen Ned, the only person in her family with a brain and a moral compass, to be the trustee in charge of managing their money. Ted was so angry he wanted ABN, anybody but Ned, to be the trustee. Unfortunately, that wasn't his call to make and his mother was no longer competent to change anything. Bummer.

But, at some point Ted's repeated calls to Bernice's lawyer wore her down. The lawyer said she felt pretty sure Bernice was not competent to make any changes. But as her attorney, she wanted to do what was best for her client. She asked Ned to call Bernice's doctor because, the attorney said if the doctor told the lawyer Bernice's dementia rendered her incapacitated to make decisions, the trustee couldn't be changed. We had been concerned about Bernice's dementia for several months. She had worsened considerably since being in the hospital last summer when we found out she had agreed to remove the DNR (do not resuscitate) order she always said she wanted. When asked about it later, she reiterated her desire not to be resuscitated so we asked why she agreed to remove the order. She didn't know she *had* agreed to remove it. It became obvious then Bernice was no longer able to comprehend complex issues. She had almost no short-term memory. One day we walked in and she told us she had watched the movie, "The Butler." When we asked her what it was about, she had no idea. (Hint: It's called, "The Butler.") A typical morning phone conversation with her went something like this:

"Hi Mom, how are you?"
"I'm fine, Honey, how are you? Where are you?"
"I'm fine. I'm at home. Did you eat breakfast yet?"
"Breakfast? I don't know. Maybe I did. Are you coming up today?"
"Probably later. I have some work to do."
"That's good. Where are you?"
"I'm at home."
"Are you coming up today?"

Bernice couldn't remember whether she had eaten breakfast and it was only 10 AM. Was she really able to make good decisions for her life and her health? It didn't seem likely so Ned spoke to the doctor many times of his concerns about his mother's ability to process and therefore to make any life or death choices. Dr. Marshall was insistent Bernice had "capacity to make medical decisions." We're not doctors but we couldn't see how he was reaching that conclusion. He had run no dementia tests as far as we knew but he kept insisting Bernice remain in charge of her choices. Years before when she was of sound mind she had chosen Ned to be her Power of Attorney for health decisions as well as financial. It seemed time for Ned to step in to help her but the doctor's insistence that she was capable kept that from happening. However, the nurses who spent much more time with Bernice than the doctor did clearly didn't think Bernice was making good health decisions. When she was very agitated and crying and upset but refusing to take any medication to alleviate her anxiety (because Anne and Nan and Ted kept telling her she was overmedicated), the nurses would call Ned and ask him to speak to his mother to get her to change her mind, which she always did after talking to him. Obviously, if the nurses thought Bernice was making good decisions they wouldn't have constantly have to call Ned to get her to change her mind.

So, when the lawyer told Ned to ask the doctor to weigh in on Bernice's capacity, Ned knew he might encounter a problem. In fact, when Ned reached out to the doctor, Dr. Marshall insisted he could not make the determination about capacity. He said it was a legal, not a medical determination. Ned asked if the doctor would simply speak to the lawyer, at the lawyer's request. The doctor refused but didn't say why. Ultimately, the lawyer decided she would draft a trustee change after all. She believed if Ted and Nan were able to change their trustees (because they were both angry with Ned) they would stop bullying and badgering their mother. Plus, as she explained to Ned, the change of trustee, while probably not a good idea for Nan who was so totally incompetent she would need significant advice and counsel after Bernice died and for the rest of her life, wouldn't really affect anyone but Ted and Nan. Her attitude was somewhat, "They're making their beds, and they'll have to lie in them." So, the lawyer had Bernice sign papers to change the trustee from Ned to Dr. Stan, a childhood friend of Ted's. We had only met Dr. Stan once and he spent the evening describing his serious love affair with smoking marijuana and also the fact that he worshipped rocker Neil Young, believing, based on his in-depth study of Young's lyrics, that Young was, in fact, God. Needless to say, we would not have picked Stan for any position of power. Stan was not someone Bernice knew or trusted but at that point it was pretty obvious Bernice didn't understand enough to care anymore. For years Bernice and Nan had fought about the trust issue. Nan argued for inheriting her money outright. Bernice stood her ground insisting (rightly so) Nan would need a trustee to help her manage life once her parents were gone. Nan was in her fifties and really hadn't worked or supported herself ever. Bernice had fought that good fight for years but now her mind was weak enough to be defeated.

During one visit with Ned Bernice released this non sequitur, "I thought I took care of everything."

She thought she had done a competent job setting up her estate equitably with provisions in place to protect Nan and Ted. But even the best plan can't stop crazy, I guess.

Chapter Twenty-Two: As Bernice Lay Dying

After Ted and Nan succeeded in having their trustee changed, I suppose they felt emboldened by their success. So, they moved on to the next goal -- moving Bernice out of the nursing home into an assisted living facility where she'd spend less money. Given Ned's promise to care for his mother and keep her safe, he couldn't let that happen. Bernice really couldn't even leave the building as a result of the breathing crises she had several times a week. She'd gasp for air and be unable to breathe until a nurse administered morphine under her tongue. As a result, if she were to go out of the building for even a little while, she'd be at risk of dying a scary and horrible death from suffocation. While she would ultimately die from her inability to breathe, at least if she were in the nursing facility she'd be sedated and comfortable during those last moments and not likely to exit this world frightened and consciously, desperately gasping for air.

The thought of Bernice's death being so ghastly did not deter Ted and Nan from being hell bent on moving her. They continued to work toward that goal. They talked to Bernice about it constantly. The nurses reported Ted called Bernice many times every day and the calls were very long. Nan left notes in Bernice's room with detailed "to do" lists for her. She needed to call the bank to get information about her money. She needed to call the lawyer or the accountant or the financial planner for information. She was no more able to make those calls than she was to fly out the window but still the notes were left for her. Sometimes they were in Nan's handwriting; other times it appeared that Bernice wrote what was dictated to her, probably by Ted on the phone. As slowly as she moved and as hard as it was for her to hear and to process and to write, those dictations must have taken hours.

As things got progressively worse and Ted and Nan's badgering and bullying of Bernice was ramping up, we desperately sought help in stopping them. Ned reached out again to Dr. Marshall for advice. We figured he was a geriatrician and must have seen families in crises like this many times. We hoped he have some helpful advice. Ned and I had a phone conference with him. He listened to Ned's description of Bernice's worsening situation. He agreed Ted and Nan were hurting her. He said Ted was "insane" and Nan was "insane and overmedicated." He also added that during the January family meeting, when he said to Ted, "You're not going to punch me, are you, Ted?" he wasn't kidding. He said he was "fearful" of Ted. But, in the end the doctor offered little in the way of advice. He reiterated his earlier contention about Bernice still being capable of making decisions but insisted she had "the right to make bad decisions." He did agree to speak to Bernice about what she wanted in terms of her ongoing care after Ned told him again that Bernice had been asking to die and had recently asked, "Why can't the doctor just give me a pill to help me die?"

We didn't hear from Dr. Marshall again but we found out later, when he spoke to Bernice about what she wanted she asked to be taken off of all medications; she was ready to die. The doctor who had insisted for months Bernice had capacity to make medical decisions must have decided in that moment she didn't because he talked her out of her decision. He described her request in her chart and indicated they reached a "shared agreement" she would continue taking all medications.

The doctor just joined the growing club of people including the social workers, the nurses, the lawyer, and the hospice personnel who would be no help in saving this poor woman from her despicable family.

One day in March or April the hospice aide who took care of her reported that Bernice had been upset that morning because her family was talking about moving her. We had heard this from the nurses many times during the past few months but on this day, we were planning to visit her anyway so we had an opportunity to talk about it with Bernice.

"Mom," we said, "we heard you told Kirsten this morning you were upset and confused about why Ted and Nan are talking about moving you. Is that true?"

"Yes," she replied. "I don't want to move. I'm comfortable here."

"Well, you don't have to move," we explained. Ned continued to assure Bernice he was working very hard to keep her in this place where she felt safe and well cared for.

"That's what I want," she said.

"Okay," we promised her, "that's what you'll have. But, you have to tell Ted and Nan how you really feel. We're arguing with them about moving you but you could help out by being honest with them."

Just then, as if by magic, the phone rang. It was Ted. Well, come to think of it, magic wasn't involved. He had been calling her twice each day for eleven years. The timing was kismet, though.

"Tell him what you want," we suggested.

"Ted, honey," she began slowly and deliberately, "I don't want to move. I want to stay here."

Her silence for several moments indicated he was speaking but we couldn't hear his end of the conversation.

"Well, yes but I don't want to move, honey," she repeated softly but somewhat firmly. "I'm happy here."

This went on for quite some time. Bernice began to get agitated. Then she had trouble breathing and started gasping for air.

She took in a huge and loud breath. As she let it out she started to weep and she begged, "Please don't do that, Ted. Please don't do that."

We could hear the edges of his voice and his tone but could not make out his words. She begged and cried for a while and then she hung up.

As soon as she hung up the receiver, it was as if a cloud lifted. Bernice immediately stopped crying and regained her composure. We asked her what Ted was threatening and what it was she was begging him not to do.

"He said he was going to call… uh…what do you call that?" She struggled to find the word. "You know, he was going to call to have you thrown out."

186

"Do you mean Security?"

"Yes, that's it. He is going to call Security to have you thrown out."

A few moments later the head of nursing came in. She saw it was Ned in the room and was a bit confused.

"Oh, it's you," she said to Ned. "Your brother called to say his brother was in here causing a disturbance and we should have you removed but we knew it couldn't be *you* he was talking about so we thought maybe there was a third brother we didn't know."

God forbid.

But she saw it was just Ned, the brother they all knew and trusted and she saw Bernice was fine so she left after speaking for a few minutes about the trouble Ted often causes when he visits or calls. Bernice's phone rang. She was pretty sure it was Ted calling back; she asked me to answer and said she wasn't up to speaking with him. I answered; it was Ted; he wasn't happy to hear my voice. He proceeded to rant about how he was coming in soon and would take over as Power of Attorney. He insisted he knew what his mother wanted and Ned was not handling things the way she wanted. He cursed me out and was quite nasty. He went on about what a lousy son Ned was and how we raised bad kids who were crappy granddaughters. He said Ned had no right to tell him what he could or could not do. He said Ned would be "out of power" soon and Ted would do as he pleased once he took over. He said he'd move his mother to another facility and take over the handling of her finances. He said Ned and I were lousy parents. I hung up in the middle of one of his rants. I wasn't going to take any more verbal abuse.

Ned and I had an honest talk with Bernice about her future and her affairs. Ned asked if she was happy with how he was handling everything. He told her Ted had been threatening to "take over."

"Oh no," Bernice said strongly, "I want you to take care of things. I picked you."

"Well, I'm trying Mom," Ned explained, "but when you tell me one thing and tell Nan and Ted something else, you make it hard."

"But I don't want them to be angry with me," she replied meekly.

"You don't have to worry about that anymore," we explained. "Nobody is going to be angry with you for saying what you want. It's time you stood up for yourself."

She smiled and lifted a fist into the air, Black Panther-style.

She talked about her car and agreed it was time for Ned to sell it. But, Nan had taken it months ago and refused to return it so Bernice told Ned to get it back and take care of it.

Just then Nan called. Bernice was feeling her oats, I guess, because with no prompting and no crying or begging this time she simply told Nan to return her car to Ned. Ned said we'd make it easy for Nan to give back Bernice's car. We'd go to Nan's house to pick it up. We had seen it in her driveway. Bernice told Nan to leave the keys in the car and the car in the driveway and we'd be there in an hour to pick it up.

Bernice thanked us for taking care of her affairs. She promised, with fist in the air again, to stand her ground with her kids. We left and headed to Nan's to pick up the car.

We arrived to find an empty driveway.

Ned called Bernice to let her know Nan had hidden the car but when he spoke to his mother, she seemed to have already lost her resolve.

"Oh, okay," was about all she said.

On the way home we spoke about how we could possibly stop these two contemptible people from continuing to bully their mother. It was unconscionable and after witnessing Bernice gasping for air, it was even more upsetting. So we searched for some leverage. We believed we needed some way to threaten Ted and Nan into backing off and letting Bernice die in peace.

188

And then we remembered Ted's felony. As part of his punishment he was ordered to pay restitution to the federal government. He owed about $450,000. He had paid virtually none of it and stopped paying at all about ten years ago. He hoped his case had fallen through the cracks and that the Feds wouldn't come after him for the money. So far it appeared his hope was well founded as no one had ever contacted him. We knew he lived in fear of that contact. In fact I think it's the only thing he feared. So we decided to use it. I wrote this email. In retrospect I'm not sure it was my best moment. Then again, maybe it was. You be the judge.

Ted,

I am so sad to have to write this note. I sincerely don't want to hurt you. But after your odious phone call on Friday in which you threatened your mother, my husband, me, and my kids, you leave me no choice.

Your mother asked you for two things on Friday:
1. Accept she didn't want to move
2. Don't call the nurses to have Ned removed from her room.

You failed her on both counts. You let her down again, cruelly and selfishly ignoring her wishes. You pressured her about moving. The nurses told your mom you phoned them anyway. (Of course they would never remove Ned.)

Hearing and seeing your mom cry and gasp for air as she begged you, "Please don't do that, Ted, please don't do that," were one of the most heartbreaking scenes I've ever witnessed. It was in that moment I realized someone had to stop you. Ironically, it's me. Your brother isn't sure I should do this but to protect people and stand up for what is right, sometimes you have to do difficult things. He understands this is what I have to do.

On Friday your mother again told us and you she wants to stay where she is. Your refusal to respect her wishes upset her greatly. She said she wants Ned to continue as POA. She said specifically she did NOT want you to take over, as you threatened. (I believe your exact words to me were "We can do this the easy way or the hard way but I'm coming in soon, I've taken most of the power already and when I come in, Ned is out." Finally, she asked Ned to get back her car and take care of it as needed. She told Nan the same and instructed her to leave the car for Ned who would pick it up in an hour. As you well know, Nan (and likely you) made sure your mother's wish was ignored.

You made it clear you won't listen to your mother. You don't care what she wants. So I'm stepping in to protect her and my family from any more issues with you and Nan. You've refused repeatedly to listen to reason so I can think of only one way to get you to stop harassing your mother and brother. At the end of this note, the choice will be yours. I have researched the Department of Justice office responsible for collecting restitution debts. The office in Southern California may be interested in learning more about you. TEL: (619) 557-5610 Or Toll Free (800) 544-1106

There are four things you must do to stop me from calling them on Friday:
1. Stop abusing your mother (already alerted Adult Protective Services).
2. Immediately stop talking about moving her.
3. Immediately stop talking about replacing the person she chose to be her POA.
4. Make certain Nan leaves your mother's car in our driveway by 6:00 PM Thursday 4/24 so Ned can do as your mother asked.

If all four of those conditions aren't met, my first call on Friday is to the phone number above. Either way, in order to protect your mother from any further liability on that car, the insurance will be canceled as of Friday. You told me you refuse to be told what to do. You may be inclined to take the risk and continue what you're doing, but for your sake I hope you don't. You will hurt only yourself. The decision is not mine, it's yours. I hope you choose the path of love and respect for your mom and agree to do as she asks. That is all Ned has ever tried to do, to give her the peace she deserves. You fought him every step of the way. Stop now. Let her have peace. She would surely do that for you.

There is no benefit to Ned in any of this. I have no idea why you, Nan, or anyone has a problem with Ned doing what's right. It seems cruel and crazy but I don't have to understand it; I just have to end it.

I repeat, because it's important, I DO NOT want to make that call, but I absolutely will if you force me. To be clear — if I ever hear that you or Nan talk any more about moving your mother, or changing anything she put into place, I can always make that call. You should also know you haven't succeeded in keeping anything you've done secret. We knew everything all along -- your vile calls and Nan's calls to Dianne, Mom's three meetings with Dianne, your calls and Nan's calls to Bob, your list of things Mom should do at the bank, and so on. We didn't expose you because, frankly, we were elated; the changing of the trustee freed Ned from a lifetime of aggravation with the two of you. I tell you this now only so you don't think you can return the car while keeping up the abuse and keep it a secret.

Don't bother to respond. This is not a negotiation. We've blocked all phone, text, and email communication from you.

In language you understand, we can do this the easy way or the hard way. The easy way is for you to just stop and this all goes away. I know that's not easy for you because you convinced yourself what you're doing is right. Somewhere along the line you made this about you; you made it a power struggle between you and your brother that your ego and pride compels you to win. Your thinking is just so twisted and it's simply wrong. Ned isn't in it to win it, there is nothing for him to win here. This is about your mother living out her time peacefully as she wants. That's all.

Finally, I feel sorry for you and Nan. Truly. And I am sorry to have to take this step. Unspeakably sorry.

Debby

He answered right away.

I really don't need to defend myself but I'll reply directly to your email:
1. *To set the record straight, I didn't threaten my mother, you, or your kids on Friday.*
2. *No one has pressured my mother to move. However, you have pressured her to not move. She can and will make her own decision regarding where she wants to be.*
3. *My mother has requested numerous things from Ned as POA which he has failed to do. She does not want her car sold or insurance cancelled until further notice. She wants Nan to continue to receive her financial support.*
4. *What you "witnessed" on Friday, was me calling after you had obviously made my mother upset by feeding her lies about Nan and I forcing her to move.*
5. *You're stepping in to protect your family? From what? Your family remains isolated and not invested as they've always been.*
6. *You're going to call the APS and the DOJ to turn me in? LMAO!!! You're the same piece of shit as your husband.*
7. *Don't lecture me about love, respect and peace for my mother. My mother knows who has it and who doesn't.*
8. *No secret about removing Ned from the trust (which only demonstrates*

how she feels about Ned), or from being POA. He's been asked repeatedly to step aside.

9. There's no power struggle here…if this were about me having power, I could have taken it a while ago. You have both lost sight of what this is about.

10. The only ones twisted here are both of you…the same twisted way you have both been since you broke away from my family more than 35 years ago and claim you were victims. What a joke!

Here are a few examples of the deplorable behavior your husband has exhibited (in case you are unaware):

1. Refusal to meet to discuss as a family what is best for my mother.

2. Refusal to comply and continue to pay for Nan's expenses as desired by my mother.

3. Bullying and humiliating Nan and calling her a moron right in front of my mother.

4. Trying to undermine my credibility by bringing a file to a meeting (which I had to force) having nothing to do with the what's in the best interest of my mother.

5. Trying to sell the car when my mother obviously didn't want that.

6. Disrespecting my mother by refusing to answer me about why he wanted her driver's license (she called me in a panic and wanted me to find out).

7. AND THE MOTHER OF THEM ALL…TELLING HER THAT SHE DOESN'T HAVE ANY MORE MONEY BECAUSE NAN AND I HAVE SPENT IT ALL. THIS SENT HER INTO A TAILSPIN AND SHE HAD TO BE SEDATED WITH MORPHINE. IT TOOK 3 DAYS FOR HER TO RETURN TO NORMALCY. THAT WAS THE SICKEST THING BY FAR.

The bottom line is that it is Ned who has caused all of the disruption to my mother and is making her anxious. I suggest you understand this and stop trying to escalate it.

All your email has done is to motivate me to do what I need to do. Any decisions should have been family decisions…not Ned and Debby decisions. This is my mother, not your Aunt Essie. Since you've taken the liberty of telling me how to care for my mother (even though you have barely had a relationship with her all these years), let me do the same on how to properly raise your children…it would have been nice if you encouraged them to finally have a relationship with their 93 year old *grandmother. It's too little too late now, but with their next grandmother maybe you should have them call or even visit a few times a year…or how about just once?! Oh yeah, there are no more grandmothers left. Don't believe me???…You might want to talk to your own friend Andy, as I listened to him remind you that my mother is "still alive" as you rambled on about what's best for her.*

Now go away. Oh yeah, you will soon, because nothing stops you from going down to NC, not even when my mother had hip surgery and couldn't walk…isn't that when Ned handed the gauntlet to Nan and allowed her to kiss his ring? Oh no, that was a different time because Nan had a breakdown, so there was no one to help my mom except me…but you didn't care!

After reading your email, there is no need to ever contact me again.

So, whether it was my finest moment or not, as you can see, it didn't go well. "LMAO." (Laughing my ass off.) That's how much he feared me turning him in to the Feds. And, while I fully intended to make good on my threat I had decided I would not do so until after Bernice's death so I guess he was calling my bluff.

As the next two weeks passed, Ned saw more notes in Bernice's room. One of them had the name of the facility Ted and Nan wanted Bernice to move to.

"Wesley, $4000, Ann's Choice $11,000"

They had convinced Bernice she should "shop around" for a cheaper facility. Ned tried to explain to his mother why she couldn't live in a $4000/month assisted living facility. He explained the difference in price was because that facility was not a skilled nursing place like the one she was in. They wouldn't provide a nurse around the clock. If Bernice had a breathing crisis there might be no one there to help her. He told his mother she would not be safe in a place like that, that she was too sick to be in a facility designed for healthier people. While Bernice still said she was happy where she was, she also said she thought a cheaper place might be better but she didn't know why. She was quite confused. It became clear she didn't even remember the conversation we had on that previous visit. The hours and hours of

Ted and Nan badgering her about moving were clearly taking a toll. The nurses continued to report Bernice's extreme distress to Ned.

It had to stop so, at the urging of the nursing home's social workers, Ned contacted Adult Protective Services to report the abuse of his mother at the hands of his siblings. They investigated and wrote a letter of recommendation to the nursing home saying Bernice should not be removed from the facility because she'd be at risk of "death or serious bodily injury." We thought that would be the end of the talk about moving Bernice anywhere or taking her out for a joy ride. We couldn't have been more wrong.

Since Ned found the name of the facility to which his siblings intended to move Bernice – Wesley -- he phoned to ask if they had heard from Ted or Nan.

"Oh, yes, your brother and sister were here looking for a spot for your mom," the woman in charge replied, "they raised a red flag with me when your brother said he was not Power of Attorney but it 'didn't matter.'"

Ned explained the entire story. The woman was sympathetic, saying she had experienced similar problems with destructive people in her family when her aging parents were ailing. Ned sent her a copy of the letter of recommendation from Adult Protective Services. She said there was no way her facility would accept Bernice, given the circumstances. Again, we thought that problem was solved. Again we were wrong.

Soon after that the woman from Wesley phoned Ned to say she had heard from Ted again. He was still seeking placement for his mother. She told him she had a copy of the Adult Protective Services letter. He told her he didn't care about that; it was not legally binding. She asked him why he wanted to move his mother so badly.

"You don't understand my brother and sister-in-law," he replied.

While that didn't answer her question in any way, he went on to say he was coming in for a visit soon and would be in touch with her again. He got belligerent when she repeated her facility would not accept his

194

mother. He also said he was "going to be Power of Attorney by tomorrow."

A few days later Ned visited Bernice. The nurse stopped him on his way in and said, "Your sister Nan was here last night with several people. They were in your mother's room and had her signing documents."

Chapter Twenty-Three: The Peoples' Court Part Deux

Ned walked into his mother's room and asked her what kind of documents Nan had her sign the night before.

"I didn't sign any documents," Bernice answered.

"Yes, Mom, you did," Ned countered. "The nurse said Nan was in here with other people and you were signing things."

"Oh, I signed something so I could go out to dinner," Bernice replied.

A few days after that Ned received a call from his mother's financial planner, Bob, the man who manages her accounts. He knows the family well and was familiar with the recent goings on.

"Ned, I'm sorry to tell you," he began, "your brother just sent us a document signed by your mother making him the new Power of Attorney."

Bob went on to explain the accounts were frozen while the legal department investigated the validity of Ted's document. It was signed by Bernice and notarized, witnessed by Nan's boyfriend and Nan's upstairs tenant. Within a day we found out Ted had sent his POA document to Bernice's banks and to the nursing home. There was one tiny problem with the document, though. Ted had sent it to Susquehanna Bank with a blank line where his name should have gone. Nan had Bernice sign a document naming a new POA but the name of the new person was not filled in. The bank manager called Ted and told him the line where the name should have been was blank so he faxed her a new page with his name filled in. That wasn't acceptable, she told him, your mother signed a blank document, you can't just send us a new page; you have to have her execute a whole new document.

That bank's refusal to accept the validity of his document didn't dissuade Ted from calling the same woman again a few days later and demanding access to his mother's checking account. She explained again why Ted was not actually POA. But, undaunted, Ted phoned the administrator of the nursing home to complain the bank wouldn't recognize him as POA. "I can't pay my mother's bills," Ted told the administrator. "Don't you want to get paid?" I have no idea what he thought the nursing home administrator could or would do about the bank but clearly Ted was desperate for someone to recognize his power.

Meanwhile, Ned contacted Bernice's attorney, Dianne. We knew weeks earlier Ted might try something like this and trick his mother into making him POA so we had discussed the possibility with the attorney before. She said Ned's only alternative was having his mother declared incompetent or incapacitated. While Dianne believed Bernice was incapacitated and no longer had the mental competence to process much, let alone to make a legal decision, she explained to Ned the process of going for guardianship was arduous and would be a lot to put Bernice through so if he didn't have to do it, he shouldn't. She suggested we wait until Ted actually did something on the off chance he wouldn't and this huge, difficult, and costly step could be avoided. Thus, when Ted did exactly as we feared he would, Dianne informed Ned the only way to protect his mother from the siblings bent on harming her was for Ned to hire an attorney and go to court to petition for guardianship of his incapacitated, demented mother.

Dianne contacted our attorney, Julie. They worked quickly to bring in an independent physician to evaluate Bernice. His report showed she suffered from moderate to severe dementia; she lacked capacity to make decisions about her welfare and had likely lacked capacity for many months prior. He said Bernice had no short-term memory. She could read but had no idea what she read. She could watch TV but could not remember what she watched just after viewing. She couldn't name the president and didn't know he was black. She was unable to process anything, partly because she couldn't retain anything long enough to process it.

The guardianship hearing was grueling. There were two attorneys, Bernice's and ours. Nan was there. Ted did not show up but he sent his lifelong friend, Ed. (Yes, you think I'm making up the trio of Ned, Ted and Ed, but I swear those names really do rhyme.) Ned was on the witness stand for almost an hour. They asked him questions about how he had been handling Bernice's affairs and what had transpired over the seven months with his siblings. They asked him to explain why he did all the things he did. He replied he was only trying to protect his mother and keep her safe where she had chosen to be for her remaining time. They asked Ned if he had his mother's driver's license. He answered affirmatively and for some reason Nan burst out laughing at that response, almost as if she thought Ned had been "caught" in some way in doing something wrong. The story behind that is this. The notary who affixed his seal to the new Power of Attorney document they tricked Bernice into signing stated he used Bernice's PA driver's license as proof of her identity. The only problem with that is that Bernice didn't have her license in May when she signed that document. Ned did. At one point a few months earlier, Bernice's attorney's paralegal suggested to Ned he should give Bernice's car to Nan, officially signing the title over to her. That way, Bernice would no longer have liability if anything happened involving that car while it was in Nan's possession since she had stolen it and refused to return it. (Given Nan's and her boyfriend Frank's level of irresponsibility, the likelihood of that car being involved in an accident was pretty high. And to our knowledge, Frank no longer had a license so if he drove it and got involved in an accident Bernice's liability could be significant.) Ned investigated how to go about the legal logistics of signing over the car to Nan. The car tag place told him he'd need Bernice's driver's license. So, sometime in April, Ned told Bernice he was going to sign the car over to Nan to protect Bernice from liability and he needed her driver's license to do so. Thus, when we saw the notary had attested he had used PA License as identification, we knew he had falsified the document. That's why the question about the license was asked in court. Not sure why Nan found it funny as it surely didn't make her look good or honest.

Then the woman from Susquehanna Bank testified about the blank POA document Ted had sent her. She also related that the week before the POA document was presented she got a call from a man who identified himself by first name only – Ted – said his mother was a resident of the nursing home, and asked for details about how one would go about changing Power of Attorney. She intuitively felt the tenor of the call was shady. While she couldn't say definitively the caller was Ted, he had the same first name and a mother at the same nursing home and within the week he sent a change of Power of Attorney. Bizarre coincidence?

The woman from Adult Protective Services testified although the investigation and results were confidential, she could confirm they had investigated an abuse allegation and had written a letter of recommendation saying Bernice should not be permitted to leave the facility because she might die.

Then the judge asked Nan if she wanted to take the stand. Nan asked if anyone would have to question her. When the judge responded she could just make a statement, she took the stand to speak about her mother's competence.

"My brother called me an idiot in front of my mother…" she began, "…well, not really in front of my mother but he was on the phone and I was in her room when he said it."

It went downhill from there. Nan exhibited the true depth of her mental and emotional problems. She was obviously a mentally deficient woman in pain.

"My mother is full of life. I bring her food and life and he…" she shot out her arm and pointed accusingly at Ned, "he brought her a banana from the other room."

A banana from the other room. I swear those were her exact words.

When our attorney asked Nan if she understood her mother was dying Nan shrugged and replied, "I don't know. That doctor," she said with a dismissive wave, "when I called him to say my mother had edema, he said, 'Your mother's edema will go away when she's DEAD!'"

When Bernice's attorney asked Nan if she thought the nursing home cost too much money, Nan sighed, "Yes, I guess so."

Then she stepped off the stand and walked by me as she returned to her seat.

"You're ugly," she spat at me under her breath.

My brother called me an idiot and *you're ugly*. Are we eight years old here or 60? I'm totally not sure anymore.

The attorneys summarized the case. Our attorney asked the judge to appoint Ned temporary guardian. Bernice's attorney agreed Bernice needed a guardian but suggested the judge appoint an independent person. (She said off the record she wanted an independent guardian in order to make things easier for Ned.)

The judge took a brief recess to ponder. He returned and appointed Ned temporary guardian for a month pending the hearing for permanent guardianship.

Ted arrived in Pennsylvania the next night. Ned worked with the administrative staff at the nursing home to put new rules in place for visiting Bernice. The first rule was no visitors after 8 PM because Bernice said she was too tired for late visitors. Ted showed up a few minutes before 9 PM. Okay, he had just gotten off the plane and was anxious to see her. Had it been me, I probably would've gone there too but when I got there and saw my mother was in bed, I would have kissed her goodnight and told her I'd be back first thing in the morning. Maybe that's just me, though because when the nurse politely asked Ted to leave and let his mother sleep, he refused, waved some papers around showing he was POA and stayed. The nurse said she'd have to call security and then the police if he didn't cooperate. He didn't. Security was called, he showed them his (fraudulent) POA document and they responded, for all intents and purposes, "Well, Ted, we'll see your POA document and raise you a court order showing your brother is guardian."

Ted left, the nurse told us, but was furious. I still don't quite get him. He knew the outcome of the hearing, he knew Ned was guardian and therefore, Ted was not (nor had he ever been) POA, but still he had to push it. Boggles the mind.

It seemed no day was without crisis at this point. Ted's visit lasted a few weeks and security had to be called repeatedly when he refused to leave, even at 9 PM. One day we got a call from Bernice's attorney who had a call from Bernice in which Bernice sounded agitated. It was on speaker with Nan and Ted in Bernice's room. They wanted the attorney's help in getting permission for them to take Bernice out of the facility to the beauty parlor (despite there being a beauty parlor right down the hall which Bernice visited every week) because, they insisted loudly, their mother's hair looked "terrible." "Mom," the attorney heard them say, "Tell her your hair looks terrible." They insisted the beauty parlor in the nursing home wasn't good enough and they were willing to risk Bernice's life by taking her out where she couldn't be dosed with morphine in a breathing crisis (which according to the nurse now happened about 5 times each week) so she could go to a different beauty parlor. Again, maybe this is just a quirk in my personality but if my 93-year-old mother were dying in a nursing home I'd cut out my own tongue before I'd tell her how awful her hair looked. The depths these folks would sink to in order to convince their mother Ned wasn't doing right by her (because he wouldn't give permission as guardian to let her go to the beauty parlor) were unfathomable.

Bernice fell and broke her wrist. The doctor explained to Ned Bernice was too weak to be taken out of the facility to see an orthopedist. Short of any kind of surgery on the wrist, which Bernice was much too frail to endure, there wasn't much to be done anyway so they wrapped her arm to immobilize it and gave her pain medication. Bernice said it didn't hurt much and didn't bother her much because it was her left hand so she was still able to use her right, her dominant hand. But Ted began calling the nursing unit insisting Bernice's X-rays be sent to his friend Stan. (trustee and also you may recall pothead doctor) Since Ned was guardian, it was up to him to give permission for the X-rays to be sent. He could see no reason for Stan to look at the X-rays as there was no recommendation Dr. Stan could make that would matter. Bernice had perfectly good doctors treating her, the injury wasn't bothering her, leave her alone. But Ted phoned Bernice repeatedly, apparently and badgered her into a frantic state. One night about 9:30 PM after just getting off the phone with Ted, Bernice called Ned in a panic, "NED, WHY CAN'T I HAVE X-RAYS?" Bernice pleaded angrily.

"Mom," Ned took a deep breath to calm his pounding heart, "you had X-rays. You fell and broke your wrist. They took X-rays and that's why your arm is wrapped. Is it hurting you? You can call the nurse for pain medicine if it hurts."

"TED SAID YOU WON'T LET ME HAVE X-RAYS! WHY CAN'T I HAVE X-RAYS? WHY CAN'T I HAVE X-RAYS?"

Ned became visibly upset. He couldn't believe his brother would torture Bernice in this way just to win some kind of victory over him. I took the phone from him thinking I could calm Bernice down because unlike Ned I was not on the verge of tears. Hearing how upset Bernice was and knowing it was for no reason other than Ted's three days of brutally beating her up verbally about X-rays made Ned astronomically angry.

"Mom, it's Debby," I began. "Are you okay?"

"Yes. I just want to have X-rays. Why won't Ned let me have X-rays?"

"Mom, you're okay. You had X-rays on Monday. You have a broken wrist. Does it hurt?"

"No."

"Do you want us to call the nurse for you and get you some pain medication?"

"No. I'm okay. I just want Ned to let me have X-rays."

"You don't need X-rays. You had them three days ago. That's how they knew your wrist was broken. That's why it's wrapped in that bandage. Are you sure you're not in pain?"

"Yes, I'm okay."

"Alright, Mom, if you're okay calm down and get some rest. You don't need any more X-rays, I promise."

"Okay, honey."

Ned called the nurses' desk to ask them to go to Bernice's room and make sure she was okay. The nurse said Ted had been on the phone badgering Bernice for 45 minutes. Bernice was bordering on hysteria when the nurse went to check on her. Ted called again. The nurse asked him to stop calling for the night; his mother needed rest. Then this very astute nurse unplugged the phone because she knew Ted could not be trusted to act in his mother's best interest.

One morning while Ted was visiting, a nurse called to report an incident from the night before. Ted, Nan, and Nan's boyfriend had been visiting and left about 8:20. A few minutes after they left, a nurse entered Bernice's room and was overcome by a chemical smell to the point of having trouble breathing (The nurse is asthmatic.). Bernice complained about her eye tearing. They quickly moved Bernice to another room and searched thoroughly for the source of the noxious odor. It wasn't anywhere else in the facility. They actually suspected Ted and Nan of having done "something" to the oxygenator or to something else in the room. They took a couple of bottles of make up and/or lotions from the room to send to Poison Control for analysis. By morning the smell dissipated. But the thought that nurses and administrators of the facility suspected her own children of trying to poison Bernice through the air was pretty chilling.

Chapter Twenty-Four: Till Death Do Us Part, Maybe

In July we reported to court for the permanent guardianship hearing with the same judge presiding. Officially Ned agreed with his mother's attorney and asked for an independent guardian to be appointed. Our attorney had said the judge was more likely to appoint a guardian if we asked for an independent. She counseled us to do so to insure the appointment of a guardian because if we had lost at court, Ted's POA could possibly have gone into effect. We couldn't let that happen. Unofficially, Ned was saddened by this turn of events. He'd promised his mother he'd take care of her through the end of her life. It was a promise he desperately wanted to keep.

But, it was not to be.

Nan showed up for the hearing, as did Anne. A few days before the hearing Anne had an attorney/friend phone our attorney to ask about the details of the case. He told our attorney Anne had only one interest in the hearing and it had nothing to do with her mother. She said she wanted to find out if her "insurances" were still in place. She was referring to the life insurance policies on her mother that would pay out upon her death to her beneficiaries – her four children. While I knew Anne didn't care much for her mother, after all she hadn't spoken to her for most of the last 13 years, I was taken aback by her willingness to tell someone she only cared about the money. Some people just make me shake my head. And then some.

Once again the judge asked Ned a few questions about why his mother needed a guardian. Once again the judge gave Nan an opportunity to speak her mind about the issue. The judge asked her, "What do you want for your mother?" She responded, "I want my bills paid." Not sure how Nan thought that answered the question about what she wanted FOR HER MOTHER, but she went on to talk about Ned and about how bad a son and brother he was. She talked about how little our daughters see their grandmother. She said she was her mother's "caretaker." Shaking my head.

The judge invited Anne to the witness stand next. He asked her what she wanted for her mother. She said she just wanted her mother to have peace. She waxed poetic about what a wonderful companion Nan was for their mother. I wondered how she could get those words out of her mouth. She wanted peace for her mom? Nan is wonderful? These were two people she hadn't included in her life for 13 years. She had spent the 20 years before that telling her mother no one else in the family loved her; that Anne was the only one who cared. She tortured her mother for 20 years telling her Nan was a drug addict because she didn't love her mother, that Ted moved to California because he didn't love his mother and that Ned ruined the family because he didn't love his mother. Now she wanted to provide peace? Shaking my head, rolling my eyes, hell I almost started screaming, "The Emperor has no clothes!"

The judge granted Ned's petition and appointed an independent guardian who was a local attorney. Outside the courtroom Alexis said quietly to Nan, "Nan I think what you're doing is really sad. I thought you were better than this."

Nan blew up. She asked Alexis, "Do you want to go outside and fight?" She meant physically; as in a fistfight outside the courthouse! Alexis politely declined. The visual of 32-year-old Alexis punching her 58-year-old aunt just didn't appeal to her somehow. Nan took the rejection politely.

"Fuck all y'all bitches," she retorted with index finger wagging in the air back and forth at all three of our daughters.

We heard little from the guardian or from Bernice's lawyer for the next few months. We heard about the myriad calls from Ted and Nan and Anne to the guardian. We heard he placated Nan by paying pretty much all of her bills and he placated Ted by not making them return their mother's car so he could drive it when he visited. He undid all the rules put in place to protect Bernice during visits. We couldn't understand why he'd cave in to the very people who were the reason Bernice needed a guardian in the first place but there was nothing we could do about any of it so we had to let it go. He did keep Bernice in the facility of her choice and we had to be satisfied with that as it was of paramount importance. Bernice's lawyer said Ted and Nan had contacted her about changing Bernice's will, which the guardian actually had the legal right to do, but the guardian said no changes would be made. Guardians have a great deal of power; it's almost unbelievable what a dastardly guardian could do.

Bernice continued her slow decline. She fell on her face and was seriously bruised. But she woke up each day and soldiered on. One Saturday in October Bernice's nurse called to say Bernice would not likely last the day. She said Ned should come to say goodbye. We had heard Ted had arrived the night before, coincidentally, not because he knew of the decline. So we knew he might be there. And he was, as were Nan and Anne. Ted's friend Billy was also in the room. Who invites a friend to his mother's death scene?

Ned approached the bed where Bernice lay breathing pretty heavily. She was conscious but not focusing. Her eyes were open but she wasn't speaking and she seemed to be in some sort of delirious state. Ned had said on the way there he planned to tell her he loved her and say goodbye but he wasn't going to stay a long time and sit vigil with his siblings. I agreed it was the appropriate choice to avoid upsetting Bernice with any sort of drama. Ted and Nan stood on either side of the bed holding Bernice's hands. Anne stood near the foot of the bed. I was standing a few feet behind Nan with Ted facing me. Out of the corner of my eye I detected Ted glaring at Ned and turning his head to mouth something to Nan. I looked away. But a moment or two later I saw Ted looking straight at me and mouthing some words. I realized he was directing this message to me, not to Nan.

"You're evil. You're evil."

Again, while I know it's not my job or responsibility to right all of the wrongs in the world, some wrongs are so glaring I can't stop myself. I couldn't stand to see him disrespect his mother's death in this manner. So I whispered to him in my most condescending tone to stop him while also letting him know he was not intimidating me, "Honey, you don't want to do this in your mother's room."

Ned bid his mother goodbye and we left the room. We stopped to speak with one of the nurses. Ned hadn't met her before but he had spoken to her on the phone a few times and she had been kind and

206

compassionate so he wanted to thank her. While we spoke to her Ted and Billy came into the hall. Ted made a beeline for my face and leaned way in to say, "You will not fucking tell me what to do."

"Ted," I began quietly, slowly, and calmly yet menacingly, "You are a disgusting person. You need to step away from me."

With that, Ned and I started down the hall to leave the facility. But Ted tried to block our way. He said to Ned, "I'll kick your ass."

Apparently, the thought of 64-year-old Ned having a fist fight with his 61-year-old brother in the hallway of the nursing home where their mother lay dying was not Ned's idea of a fun time (like father, like daughter) so he simply took out his cell and said, "I'm calling 911."

"You don't have to do that," I said quietly as I touched him gently on the arm to lead him toward the door at the end of the hall, "we are just leaving." I simply could not abide this scene outside Bernice's room and knew if Ned had a moment to think he wouldn't want that either. We walked down the hall. Ted tried to block us for a few more steps but we walked quickly past him and left.

The next morning Ned phoned the nurse to find out how his mother was. We figured it might take a day or so for her to die. He didn't want to return and deal with his siblings again but he did want to know how she was. The nurse said Bernice was awake but confused.

She was confused? No, *I* was confused. How could Bernice even be conscious enough to be confused? Turned out, she rallied and lived to see another day. In fact, unfortunately for that poor woman, she saw many other days.

Chapter Twenty-Five: The Fourth Death: Bad Funeral Behavior

Months earlier, in June, the one month Ned served as temporary guardian for his mother, he had paid a few bills. He paid her insurance bill, her drug bill, the bill for the nursing home, the bill for her therapist and last but most definitely not least, the bill for the attorney who handled the guardianship case for us. When we first concluded Ned would have to seek guardianship of his mother in order to protect her from his siblings, her attorney Dianne explained the process to us. She said she could not represent Ned as the petitioner for guardianship because even though she was the one who told Ned to seek guardianship, Dianne had to represent Bernice. She explained we'd need to retain an attorney and it was going to be expensive but the way it works is this, generally. If you seek guardianship and win, that is if the court rules the person *does* need a guardian, the attorney expense can legitimately be paid for by the "ward," in this case, Bernice. If, however, the court rules against guardianship, you would have to pay the attorney's fees out of your pocket. So, when we chose to pursue this matter we risked having to pay the attorney's fees ourselves. And they were substantial -- $20,000+. Lawyers are definitely the big winners in these situations because whether the client wins or loses, the lawyers get paid -- Big Time!

Furthermore, unbeknownst to us, any business the guardian conducts for the ward, for example, paying her bills, is overseen by the judge who appointed the guardian. This makes a great deal of sense because it protects the ward from any potential financial misconduct on the part of the guardian. But we didn't know that meant Ned would have to appear in court to have the judge "ratify" the bills he had paid in June. But, sometime in October we learned about this hearing and it was scheduled for December 9. The attorney explained it was not a big deal. (Again, the lawyer wins because even in this simple procedure the guardian cannot go to court unless accompanied by a lawyer. Ka-ching!) Basically the judge would ask Ned what bills were paid and what they were for. The guardian would be there too and Ned's siblings, considered "interested parties" in this matter, would also be invited. But, overall, the hearing wasn't much more than a formality.

Ned had paid a few bills but none was controversial. Then again, we are dealing with some twisted siblings here so we couldn't be sure no dramatics were in the offing.

At 10:00 on December 9 (coincidentally Nan's birthday), the hearing began. No siblings were present. The judge asked Ned to describe the bills he paid. He asked if all the bills were for Bernice's benefit. He asked the guardian if he felt Ned paid the bills appropriately. The guardian agreed Ned had handled everything as he should have and that would have been it except… 20 minutes into the hearing Nan arrived. The judge summarized what had transpired and asked if she had anything to say. Of course she did. She took the stand and began her angry diatribe.

"This is outrageous."

Nan proceeded to describe how awful a man Ned is. "He's a dictator, a tyrant," she spat out in anger. She went on to talk about how her mother didn't need a guardian in the first place and the whole plan was a devious and dastardly act orchestrated by Ned who was on a destructive power trip according to Nan. (Not that she used the words devious or dastardly as I'm sure those are beyond her vocabulary skills.) Following her logic no bills should be paid fostering the guardianship. There was only one fly in Nan's ointment, one bit of logic she didn't think through. The judge at this hearing was the same judge who ruled not once but twice already that Bernice was incapacitated and needed a guardian. So, here's Nan thinking she's trashing her brother by saying what a bad guy Ned is, but really, what she's doing in her testimony is telling the judge how wrong *he* was in ruling for guardianship in the first place. Maybe not her best plan of attack.

But she went on. Our lawyer passed Ned a note, "The judge isn't listening." I guess she deduced that from his decidedly disinterested body language and facial expression. He was leaning to one side, resting his head on his hand and kind of staring downward toward his desk. He didn't look like he was registering anything Nan was saying; it's true. But this was not his first time at the Nan rodeo. He had heard her wacky testimony twice before and she wasn't really bringing anything new to the act so it's understandable his mind might have wandered.

Then Nan announced she wanted to read a letter written by her brother Ted who "couldn't be here." It's funny how with all of Ted's trips to Philadelphia and his extended stays during each of those trips, a total of about 8 weeks this year, (None of which he ever paid a penny for because his friend Ed provides him with free tickets, he drives his mother's car, and he stayed with us or with a friend.) whenever a court hearing took place Ted was nowhere to be found. The judge refused to allow Nan to read the letter. Undaunted she pressed and whined. He refused again but she whined some more. The judge asked how long was the letter. Nan said it was a "few pages." The judge relented and said she could read a bit of it.

The letter started out with an insane pack of lies, pretty much the same as the rest of Nan's testimony. Ned's a bad guy, he had ruined their family, the parents didn't trust him and only put him in charge because of birth order (clearly not true as Ned isn't the oldest), etc. Ted said Ned didn't want Bernice to have the hip surgery that "saved her life" a few years earlier. (a bizarre lie)

What we learned from listening to Ted's pathetic letter was this. He really needed to prove to someone, most likely himself, that his mother really did like him best. The overall theme of the letter was that Ned was bad while Ted was good. Yes, Bernice had picked Ned to take care of things but according to Ted, she had really wanted *him* all along because he was just a better guy than his brother. Ted had lots of things to feel guilty about when it came to his relationship with his mother. Not only had he let her down by committing a felony, since that time he had taken at least $100,000 in support from her. My amateur psychology degree tells me he may have felt pretty lousy about himself, although he would never admit it. In his heart, though, he knew what we all knew: his mother recognized Ted for the loser he was. He had only a short time left to prove to his mother and the world he was the best son after all. That's part of the reason he resorted to such desperate measures to take over her affairs. While it's true he wanted her to spend less money leaving more for him to inherit, he also wanted to be the one in charge so that everyone would understand he was the best of her four children after all.

Nan continued to read. At one point, she glanced up at us with a supercilious gleam in her eye as she read deliberately, "Ned was removed from his job as a school principal because he is a racist."

There's only one problem with that statement. Well, two problems really. First, it's not true. In the 90s Ned was a principal at an inner city elementary school. It was a fractious place, a school that had had five principals in as many years. Much of the staff was white and all of the kids were black. There was a small group of vocal but destructive parents who tried like hell to take over the building insisting that whites should not be teaching their kids and/or running their school. They did some protesting, they did some threatening of the staff and finally, they did accuse several staff members of being racist. White the school district investigated and found no wrongdoing on anyone's part ultimately, and quite sadly and reluctantly, Ned and many of the wonderfully dedicated staff members chose to leave as they weren't safe there. Nan and Ted knew the truth about what happened at the school so they knew their statement in the letter was a malicious lie. So that was one problem with what they said. Secondly, it has nothing to do with the issue of the guardianship of Bernice. Even if Ned were a racist, how would that be relevant? His mother is not the least bit black!

Our lawyer stood and said, "Your Honor, I have no problem with listening to testimony of the matter at hand, but..." and she pretty much shrugged her shoulders and put up her hands as if to ask, "Really?"

The judge said he agreed wholeheartedly. He told Nan to stop reading the letter. She started to argue with him. He put his hand up in a gesture that said clearly, "STOP." He told her she was NOT to interrupt him again. She insisted on reading more of the letter and he said she'd have to skip the part she had been reading and could quickly paraphrase the rest and wrap it up. She did. She stepped off the witness stand and this time as she passed me she murmured under her breath, "Bitch." I figured that meant I was going up in her estimation because at the last hearing she was calling me "Ugly." I figured "bitch" was an improvement. But then again, maybe not.

The judge ruled in Ned's favor and agreed the bills were legitimate.

That night, in the middle of the night at about 3:30 AM, the phone rang. It was Bernice's nurse reporting Bernice had declined rapidly. She suggested it was time for Ned to come say goodbye. (It seems crass to say "again" here but let's face it, this is the third "come and say goodbye" call we had.) Ned asked if the nurse had phoned anyone else. He did want to say goodbye to his mother if these were in fact her last moments. But Ned was reluctant to run into those siblings again (although to our knowledge Ted was not in town.). But the nurse said she had only called Ned. She had checked the chart and chosen to call just Ned after seeing, I guess, that Ned had been the Power of Attorney/contact person. Officially she should have called the guardian. Once we arrived the nurse said she had also called the guardian after she called Ned. It was just wonderful and very kind of her to call Ned at all. I think she knew, like most of the staff at the nursing home, that Ned was a good and kind man who wanted to do right by his mother. They had seen enough of what the other three siblings were up to. They knew the truth.

We got there in about 20 minutes. Ned approached the bed. Bernice was conscious and seemed to know what was going on. She reached out and said, "Ned, hold my hand." He did. She said, "Nothing is happening, nothing is happening." Ned just held her hand and comforted her. He told her she'd see Jack and her sisters again, knowing that would make her happy. Then, worrying that the guardian had called Nan and Anne by that time, and not wanting his mother to have to endure any kind of scene on her deathbed, Ned stayed a bit and then we left.

Bernice died about 48 hours later in the middle of the night with Nan and Nan's boyfriend Frank by her side and Ted on the phone. I still feel badly about that. It's appropriate that Nan was there with her mom. They had shared a long life together and although they had quite a codependent and unhealthy relationship I do believe they loved each other. But Nan's boyfriend Frank is, in a word, creepy. If you saw him walking toward you on the street your instincts would compel you to cross to the other side. He and Nan have been together on and off about 20 years and at no time has Bernice expressed being comfortable or happy with his presence in her life or her daughter's. He's been an addict, he's been abusive, he and Nan have had a very contentious relationship and he's just not someone you want in your life or in the life of anyone you care about. If Bernice could choose the cast for her death scene I feel very sure Frank would not have made the cut.

But at least she had a death scene, finally. It had been a torturous 14-month ordeal for all. It seemed like an eternity to us and we weren't the ones suffering in a nursing home for more than a year.

With Bernice's death the guardian lost his job and Ned was back on duty, this time as executor. It fell to him to arrange the funeral. Bernice had planned and prepaid her funeral so all Ned had to do was to call the funeral home and alert her friends and family. Given that she had died in the early morning hours of Friday it made sense to arrange her funeral for Sunday. That way there would be two days to take care of anything that needed to be arranged but we'd still be within the quick timeframe in which Jewish people bury their dead. Orthodox Jews bury within 24 hours but even those who are less observant bury usually within two days. Knowing that Sunday is a popular day for funerals so that attendees don't have to take a day off from work, Ned was anxious to secure a time so he called the funeral home right after he got the call telling him his mom had died. They already had some bookings for Sunday and Ned couldn't get his first choice of time slot so he chose 9:30 AM.

Early Friday morning Ned sent out a polite and businesslike email to alert his siblings to the arrangements he had made and to let them know the limo would be picking up at Anne's house, as Bernice had arranged for two limos years earlier.

Anne, Ted and Nan,
Mom's funeral is, as she selected, at Goldstein's Southampton at 9:30 AM Sunday, December 14. A limo will pick up at School Road, probably 8:15 but will send confirmation email as soon as the time is confirmed. They say it seats 7 people.

All pallbearers have been contacted with the exception of Ed.
Flowers have been ordered, per Mom's request.
Everyone on Mom's list has been contacted except people out West. Will phone them later.

Ned

Within minutes of sending that email Ned spoke to the guardian on the phone. He told Ned Anne was furious Ned arranged the funeral without consulting them. Given that Anne hadn't spoken to Ned for most of the last 30 years and just two days earlier Nan had read Ted's letter in court calling Ned a racist, was it really reasonable (or sane?) to think Ned should call any of these people and say, "So, what's good for you, Honey?" Yes, they were dysfunctional right up to the moment of Bernice's death and now they were taking it just one step further. To death and beyond!

Apparently, Anne had told the guardian Ted could not get into town by Sunday. Then she called the funeral director and insisted the funeral be changed to Monday. She told him her brother couldn't get from California to Philadelphia in two days. She never, however, told either of these men why Ted couldn't get there in two days. If it were true there had to be a reason. After all, anyone can fly from the West Coast to the East Coast in a few hours, and certainly within two days. The funeral director told Anne she'd have to speak to her brother Ned; only the executor could change the funeral. Perhaps if we had believed Ted couldn't get there Ned would have changed the funeral day. But two things, let's call them logic and history, told us this claim was bullshit. We knew they wanted the funeral to be Monday, we just didn't know why. Later that day Ted texted Ned (using a borrowed phone as Ned had long ago blocked all communication from Ted's phone) and said Ned was "inconsiderate" and that "Mom would have wanted her family to be at her funeral." That's when we knew for sure the claim was untrue. If Ted truly couldn't get to his mother's funeral and Ned was to blame, calling him "inconsiderate" would not have been Ted's choice of epithet. At that point we felt sure Ted would be at the funeral. We never did find out what the reason was for Anne insisting the funeral be rescheduled. It became obvious it had nothing to do with Ted's inability to get there. We learned a friend of Ted's couldn't get there until Monday and maybe that was the reason but then why would Anne get involved? Ted never actually made any of the calls himself and that is not like him at all. He lives to call people and yell at them. It makes more sense there was something about Sunday that didn't work for Anne's schedule and she was merely using Ted as her excuse. He was going along just for the sport of annoying Ned. She does run her annual charity event that was scheduled for Saturday, the day before the funeral. Maybe, we guessed, she just didn't want to get up so early the next day.

Later that day we spoke to the rabbi who was to officiate at the funeral. We gave him the backstory on the family saga so that he'd be prepared for a possibility of drama at the funeral. He was comforting and compassionate. He made a suggestion, too, upon learning of our long-term difficulties with Ned's parents. He suggested Ned and I and our daughters write our feelings on a piece of paper and throw it into the grave, literally and figuratively leaving our hurt, our regrets, and our sorrow about what was never to be behind us so that we could all move on. We loved the idea and later that night, most of us wrote something. We also told the rabbi about Anne and Ted's insistence that Ted couldn't be at the funeral but after speaking to both of them he called us back to say neither had mentioned it and Ted would in fact be attending. Of course.

Sunday dawned and it was time to head to the funeral. I told our daughters that if any of the family ~~nutjobs~~ members approached them or us and said anything nasty we would have only one response, "Sorry for your loss." Then we'd walk away. That was the plan and we promised (Although somewhat reluctantly as some of us really, really, really wanted to decimate these folks with just the right words.) to stick to it.

Moments after we arrived at the funeral home we saw Ted and his sons down the hall. One of the boys nodded at Alexis and she returned the gesture. We were ushered into separate rooms. The family members who wished to view Bernice's body were permitted to do so and then we waited for the service to begin. Eventually we saw Anne, Nan, and Ted but we didn't speak. They were seated to the right of the aisle on the front row; we were seated on the left. But Ted's sons did come over to hug Ned, our daughters, and me. No one really said much but there was sincere hugging. Then the attendees began filing up the side aisle to our left and moving past us to express condolences and continuing across the row to the "other side." (Literally, with multiple meanings) Our friends extended condolences to us and as far as we know, also to Ted, Nan, and Anne. Anne's closest friends, many of whom have known Ned for 40 years, avoided our side, one of them even going so far as to argue with the funeral director who was standing at the door ushering everyone down the side aisle so they'd have to pass all the mourners. She insisted on going in the opposite direction. So, some of Anne's friends expressed no sorrow for Ned's loss. I swear I don't understand people. How does anyone go to a funeral and plan NOT to extend condolences? If you are going to do that, don't attend. It's disrespectful to the person who has died as well as to the living. But, given that is exactly what Anne did 40 years earlier at my mother's funeral, it should have come as no surprise.

Ned had asked the rabbi to keep the focus on Bernice and he did a great job of doing exactly that in the service. After the rabbi said a few words about Bernice, he called up Bernice's granddaughter, Anne's daughter Beth, who delivered a nice eulogy about her grandmother. She even mentioned the elephant in the room by referencing the "vision" her grandmother had for her family that she failed to achieve. Then Ted spoke for about five minutes describing how much he loved his mother and even more so how much she loved him, how he'd never know a love that good in his life, how she loved him unconditionally and how she was the finest person ever to walk the planet. I may not be objective here but I found the whole thing a tad off. To speak at that length about how much his mother loved him, as if he had to prove to the attendees that "Mom really had loved him best" was a bit too much for comfort. But, I'll let that go, he loved her, she loved him, he's grieving, I get it.

Next it was Ned's turn to deliver the eulogy he'd written. I'd read it before so I knew what he'd written and it was perfect. He focused on better days when his mom was younger and happier. He'd written about how she and his father were the loves of each other's life. He lovingly described the days when the family was happy and Bernice was taking care of all of them. He was about to share a beautiful eulogy. He stepped to the podium to begin but before Ned could speak, Ted got up from his seat on the front row, turned and proceeded down the length of the center aisle in full view of all in attendance and WALKED OUT OF HIS MOTHER'S FUNERAL. There was an audible gasp in the room. Nan doubled over as if in pain, then she began to rock and then she too got up and walked the length of the aisle but upon reaching the door she turned and sat in the back. My guess is this: The dastardly duo planned to do this together to make a protest statement of some kind while Ned spoke. Ted was able to execute the plan; Nan just couldn't bring herself to follow through. I believe they thought they'd shame and embarrass Ned with this action but they were unable to see they shamed only themselves. Here was Ted, a man who just bore witness to how much he loved his mother and then disrespected her in the most offensive way. Sad.

After the service, surprisingly, Anne approached Ned and said she liked what he had said. He put his arm around her and said gently, "It didn't have to be this way." Not surprisingly she glared at him with ice in her voice and spat out, "You made choices, Ned. Let it go." He will. I was already over it, and her.

At the cemetery, following the brief service, during which Anne insisted the rabbi talk about how much Bernice loved the charity Anne runs, (Despite the fact her mother had nothing to do with it for at least the last 12 years, but okay, I'm letting that go too.). Ned began covering the casket with dirt. In Judaism, the highest honor, the last "mitzvah" or good deed you can perform for a person is to bury them, to literally cover the casket with dirt until it is no longer visible. The reason it's considered such a good deed is because it's the only act you can perform for a person when they will not be able to repay the kindness. You do this purely to do "good" and not in any way to be paid back. So, Ned began the burial and at one point Anne's son Rob who hasn't spoken to us in about 20 years, per his mother's instructions (Her children aren't permitted to speak to us or to our daughters, their cousins.), picked up a second shovel and worked with Ned to put in the dirt. Afterwards they hugged. Both Beth and Rob spoke to our daughters. Our daughters expressed openness to having relationships with them. We'll see if Beth and Rob respond. This isn't the first time our daughters have broached the subject. In the past their cousins have rebuffed them. Ned urged Beth not to let this estrangement go to another generation. But that is out of our hands.

And as the sun set on that Sunday, the saga of our twisted sisters (and one horribly perverse brother) was put to rest.

We felt some sadness in the end, but mostly we just felt free.

Chapter Twenty-Six: Through Thick and Thin

When we were young my friend Patti and I planned to become "blood sisters." We figured we'd prick our fingers with pins just enough to draw a tiny droplet of blood. Then we'd touch each other's fingers so the blood could mingle. We thought the blood tie created sisters. They say "blood is thicker than water," which we're taught means the connection with family should take precedence over the connection with friends who are somehow in that proverb represented by water. (I'd have chosen vodka to represent friends, not as thick as blood but ever so much more interesting.) The viscosity of the liquid is not what binds people, though. These dynamics form the bond: time, desire, honesty, and love.

Those are the quintessential quartet of successful relationships. Be they family or friends, without those four, relationships lack depth. Strong relationships don't just happen. You have to want them and work to build them. One difference between family and friends is worth noting. With your friends, your chosen "family," the death of your parents isn't likely to put your relationship asunder. That only happens with real family.

Ned and I have spent years and literally thousands of hours dissecting and discovering how our families dissolved. We want to understand. We want to know who is responsible. In this book I have pointed fingers. They say when you point a finger at someone, three of your fingers point back at you, meaning when you blame others for your troubles you also implicate yourself. That's as it should be because you must be accountable for the things that happen in your life. You are a contributor to your destiny. Consequently, I ask what did I do, what did Ned do, to become estranged from our siblings? I will try to answer those questions, but first let me explain the fingers I've pointed at others and summarize what I believe they did wrong. (Ever so much easier than figuring out where I went wrong.)

The adult children in Ned's family got embroiled in a power struggle; but I think they really just wanted to be loved. The need for love got sublimated somehow as they became more and more caught up in competing for their parents' attention and money. That battle took precedence over everything else. Bernice and Jack set this up by using money as the lure to garner their adult children's love and affection. They also just wanted to be loved but I don't believe they had the requisite faith in themselves to trust their children would love them no matter what. They had never woven honesty and unconditional love into the foundation of the family. Without honesty there can be no trust. Without trust, closeness is unattainable. To teach children how to trust and be trusted, parents must provide opportunities for children to earn trust while demonstrating that the parents can be counted on. In Ned's family, trust was fleeting and conditional. Jack was a good man at heart but he was insecure and perhaps afraid people wouldn't love him just as he was. He didn't know how to obtain love in a healthy way. He wasn't articulate so he was unable to communicate effectively. Thus, he sought to earn and maintain love through control. His fear manifested itself in anger. When he was angry he might hit the kids, and that threat was palpable at all times. Bernice and the children became skilled at lying and shifting blame to avoid his anger and the resulting violence.

Children must respect parents but there is a difference between respect and fear. Everyone in Ned's family was afraid of Jack's volatile temper. That fear takes a toll on a family and results in a lack of trust. It's unhealthy to grow up believing you can't rely on your parents. It also resulted in a competition between the children. No one wanted to be the one who made Jack angry. If the children could deflect the anger onto a sibling, that is what they did. They didn't learn to band together to cope with Jack's anger; they learned to compete to avoid it personally. Above all, nothing was ever their fault. Their fingers always had to point elsewhere.

Bernice loved deeply but she was also frightened and insecure. She couldn't handle confrontation and learned it was easier to acquiesce to pressure or to lie in order to save herself the pain of conflict. She wanted to be a good wife and mother but she was not strong enough to stand up to her husband and later to her daughter to protect her family. Instead, she manipulated Jack and others with deception and taught her children to do the same, saying occasionally that keeping the truth from someone was a "white" lie because no one got hurt. So, if something happened that had the potential to make Jack angry, Bernice just wouldn't tell him about it. She couldn't trust her husband to keep the kids safe, the kids couldn't trust her to protect them if the truth came out, and they couldn't trust each other because your sibling could tattle on you with information that might get you into trouble. The kids learned lying was a good way to manipulate people. Some of them took that strategy into adulthood.

Children must grow up believing their parents love them unconditionally. They must know making mistakes won't cost them their parents' love and affection. Family members must be able to believe saying "I'm sorry" and changing the behavior are enough to enable everyone to move on.

Here's an episode that illustrates the problem brewing in Ned's family. When Ned was about 16 and Anne about 20, they were having an argument. After it was over, Ned was sitting at the kitchen table sketching. Anne came up behind him, stealthily picked up the telephone receiver from the wall phone and slammed it as hard as she could into Ned's back. In those days the phone receiver was a hard and weighty piece of equipment. Being struck with one was not unlike being hit with a small hammer. Shocked and enraged Ned jumped up and hit Anne back. When Jack heard the story, he blamed Ned and punished him severely. Ned was scheduled to take a trip with his friends that weekend. He had been planning it for a year. Once Anne told her story, Jack told Ned he was not allowed to go on his trip. Ned explained he had been physically attacked after their argument had ended, but his mother wouldn't take his side and his father punished him but not Anne. Ned did ultimately go on part of the trip but the story provides insight into the family dynamic.

Jack couldn't use violence to control his adult children so he used money and attention as the carrot and the stick. When he approved of what his kids did, he gave them money. When he didn't approve, he cut them off. When 20-year-old Nan moved in with a boyfriend of another religion, Jack said he didn't plan to speak to her again—ever— and he didn't for quite a while. When Anne married and her husband became a lawyer, Jack paid to have their roof replaced. When he was angry with Ned for displeasing Anne, he reduced his share of the inheritance. Good behavior = money. Bad behavior = less money or no contact.

Ned's family dynamic was further complicated by mental illness. Nan was diagnosed as bipolar with severe emotional disturbance. She also suffered with addictions. Her illness, which she has never succeeded in getting fully under control, affected her ability to care about anyone but herself. Anne and Ted have never been diagnosed with any mental impairment, but in my humble non-medical opinion they are typical of people with narcissistic personality disorder. They are unable to see the world from any perspective other than their own, they have a sense of entitlement that guides their lives and they never, and I mean never, think anything is their fault. When Anne got divorced, it had to be 100% Stuart's fault. When she was diagnosed with MS, it had to be the fault of her parents for putting too much stress on her (Not that developing MS was her fault. My point is it wasn't anyone's fault but Anne had to assign blame to her parents using her illness as a weapon.). When Ted was convicted of a felony, it wasn't because he chose to defraud people; it was because he was the innocent dupe of the "bad guy" he picked for a partner. When his marriage fell apart it was because his wife was an alcoholic, not because he was involved in a criminal enterprise and was a lousy husband and father. Anne and Ted both have a history of awful relationships. They react to everything defensively and with anger when they don't get their way. If you disagree with either of them on any point, they see it as black and white. You are against them, your viewpoint has no validity, they are angry, and their anger is never moderate. Most frustrating of all, they do not recognize they have a problem in this area so they aren't likely to understand they are narcissists.

Finally, potential mental illnesses aside, there are the ways in which the children in Ned's family modeled their parents' behavior. Much like Jack, Anne controls the people she "loves." They are afraid of her and of losing her affection so they do what she asks. When she can no longer control them she cuts them out of her life. She did it to her first husband, her daughter, her son, her siblings, some of her friends, and ultimately her parents. Sad.

Nan is not strong; she is like Bernice in that way. She withdraws from life because it overwhelms her. She protects herself through that withdrawal and by convincing herself no one cares about her while living in a way that makes her difficult to love because she is so detached. A lifetime of that has left her selfish and mean. Sad.

Ted doesn't make connections with many people. He's extremely private and trusts no one. He has anger management issues similar to those his father had. He absolutely cannot respect authority. He got into trouble as a teen and flunked out of high school as a result of his refusal to follow rules. (Although to his credit he did later earn a GED and a college degree.) He's an unhappy and lonely person. He once told me he didn't know if he had ever been happy. He's not devoid of positive attributes, though. Like his mother, he's creative and talented. He can be charming. He had potential to live a good life but didn't or couldn't choose a pathway to peace. Sad.

As a result of these behavior traits and choices, no one in Ned's family trusted anyone else. In order to trust others, you must be trustworthy yourself. If you know you are a liar, a schemer, and someone on whom others cannot depend, you see the world through your own looking glass. People who cannot be trusted, whether due to their weakness, their ineptitude, or their lack of moral compass, cannot trust others either. They believe inherently everyone is like them. In contrast, people who are dependable and honest are likely to trust others to behave in a similar manner.

Ned works hard to make peace with his past. He recognizes his own anger issues and works hard to mitigate them. He puts time and energy into his friendships and his family affairs in order to have meaningful interactions. He is trustworthy and as such, he is able to have reciprocal relationships, unlike his siblings.

Earlier in this story I said I was supposed to be the heroine of this tale. It was a joke. I know I am not the heroine, just the narrator and one of the players. I understand I am not blameless. I am a vengeful person. I admit this with no pride; I'm just acknowledging one of my character traits. During the years when Anne would hurt me or my husband or my kids I'd plot ways to hurt her back. I never actually put any of those into practice but I must confess I've spent countless moments enjoying constructing ways to make her squirm emotionally. It's not like I planned to hit her with my car, although...

Maybe I could have reached out more compassionately to her over the years. If her marriage broke up over an affair her husband had and she kept that truth from us, I think that dishonesty probably made the whole situation worse. If we had known someone she loved betrayed her, we could have handled things differently. (Although, we still believe staying civil for the sake of the children is a must in any divorce.) We could only react to what Anne shared at the time: that she was unhappy and bored with Stuart. But, truth notwithstanding, maybe I could have tried harder to grasp what she needed. The same goes for my relationships with Jack and Bernice. I had no respect for the way they raised their kids or treated my husband, my daughters, or me. I didn't love them and because they hurt so many people I cared about I wasn't motivated to bridge the divide and find common ground on which to start again and build stronger bonds. I didn't trust them. I didn't try very hard to rebuild that trust once the truth of their betrayal of us was revealed. Maybe I should have had more sympathy for the rock and the hard place they lived between in the battle of Anne versus the rest of their family.

On my family's side of the dysfunction junction, I am stymied. My sister was never forthcoming about what really motivated her anger toward me. I can only guess. I know I could have tried harder to communicate with her. Perhaps I could have respected who she was more than I did. While I sent letters and called a few times in the first couple of years after Dad died, after the lawsuit debacle I got deeply discouraged so I surrendered and stayed away. I could have and perhaps should have gone to New York and knocked on her door, imploring her to talk to me about what I did that was so hurtful to her. I know in her mind I did something heinous. I just don't know what it is. That's a poor excuse for me, I am aware of that. Maybe I should have handed over the train set.

Finger pointing wise, what did my parents do to raise such disconnected daughters? That is a difficult question to answer. They modeled reasonably healthy sibling relationships. My mother had a brother she loved and she was close with him and with his family. She was kind to them; she visited often although they lived in a different state. She even invited her niece to spend a summer with us so she could attend camp. My mother spoke lovingly about her brothers and her parents throughout her life.

My dad also modeled adequate sibling behavior, given his quiet and private nature. Despite the fact his brother lived several states away, they spoke (Okay, I use the term "spoke" lightly as neither said much.) on the phone and we saw them a few times a year. My uncle and aunt did not have kids, nor did my father's sister so Dad didn't have nieces or nephews. But he was close with his cousins. We saw them often and they are still an important part of my life. I grew up with parents who valued family.

But I don't recall either of my parents ever talking to my sister or me about the importance of our relationship. They could see we didn't play together often. Maybe they thought we were too many years apart or maybe they didn't think this was something they should worry about. I don't know if they thought my sister was socially odd. They never said. I don't know if they worried about Linda's lack of friends. If I have to point a finger at something they did wrong in raising us, I'd have to say it was in not talking more or at all about the types of siblings we were or should be.

Parents can nurture healthier sibling relationships. They can encourage their children to do things together and teach children how to handle conflict in healthy ways. Both my parents and Ned's could have done a much better job in this area. I understand parents want harmony in the home but conflict and its resolution should not be the enemy of harmony. If anything, teaching children how to clash with siblings in healthy ways during childhood is a great strategy to build strong long-lasting relationships. Sibling rivalry is an integral part of development. It's imperative to teach children how to handle it rather than to teach them to pretend it doesn't exist. Some parents have difficulty acknowledging their children fight because they believe it's a poor reflection on their parenting skills. They may think if the kids argue, it means the parents aren't treating all children equally. In fact the opposite is true. When parents teach children strategies for clashing with siblings, working it out, and ultimately resolving the problem, they are teaching them a skill they can employ well into adulthood. The truth is if my parents and Ned's had helped us build strong sibling relationships when we were children, we could have grown up with strategies in place. If Ned's parents taught their children how to process problems with their siblings when they were kids, the likelihood is when they argued as adults, they might have had the skills to "fight fairly" and then been able to move on with stronger bonds.

Were my parents and Ned's bad parents because their children are estranged? I believe good people with flawed skills would be a more apt description. As it is with any relationship, there are no simple answers. Things are not all black and white.

What I have concluded is we need familial relationships in order to be happy. When we don't have them with our blood relatives, we can build them with friends. Ned has deep and abiding friendships with men he regards as brothers. My friends have become my sisters. These are friendships built over the years that have a basis in deeply rooted trust. We support each other in good times and bad. They are the people I reach out to when I need a good laugh or a good cry.

What would I tell someone who is experiencing a similar situation with their own "bad sibling"? I'd say if you have tried understanding and compassion and support, if you've been to therapy hell and back and if you still simply cannot work it out so you and your siblings can live in peace and harmony, you may have to give up. Literally. You may have to choose to let that person or persons go from your life. Blood is not a reason to keep a genuinely toxic person in your life or in your family's life. It's not easy to let someone go. But if the pain of being involved with that person is too great a burden to bear, sometimes the responsible choice, the healthy choice, and maybe the only choice is to let her go. If someone is blocking your path to happiness, you may have to step around him and just keep walking. Letting go comes in many levels, however. If you are eschewing just one family member you may have to do it in such a way so as to not to destroy your entire family. Don't ask others to take sides, just cut back on your interactions with that person. Letting go might just be an emotional surrender. In other words, you could still attend family events involving that person or persons; just keep your interaction to a minimum.

If any members of your family bring you down and are judgmental about your life, your choices, and your circumstances, if they are filled with envy and resentment toward you, if they are deceitful in their dealings with you, why continue to spend time, energy, and resources on them? Imagine how much happier you could be by gravitating to people who share interests and values with you. Imagine working together to achieve goals. Imagine being enveloped by people who love you. After all, isn't that what family is supposed to be?

Surround yourself with people you love and trust if you weren't born into a family that provides you with the close connections you require to live a fulfilled and happy life. They may be friends or mentors or neighbors. These are the people who will be there for you at the times of your life—birth, death, joy, illness, good times, bad times, and everything in between. To consciously create your own support group is a very healthy way to react to family dysfunction. Just be emotionally prepared for the potential return of those real family members when your parents die. But in the meantime, move on, move forward, and do whatever it takes to live a good life.

Epilogue: Life Before Death Revisited

We have concluded family is not necessarily a reason to keep certain people in your life. But, whether you keep the dysfunctional family members around or cut them off, when death of a parent is at the door, it brings all the cast members back into the story of your life. And when they return they will bring with them a lifetime of changes so you may not even easily recognize them as the same people they were before. If you didn't work well as a family unit previously, it may be even more difficult after so many years. Plus, they may add even more people and personalities to the mix as they might have spouses and children who will add their opinions into an already difficult situation.

We have spoken to countless people about our saga. It is astounding how many come back to us with a story of their own involving a death in the family. While I don't pretend to be a psychologist or therapist of any kind, I do, unfortunately, know a great deal about dealing with death in the family. If you believe, as I do, that lessons learned through experience can be valuable, then I invite you to learn from my experience. Why tell this story? Forewarned is forearmed, perhaps, but more importantly you can stave off some of the pain of dealing with a parent's death only by living proactively early enough to detour death's divisiveness.

They say people die the way they live. If they lived as our parents did with things unsaid and wishes unclear, their deaths are more likely to be problematic to their families. I suggest family members work together far in advance to understand this "death checklist." Following these suggestions won't be the difference between life and death but it could mean the difference between a good and peaceful death and a bad and torturous one for your family. Whether dealing with the death of your parent or your own upcoming demise, these suggestions may help.

1. Reinvent death: Perhaps death needs a snappy slogan: *Death: It's not all bad. Death: New beginnings for an old life. Death: The ultimate in stress relief.* The point is to find a way to talk about death openly. Why not? It's going to happen, we all know it.

Talking about death isn't going to make it happen any sooner. If you superstitiously believe talking about death is bad luck, let that go. Newsflash: You and everyone you love is going to die whether you speak about it or not. Your words don't have the power to make death come or go. People don't love talking about death so it may take some work to get this ball rolling. Don't give up. Don't be put off when your parents or adult children ask to talk about something more pleasant. Break out your snappy slogan and press on. A parent's death brings many adult children back to childhood and not in a good way. Old hurts and resentments resurface as people scramble to right any leftover wrongs or to heal old wounds still festering beneath the surface. It's not rational; it's emotional and desperate. The more talking you can do in advance, while the parent is alive and somewhat well, the better.

2. Talk about money. Besides death the subject of money is also one people loath discussing. In families money can easily become the currency of love. If you talk about money openly, that will help to alleviate that problem. If there are siblings with greater need, talk about that before wills are written. And know in your own heart the difference between love and money.

3. Talk about love. Family battles involving death and money are ultimately about love. Airing your feelings exposes them to the light of understanding.

4. Listen to your parents and make sure your adult children listen to you. If your parents are willing to speak about their deaths, you must listen. Don't withdraw because death is upsetting to think about. Encourage your parents to verbalize their thoughts and their fears. Let them know you are supportive. If you are the aging parent, insist your adult children listen to you.

5. Embrace openness. Once the death discussion is on the table it opens the door for a solid talk about the future. Avoiding the battles over the inheritance and the estate depends on the ability of the family members to speak openly about the future. Everyone must put cards on the table, that is, everyone should know everything about the family estate before the parents die. Parents should make their wills part of an "open book" exhibit. If there is something in your will you wouldn't want someone in your family to know about until after you are dead that is a red flag. If your gut sense is that anything in your will might be

problematic, it shouldn't be included. Money isn't the only issue. Possessions should be documented and distributed per the wishes of the owner. Everyone in the family should be apprised about who gets what and why. My highest recommendation would be to gather as a family at some point and allow each person to verbalize what he or she would most like to have. Then be sure everyone in the family knows who is getting what and why.

6. Appoint a point person and a back up choice in case that person can't do the job. You need a person to serve as Power of Attorney. The Power of Attorney steps in while you're alive but unable to handle your affairs. He or she may make decisions for you and will have access to your finances. It is imperative you choose wisely. You must choose a person you can trust who has a backbone and will advocate strongly for you. Choose one person, not a committee or co-powers. You may think they'll get along and make decisions together but you are creating scenario for trouble if you don't choose just one person who has the ultimate power. You can tell that person you'd like him or her to take family needs and opinions into consideration but be sure everyone knows the point person has the final decision-making power.

7. When you are getting ready to write a will (Which you should do if you haven't already. Dying without a will could result in your family losing much of what is yours to your state, depending on the laws in the state where you live.), choose an executor with the same qualities you looked for in a Power of Attorney. The executor is the person who will take care of the affairs that need to be wrapped up after you die. Again, my strong recommendation is not to choose more than one person to serve at one time. If you already have dissent in the family or members of your immediate family who don't speak to each other, don't choose one of them to be executor. Choose an impartial person or a bank to manage your estate.

8. Think about your last days and the quality of life you want. Do you want to be kept alive at all costs? Do you want to be hooked up to machines that may feed you and help you breathe? Do you want to be given antibiotics if you develop an infection after you already have a terminal condition? These are decisions you should make now and then be sure to put your

choices in writing in a Living Will or an Advanced Medical Directive. Also choose someone to be your Power of Attorney for health issues. It doesn't have to be the same person you choose for financial affairs. Make sure every member of your family knows your choices. You may not always be able to communicate those wishes so you must do so in a way that makes your wishes known before you are not able to do so yourself.

9. Assume nothing. If you have a loving family that's wonderful but it's not a guarantee of peace when it comes to settling an estate. No family is off limits when it comes to the toll death takes on family relationships. If you have a strong and supportive family that's all the more reason to make sure it stays that way.

10. Seek professional help. Wills should not be weapons. Check in with a lawyer and a financial planner. Leave a legacy of love, not an instrument of retribution. No one should find out after a death the deceased had unresolved feelings of anger. That shouldn't be anyone's last communication with the living. Communicate while you're alive. When communication becomes a one-way street it goes nowhere. If you are in the midst of a family battle, seek a professional mediator before it's too late. Look for a geriatric manager. They have associations in every state.

Post Mortem

E arlier in the story I said if I could have a few minutes to live over, I'd choose a few moments with my mom. But I wondered what if I could have just a few seconds with each of these dead parents? Here are my thoughts about what I'd say:

To My Dad: Thanks. I'm grateful every day for having you as a father.

To My Mom: I love you. You said you hoped someday I'd have a daughter just like me. I have three. I hope you can see how I passed along your legacy of love. You'd be so proud of them and they would have been honored to know you. And, I hope you really weren't embarrassed about the way I turned out.

To Jack: What were you so angry about? You had a pretty good life, after all.

To Bernice: I'm sorry. I'm unspeakably sorry. I wish things had turned out differently for you.

Made in the USA
San Bernardino, CA
07 September 2016